VITAL
BIBLICAL
ISSUES

THE VITAL ISSUES SERIES

VITAL ISSUES SERIES

VITAL BIBLICAL ISSUES

*Examining Problem
Passages of the Bible*

ROY B. ZUCK
GENERAL EDITOR

Grand Rapids, MI 49501

Vital Biblical Issues by Roy B. Zuck, general editor.

Copyright © 1994 by Dallas Theological Seminary.

Published by Kregel Resources, an imprint of Kregel Publications, P.O. Box 2607, Grand Rapids, MI 49501. Kregel Resources provides timely and relevant resources for Christian life and service. Your comments and suggestions are valued.

Unless otherwise noted, all Scripture quotations are from the *New American Standard Bible* © 1960, 1962, 1963, 1968, 1971, 1972, 1973, 1975, 1977 by The Lockman Foundation, a corporation not for profit, La Habra, CA and are used by permission.

Cover Design: Sarah Slattery
Book Design: Alan G. Hartman

Library of Congress Cataloging-in-Publication Data
Roy B. Zuck.
Vital biblical issues: examining problem passages of the Bible / Roy B. Zuck, gen. ed.
    p.   cm. (Vital Issues Series; v. 3)
    1. Bible—Criticism, interpretation, etc. I. Zuck, Roy B.
II. Series: Zuck, Roy B. Vital Issues Series.
BS511.2.V58   1994   220.6—dc20   94-31339
                                                  CIP
ISBN 0-8254-4072-6 (paperback)

1 2 3 4 5 Printing / Year 98 97 96 95 94

Printed in the United States of America

Contents

Contributors

Gleason L. Archer, Jr.
> Professor of Old Testament and Semitic Languages, Emeritus, Trinity Evangelical Divinity School, Deerfield, Illinois

Robert B. Chisholm, Jr.
> Professor of Old Testament Studies, Dallas Theological Seminary, Dallas, Texas

Joseph C. Dillow
> President, Biblical Education by Extension, International, Shatin, New Territories, Hong Kong

Duane A. Dunham
> Professor of New Testament Language and Literature, Western Conservative Baptist Seminary, Portland, Oregon

Charles Lee Feinberg
> Dean, Emeritus, and Professor of Semitics and Old Testament, Emeritus, Talbot School of Theology, La Mirada, California

Ed Glasscock
> Associate Professor, Moody Graduate School, Chicago, Illinois

Michael P. Green
> Associate Professor, Moody Graduate School, Chicago, Illinois

D. Edmond Hiebert
> Late Professor of New Testament, Mennonite Brethren Biblical Seminary, Fresno, California

Tracy L. Howard
> Attorney, Vinson and Elkins, The Woodlands, Texas

S. Lewis Johnson, Jr.
> Professor of New Testament Studies, Emeritus, Dallas Theological Seminary, Dallas Texas, and Teacher, Believers Chapel, Dallas, Texas

J. Carl Laney
    Professor of Biblical Literature, Western Conservative
    Baptist Seminary, Portland, Oregon

Eugene H. Merrill
    Professor of Old Testament Studies, Dallas Theological
    Seminary, Dallas, Texas

Thomas Kem Oberholtzer
    Associate Professor of Bible Exposition, Western
    Seminary—Phoenix, Phoenix, Arizona

J. Barton Payne
    Late Professor of Old Testament, Emeritus, Wheaton
    College, Wheaton, Illinois

Allen P. Ross
    Associate Professor of Biblical Studies, Trinity Episcopal
    School for Ministry, Ambridge, Pennsylvania

Charles C. Ryrie
    Professor of Systematic Theology, Emeritus, Dallas
    Theological Seminary, Dallas, Texas

Stanley D. Toussaint
    Professor of Bible Exposition, Emeritus, Dallas Theological
    Seminary, Dallas, Texas

Merrill F. Unger
    Late Professor of Old Testament, Dallas Theological
    Seminary, Dallas, Texas

Kenneth T. Wilson
    Instructor in Bible and Theology, Colorado Christian
    University, Denver, Colorado

Preface

Every Bible student recognizes the life-giving power of God's Word. The authoritative, inerrant Scriptures provide spiritual birth (1 Peter 1:23) and offer spiritual nourishment and growth (1 Peter 2:2). No one can read the Bible without acknowledging its uniqueness as God's divine truth, given by the inspiration of the Holy Spirit.

While the Bible—as God's message to mankind—stands in its simplicity as a book easily understood by children, youth, and adults, it also challenges the most astute, scholarly minds.

Is this surprising? Not really—its profundity of thought testifies to its divine origin. How can humans fully comprehend God? Seeking to plumb the unfathomable depths of Scripture is like a child trying to measure the ocean by his bucket on the shore.

The chapters in this book address some of the problem passages in the Bible. Why did Noah curse Canaan? Did God change his will about Israel having a king? Why did the psalmists pray for vengeance on their enemies? Is the book of Daniel a fraud? What did Jesus mean when He commanded His followers to take up their own crosses? What does abiding in Christ mean? In what sense did God "give up" sinners? Did Paul teach that women should wear head coverings? In what sense is the church a "mystery"? What is the meaning of the phrase "the husband of one wife"?

The writers of these chapters, reprinted from *Bibliotheca Sacra*, Dallas Seminary's quarterly journal, suggest answers to these and other difficulties in the Scriptures. Hopefully these studies will enhance reader's understanding of the Bible while at the same time providing spiritual nourishment for the soul.

ROY B. ZUCK

About *Bibliotheca Sacra*

A flood is rampant—an engulfing deluge of literature far beyond any one person's ability to read it all. Presses continue to churn out thousands of journals and magazines like a roiling, raging river.

Among these numberless publications, one stands tall and singular—*Bibliotheca Sacra*—a strange name (meaning "Sacred Library") but a journal familiar to many pastors, teachers, and Bible students.

How is *Bibliotheca Sacra* unique in the world of publishing? By being the oldest continuously published journal in the Western Hemisphere—1993 marked its 150th anniversary—and by being published by one school for sixty years—1994 marks its diamond anniversary of being released by Dallas Seminary.

Bib Sac, to use its shortened sobriquet, was founded in New York City in 1843 and was purchased by Dallas Theological Seminary in 1934, ten years after the school's founding. The quarterly's one-hundred and fifty year history boasts only nine editors. Through those years it has maintained a vibrant stance of biblical conservatism and a strong commitment to the Scriptures as God's infallible Word.

I am grateful to Kregel Publications for producing a series of volumes, being released this year and next, commemorating both the journal's sesquicentennial (1843–1993) and its diamond anniversary (1934–1994). Each volume in the Kregel *Vital Issues Series* includes carefully selected articles from the thirties to the present—articles of enduring quality, articles by leading evangelicals whose topics are as relevant today as when they were first produced. The chapters have been edited slightly to provide conformity of style. As Dallas Seminary and Kregel Publications jointly commemorate these anniversaries of *Bibliotheca Sacra*, we trust these anthologies will enrich the spiritual lives and Christian ministries of many more readers.

ROY B. ZUCK, EDITOR
Bibliotheca Sacra

For *Bibliotheca Sacra* subscription information, call Dallas Seminary, 1–800–992-0998.

CHAPTER 1

The Curse of Canaan

Allen P. Ross

The bizarre little story in Genesis 9:18–27 about Noah's drunkenness and exposure along with the resultant cursing of Canaan has perplexed students of Genesis for some time. Why does Noah, the spiritual giant of the Flood, appear in such a bad light? What exactly did Ham do to Noah? Who was Canaan and why should he have been cursed for something he did not do? Though problems like these preoccupy much of the study of this passage, their solutions are related to the more basic question of the purpose of the account in the theological argument of Genesis.

Genesis, the book of beginnings, is primarily concerned with tracing the development of God's program of blessing. Blessing was pronounced on God's creation, but sin (with its subsequent curse) brought deterioration and decay. After the Flood there was a new beginning with a renewal of the decrees of blessing, but once again corruption and rebellion left the human race alienated and scattered across the face of the earth. Against this backdrop God began His program of blessing again, promising blessing to those obedient in faith and cursing to those who rebel. The rest of the book explains how this blessing developed: God's chosen people would become a great nation and inherit the land of Canaan. So throughout Genesis the motifs of blessing and cursing occur again and again in connection with those who are chosen and those who are not.

An important foundation for these motifs is found in the oracle of Noah. Ham's impropriety toward the nakedness of his father prompted an oracle with far-reaching implications. Canaan was cursed; but Shem, the ancestor of Israel, and Japheth were blessed. It seems almost incredible that a relatively minor event would have such major repercussions. But consistently in the narratives of Genesis, one finds that the fate of both men and nations is determined by occurrences that seem trivial and commonplace.

The main characters of these stories acted on natural impulse in their own interests, but the narrator is concerned with the greater significance of their actions. Thus it becomes evident that out of the virtues and vices of Noah's sons come the virtues and vices of the families of the world.[1]

The purpose of this section in Genesis, then, is to portray the characteristics of the three branches of the human race in relation to blessing and cursing. In pronouncing the oracle, Noah discerned the traits of his sons and, in a moment of insight, determined that the attributes of their descendants were embodied in their personalities.[2] Because these sons were primogenitors of the families of the earth, the narrator is more interested in the greater meaning of the oracle with respect to tribes and nations in his day than with the children of Shem, Ham, and Japheth.[3]

Shem, the ancestor of the Shemites to whom the Hebrews belonged, acted in good taste and was blessed with the possession of the knowledge of the true God, Yahweh. Japheth, the ancestor of the far-flung northern tribes which include the Hellenic peoples,[4] also acted properly and thus shared in the blessing of Shem and was promised geographical expansion. In contrast, Ham, represented most clearly to Israel by the Egyptians and Canaanites, acted wrongly in violating sexual customs regarded as sacred and as a result had one line of his descendants cursed with subjugation.[5]

So the oracle of Noah, far from being concerned simply with the fortunes of the immediate family, actually pertains to vast movements of ancient peoples.[6] Portraying their tendencies as originating in individual ancestors, the book of beginnings anticipates the expected destinies of these tribes and nations. Vos fittingly notes that it occurred at a time when no event could fail to influence history.[7]

The Prologue (Gen. 9:18–19)

Genesis 9:18–19 provides not only an introduction to this narrative but also a literary bridge between the Flood narrative and the table of nations. The reader of Genesis is already familiar with the listing of the main characters of this story: Noah and his three sons Shem, Ham, and Japheth (5:32; 6:10; 7:13; 9:1; and later in 10:1). But in this passage two qualifications are supplied. They were the sons of Noah who came out of the ark, and they were the progenitors from whom all the nations of the earth originated. The first description connects the characters to the

Flood account, and the second relates them to the table of nations.

Of greater significance for the present narrative, however, is the circumstantial clause in verse 18, "Now Ham was the father of Canaan." Many have thought that this is a primary example of a redactor's attempt to harmonize the deed of Ham and the curse of Canaan portions of this narrative.[8] If that were the case, it could have been done more effectively without leaving such a rough trace. The point of this clause seems rather to show the connection of Canaan with Ham. However, far from being merely a genealogical note, which would be superfluous in view of chapter 10, the narrative is tracing the beginnings of the family and shows that Ham, acting as he did, revealed himself as the true father of Canaan.[9] The immediate transfer of the reference to Canaan would call to the Israelite mind a number of unfavorable images about these people they knew, for anyone familiar with the Canaanites would see the same tendencies in their ancestor from this decisive beginning. So this little additional note anticipates the proper direction in the story.

The Event (Gen. 9:20–23)

NOAH'S BEHAVIOR

The behavior of Noah after the Flood provided the occasion for the violation of Ham. Noah then acted so differently from before the Flood that some commentators have suggested that a different person is in view here.[10] But the text simply presents one person. The man who watched in righteousness over a wicked world then planted a vineyard, became drunk, and lay naked in his tent. Or, as Francisco said it, "With the opportunity to start an ideal society Noah was found drunk in his tent."[11]

This deterioration of character seems to be consistent with the thematic arrangement of at least the early portion of Genesis, if not all of the book. Each major section of the book has the heading אֵלֶּה תוֹלְדֹה, commonly translated "these are the generations of." The narratives that follow each heading provide the particulars about the person, telling what became of him and his descendants. In each case there is a deterioration from beginning to end. In fact the entire Book of Genesis presents the same pattern: The book begins with man (Adam) in the garden under the blessing of God, but ends with a man (Joseph) in a coffin in Egypt. The תוֹלְדוֹת of

Noah began in 6:9 with the note that Noah was righteous and blameless before the Lord, and ended in 9:18–27 with Noah in a degraded condition. But it was a low experience from which God would bring brighter prospects in the future.

Noah, described as a "man of the soil" (9:20), began by planting a vineyard. This epithet (אִישׁ הָאֲדָמָה) is probably designed to say more than that he was a human farmer. In view of the fact that he is presented as the patriarch of the survivors of the Flood, Noah would be considered as the master of the earth, or as Rashi understood it, the lord of the earth.[12]

The two verbs (וַיָּחֶל . . . וַיִּטַּע) in the sentence are best taken as a verbal hendiadys, "he proceeded to plant" a vineyard. Whether he was the first man in history to have done so is not stated, but he was the first to do so after the Flood. The head of the only family of the earth then produced the vine from the ground that previously produced minimal sustenance amid thorns.

The antediluvian narratives represent various beginnings, none of which appear particularly virtuous. Besides Noah's beginning in viticulture, the first "hunter" is mentioned in 10:8. Nimrod was the first (הֵחֵל) "to be a mighty warrior on the earth." And in 11:6, concerning the activities of Babel, the text reads, "they have begun (הַחִלָּם) to do this." The use of the same verb in all these passages provides an ominous note to the stories.

The planting of the vineyard, however, appears to be for Noah a step forward from the cursed ground. Since Lamech, Noah's father, toiled under the curse,[13] he hoped that his son would be able to bring about some comfort (5:29) and so he called him Noah, which means "comfort." Perhaps Noah hoped that cheer and comfort would come from this new venture.

The vine in the Bible is considered noble. The psalmist described the vine as God's provision, stating that it "gladdens the heart of man" (104:15). A parable in Judges has a vine saying, "Should I give up my wine, which cheers both gods and men?" (9:13). Not only did the fruit of the vine alleviate the pain of the cursed, but also it is the symbol of coming bliss in the Messianic age. Zechariah 8:12 and Isaiah 25:6 describe the future age by employing this idea.[14]

But while it may be that wine alleviates to some degree the painful toll of the ground, the Old Testament often warns of the moral dangers attending this new step in human development. Those taking strong vows were prohibited from drinking wine

(Num. 6); and those assuming responsible positions of rulership were given the proverbial instruction that strong drink is not for kings, but for those about to die (Prov. 31:4–5).

The story of Noah shows the degrading effects of the wine—drunkenness and nakedness. No blame is attached in this telling of the event, but it is difficult to ignore the prophetic oracles that use nakedness and drunkenness quite forcefully. Habakkuk, for one, announced, "Woe to him who gives drink to his neighbors, pouring it from the wineskin till they are drunk, so that he can gaze on their naked bodies" (2:15). Jeremiah also used the imagery for shame and susceptibility to violation and exploitation, lamenting, "You will be drunk and stripped naked" (Lam. 4:21).

Since the prophets view drunkenness and nakedness as signs of weakness and susceptibility to shameful destruction, many have condemned Noah's activities. The Talmud records that Noah was to be considered righteous only when compared with his wicked generation.[15] All that Rashi would say was that Noah degraded himself by not planting something else.[16] Most commentators at least view it as an ironic contrast in Noah's character[17] if not an activity that is in actual disharmony with the picture of the man given earlier.[18]

On the other hand there have been many who have attempted to exonerate Noah in one way or another. Medieval Jews took it in an idealistic way, saying that Noah planted the vine in order to understand sin in a better way and thus to be able to warn the world of its effects.[19] Various scholars have tried to free Noah from blame by viewing the passage as an "inventor saga."[20] Noah, the inventor of wine, was overpowered by the unsuspected force of the fruit and experienced the degradation of the discovery.[21]

Cohen takes the exoneration a step further. Observing that the motif of wine in the ancient world was associated with sexuality, he argues that Noah was attempting to maintain his procreative ability to obey the new commission to populate the earth. To substantiate his view, Cohen drew on the analogy of Lot with his daughters (Gen. 19:30–38) and David with Uriah and Bathsheba (2 Sam. 11:12–13), since wine was used in each case to promote sexual activity.[22] Cohen acclaims the old man for playing the role so well.

It cannot be denied that wine has been used in connection with sex. However, Cohen's theory, no matter how fascinating, must be rejected as a highly speculative interpretation. It is more plausible to proceed on clear evidence and to take a normal, sensible approach. Later biblical allusions show drunkenness and nakedness to be shameful weaknesses, often used figuratively for susceptibility before enemies. Noah is thus not presented in a good light.

In view of this, it appears that along with the primary intent of the narrative to set the stage for the oracle, the passage also presents a polemic against pagan mythology.[23] The old world saw Armenia as the original home of wine, but Egyptian literature attributed the invention of wine to the god Osiris, and Greek literature attributed it to Dionysius. The Genesis account, by contrast, considers the beginning of wine and its effect on man as less than divine. It has the trappings of depravity. Cursing and slavery, rather than festive joy, proceed from its introduction into the world. Any nation delighting in the vices of wine and nakedness, this polemic implies, is already in slavery.

HAM'S VIOLATION

Noah's condition prompted the sin of his son Ham. Ham, who again is said to be the father of Canaan, "saw his father's nakedness and told his two brothers outside" (9:22). They in response carefully came in and covered the old man. When Noah learned what Ham had done to him, he cursed Canaan but he blessed Shem and Japheth.

What did Ham do that was serious enough to warrant such a response? One answer is that Ham did nothing at all to deserve such a blistering curse. Many writers believe that two traditions have been pieced together here, one about Ham and another about Canaan. Rice asserts, "All the tensions of Genesis 9:18–27 are resolved when it is recognized that this passage contains two parallel but different traditions of Noah's family."[24] In fact he states that no interpretation that considers the story to be a unity can do justice to the text. But it must be noted in passing that positing two traditions in no way solves the tension; instead it raises another. If the parts of the story were from two irreconcilable traditions, what caused them to be united? To assert that two differing accounts were used does not do justice to the final, fixed form of the text. The event was obviously understood to be the basis of the oracle that follows in 9:24–27.

Some commentators attempt to reconstruct what took place. Figart suggests that Ham and his brothers came to see Noah, and that Ham went in alone, discovered his father's condition, and reported it to his brothers who remedied the situation. Figart's point is that there was no sin by Ham.[25] He suggests that Canaan, the youngest, must have been responsible for the deed that incurred the curse.

But it seems clear enough that the story is contrasting Ham, the father of Canaan, with Shem and Japheth regarding seeing or not seeing the nakedness. The oracle curses Ham's descendant, but blesses the descendants of Shem and Japheth. If Canaan rather than Ham were the guilty one, why was Ham not included in the blessing? Shufelt, suggesting also that Canaan was the violator, reckons that Ham was reckless.[28] But it seems that the narrative is placing the violation on Ham.

Many theories have been put forward concerning this violation of Ham. Several writers have felt that the expression "he saw his nakedness" is a euphemism for a gross violation. Cassuto speculates that the pre-Torah account may have been uglier but was reduced to minimal proportions.[27] Greek and Semitic stories occasionally tell how castration was used to prevent procreation in order to seize the power to populate the earth.[28] The Talmud records that this view was considered by the rabbis: "Rab and Samuel [differ], one maintaining that he castrated him, and the other that he abused him sexually."[29] The only possible textual evidence to support such a crime would come from Genesis 9:24, which says that Noah "found out what his youngest son had done to him." But the remedy for Ham's "deed" is the covering of Noah's nakedness. How would throwing the garment over him without looking undo such a deed and merit the blessing?

Bassett presents a view based on the idiomatic use of the words "uncover the nakedness."[30] He suggests that Ham engaged in sexual intercourse with Noah's wife, and that Canaan was cursed because he was the fruit of that union. He attempts to show that to "see another's nakedness" is the same as sexual intercourse, and that a later redactor who missed the idiomatic meaning added the words in 9:23.

But the evidence for this interpretation is minimal. The expression רָאָה עֶרְוָה is used in Scripture for shameful exposure, mostly of a woman or as a figure of a city in shameful punishment, exposed and defenseless. This is quite different from the idiom used for sexual violation, גִּלָּה עֶרְוָה, "he uncovered the nakedness." This construction is used throughout Leviticus 18 and 20 to describe the evil sexual conduct of the Canaanites. Leviticus

20:17 is the only occurrence where רָאָה is used, but even that is in a parallel construction with גָּלָה, explaining the incident. This one usage cannot be made to support Bassett's claim of an idiomatic force meaning sexual intercourse.

According to Genesis 9 Noah uncovered himself (the stem is reflexive). If there had been any occurrence of sexual violation, one would expect the idiom to say, "Ham uncovered his father's nakedness." Moreover, Rice observes that if Ham had committed incest with his mother, he would not likely have told his two brothers, nor would the Torah pass over such an inauspicious beginning for the detested Canaanites (see Gen. 19:30–38).[31]

So there is no clear evidence that Ham actually did anything other than see the nakedness of his uncovered father. To the writer of the narrative this was apparently serious enough to incur the oracle on Canaan (who might be openly guilty in their customs of what Ham had been suspected of doing).

It is difficult for someone living in the modern world to understand the modesty and discretion of privacy called for in ancient morality.[32] Nakedness in the Old Testament was from the beginning a thing of shame for fallen man. As a result of the Fall, the eyes of Adam and Eve were opened, and, knowing they were naked, they covered themselves. To them as sinners the state of nakedness was both undignified and vulnerable.[33] The covering of nakedness was a sound instinct for it provided a boundary for fallen human relations.

Nakedness thereafter represented the loss of human and social dignity. To be exposed meant to be unprotected; this can be seen by the fact that the horrors of the Exile are couched in the image of shameful nakedness (Hab. 3:13; Lam. 1:8; 4:21). To see someone uncovered was to bring dishonor and to gain advantage for potential exploitation.

By mentioning that Ham entered and saw his father's nakedness the text wishes to impress that seeing is the disgusting thing.[34] Ham's frivolous looking, a moral flaw, represents the first step in the abandonment of a moral code. Moreover this violation of a boundary destroyed the honor of Noah.

There seems to be a taboo in the Old Testament against such "looking" that suggests an overstepping of the set limits by identification with the object seen (Gen. 19:26; Ex. 33:20; Judg. 13:22; 1 Sam. 6:19). Ham desecrated a natural and sacred barrier by seeing his father's nakedness. His going out to tell his brothers about it without thinking to cover the naked man aggravated the unfilial act.[35]

Within the boundaries of honor, seeing the nakedness was considered shameful and impious. The action of Ham was an affront to the dignity of his father. It was a transgression of sexual morality against filial piety.[36] Because of this breach of domestic propriety, Ham could expect nothing less than the oracle against his own family honor.[37]

SHEM'S AND JAPHETH'S REVERENCE

Shem and Japheth acted to preserve the honor of their father by covering him with the garment (Gen. 9:23). The impression is that Ham completed the nakedness by bringing the garment out to his brothers.

The text is very careful to state that the brothers did not see their father's nakedness. Their approach was cautious, their backs turned to Noah with the garments on their shoulders. In contrast to the brevity of the narrative as a whole this verse draws out the story in great detail in order to dramatize their sensitivity and piety. The point cannot be missed—this is the antithesis of the hubris of Ham.

The Oracle (Gen. 9:24–27)

With the brief notice that Noah knew what his youngest son[30] had done to him, the narrative bridges the event and the oracle. The verb יָדַע would suggest either that Noah found out what had transpired or that he knew intuitively. Jacob suggests that "the different ways of his sons must have been known to him."[39] Certainly Noah knew enough to deliver the oracle, as Jacob much later had such knowledge about his sons (Gen. 49).

The essence of the oracle is the cursing of Canaan: "Cursed be Canaan! The lowest of slaves will he be to his brothers." Even when the blessings are declared for the brothers, the theme of Canaan's servitude is repeated both times.

The very idea of someone cursing another raises certain questions as to the nature of the activity. Scharbert points out that (a) the curse was the reaction of someone to the misbehavior of another in order to keep vigorously aloof from that one and his deed; (b) the one cursed was a subordinate who by the cursing would be removed from the community relationship in which he had enjoyed security, justice, and success; (c) the curse was no personal vendetta but was used to defend sacral, social, and national regulations and customs; and (d) the curse was effected by divine intervention.[40]

In the ancient world the curse was only as powerful as the one making it. Anyone could imprecate, but imprecation was the strongest when supernatural powers were invoked.[41] The Torah had no magical ideas such as sorcery and divination (Ex. 22:17–18). The curse found its way into Israel as part of an oath to protect its institutions. One who committed a serious transgression against covenant stipulations was delivered up to misfortune, the activation of which was Yahweh's (Deut. 28; Josh. 6:26; 1 Sam. 26:19).

So the curse was a means of seeing that the will of Yahweh was executed in divine judgment on anyone profaning what was sacred. It is an expression of faith in the just rule of God, for one who curses has no other resource. The word had no power in itself unless Yahweh performed it.[42] Thus it was in every sense an oracle. God Himself would place the ban on the individual, thus bringing about a paralysis of movement or other capabilities normally associated with a blessing.[43]

In this passage the honor of Noah and the sanctity of the family, one of God's earliest institutions, are treated lightly and in effect desecrated. Noah, the man of the earth, pronounced the oracle of cursing. It is right, and Yahweh would fulfill it.

The second part of verse 25 specifies the result of the curse— abject slavery. This meant certain subjugation, loss of freedom for autonomous rule, and reduction to bondage.[44] A victor in war would gain dominion over the subjugated people so that they might be used as he pleased. However, in the Old Testament slaves were to be treated favorably, protected by law, and even freed in the sabbatical year (Ex. 21:2, 20).

But Noah was not content to give a simple pronouncement of Canaan's slavery. By using the superlative genitive עֶבֶד עֲבָדִים ("servant of servants"), he declared that the one who is cursed is to be in the most abject slavery. Canaan would serve his "brothers" (normally understood to refer to Shem and Japheth since the main idea of the curse is repeated in the next lines).

The fact that Canaan, and not Ham, received the curse has prompted various explanations. Of course there are those, as already discussed, who posit separate traditions and see two distinct stories that were later fused into a single account. Others have found reason for excusing Ham on the basis of the blessing in 9:1. Not only would it be unusual for a person to curse what God had blessed, but also one would not normally curse his own son.[45] While this may partially explain Noah's choice, it cannot be the whole explanation.

Kidner sees the principle of talionic justice in the passage. For Ham's breach of family, his own family would falter and that through the youngest.[46] But is it right to curse one for the action of another?

The Torah does incorporate this measure-for-measure judgment from one generation to another, but in such cases the one judged is receiving what he deserves. A visitation of the sins of the fathers on later generations will be on those who hate Yahweh (Ex. 20:4). A later generation may be judged for the sin of an ancestor if they are of like mind and deed. Otherwise they may simply bear the fruit of some ancestor's sin.

It is unlikely that Canaan was picked out for cursing just because he was the youngest son of Ham. On the contrary, the Torah, which shows that God deals justly with all men, suggests that Noah saw in him the evil traits that marked his father Ham. The text has prepared the reader for this by twice pointing out that Ham was the father of Canaan. Even though the oracle would weigh heavily on Ham as he saw his family marred, it was directed to his descendants who retained the traits.

In this regard it must be clarified that Canaan the people, not the man, are in view for the fulfillment of the oracle. The names Canaan, Shem, and Japheth all represent the people who were considered their descendants. So by this extension the oracle predicts the curse on the Canaanites and is much wider than a son's being cursed for his father, although the oracle springs from that incident in the family. Therefore the oracle is a prophetic announcement concerning the future nations. To the Hebrew mind, the Canaanites were the most natural embodiment of Ham.[47] Everything they did in their pagan existence was symbolized in the attitude of Ham. From the moment the patriarchs entered the land, these tribes were there with their corrupting influence (Gen. 13:18; 15:16; 18:32; 19:38).

The Torah warned the people of the Exodus about the wickedness of the Canaanites in terms that call to mind the violation of Ham (Lev. 18:2–6). There follows a lengthy listing of such vile practices of the Canaanites (18:7–23) that the text must employ euphemisms to represent their deeds ("nakedness" alone is used 24 times). Because of these sins the Canaanites were defiled and were to be driven out before the Israelites.

The constant references to "nakedness" and "uncovering" and even "seeing" in this passage, designating the people of Canaan as a people enslaved sexually, clearly reminds the reader of the action of Ham, the father of Canaan. No Israelite who knew the culture of the Canaanites could read the story of their ancestor Canaan without making the connection. But these descendants of Ham had advanced far beyond his violation. The attitude that led to the deed of Ham came to full fruition in them.

Archaeology has graphically illustrated just how debased these people were. Bright writes, "Canaanite religion presents us with no pretty picture. . . . Numerous debasing practices, including sacred prostitution, homosexuality, and various orgiastic rites, were prevalent."[48] Wright and Filson add that "the amazing thing about the gods, as they were conceived in Canaan, is that they had no moral character whatever. In fact, their conduct was on a much lower level than that of society as a whole, if we can judge from ancient codes of law. . . . Worship of these gods carried with it some of the most demoralizing practices then in existence."[49] Albright appropriately adds to this observation.

> It was fortunate for the future of monotheism that the Israelites of the conquest were a wild folk, endowed with primitive energy and ruthless will to exist, since the resulting decimation of the Canaanites prevented the complete fusion of the two kindred folk which would almost inevitably have depressed Yahwistic standards to a point where recovery was impossible. Thus, the Canaanites, with their orgiastic nature worship, their cult of fertility in the form of serpent symbols and sensuous nudity, and their gross mythology, were replaced by Israel, with its nomadic simplicity and purity of life, its lofty monotheism, and its severe code of ethics.[50]

So the text is informing the reader that the Canaanite people, known for their shameless depravity in sexual matters and posing a continual threat to Israel's purity, found their actual and characteristic beginning in Ham. Yet these descendants were not cursed because of what Ham did; they were cursed because they acted exactly as their ancestor had. That moral abandon is fully developed in the Canaanites. The oracle announces the curse for this.

In actual fact Noah was supplicating God to deal with each group of people as they deserved, to the ancestor and descendants alike. Since this request was in harmony with God's will for the preservation of moral purity, He granted it.[51] If the request had not been in harmony, Noah's curse would have had no result.

Canaan, then, is the prototype of the population that succumbed to enervating influences and was doomed by its vices to enslavement at the hands of hardier and more virtuous races.[52] Because Ham, the "father" of Canaan, had desecrated the honor of his father by seeing his uncovered nakedness, this divine and prophetic oracle is pronounced on the people who would be known for their immorality in a shameful way, a trait discernible in this little story in the history of beginnings.

The blessing aspect is given to Shem, but the wording is unexpected: "Blessed be the LORD [Yahweh], the God of Shem." The emphasis on the possession of God by his name is strengthened in this line in a subtle way. Delitzsch says, "Yahweh makes Himself a name in becoming the God of Shem, and thus entwines His name with that of Shem, which means 'name.'"[53]

By blessing one's God, the man himself is blessed. The idea is that Shem will ascribe his good fortune to Yahweh his God, for his advantage is not personal merit; his portion is Yahweh.[54] The great line of blessing will be continued through Shem from Noah to Abram, the man of promise.

Here again, however, the point of the oracle looks to the descendants. It would then be clear to Israel, who found themselves in such a personal, covenantal relationship with Yahweh that they were the heirs of this blessing.

The announcement of Japheth's share in the blessing of Shem is strengthened by the play on his name "Japheth" (יֶפֶת) from the verb "to enlarge" (פָּתָה). Here too the descendants are in mind, for they would expand and spread out in the world. The second part of this verse is the resultant wish that Japheth would dwell in the tents of Shem. This is most likely an expression of the prospect of peaceful cohabitation.[55] Certainly the prospect of this unification is based on the harmony of the ancestors in the story. As a partner in covering up Noah, Japheth's descendants are granted alliance with Shem in the subjugation of Canaan.

The church fathers saw this as the first sign of the grafting in of the Gentiles in spiritual blessings, but later revelation speaks more of that. All that can be said of Genesis 9:27 in the oracle is that peaceful tenting of Japheth with Shem was a step toward that further ideal blessing.

The Epilogue (Gen. 9:28–29)

The narrative, as well as the תּוֹלְדוֹת, ends with verses 28 and 29 supplying the final note of the genealogy of Noah, the last name on the table of Genesis 5. A new תּוֹלְדוֹת begins in chapter 10.

The essential part of this narrative is most certainly the oracle, and the dominant feature of that oracle is the cursing of the Canaanites.[56] They are doomed to perpetual slavery because they followed in the moral abandon of their distant ancestor. Their subjugation would be contrasted by the blessing on the others: Shem has spiritual blessings by virtue of knowing Yahweh; Japheth has temporal blessings with the prospect of participation with Shem.

The curse narrative of Genesis 9 immediately precedes the listing of the families and their descendants in Genesis 10; if there were any question as to whom the narrator had in mind, the lines could be traced immediately.

Japheth, whose expansion was already anticipated in the oracle, represented the people who dominated the great northern frontier from the Aegean Sea to the highlands of Iran and northward to the steppes beyond the shores of the Black Sea. Those best known to the writer were the Hellenic peoples of the Aegean coastlands.[57]

Shem also is pictured as expanding, dwelling in tents. The oracle looks beyond the ancestor to his descendants, among whom were the Hebrews. It would be difficult to understand the narrator's assuming Yahweh to be covenanted with any other people. The possession of the blessing would be at the expense of the Canaanites whom Israel would subjugate, thus actualizing the oracle.

Canaan represents the tribes of the Canaanites who were considered to be ethnically related to the other Hamites, but were singled out for judgment because of their perverse activities. The curse announced that they would be enslaved by other tribes, a subjugation normally accomplished through warfare.

On the whole, this brief passage expresses the recoiling of Israelite morality at the licentious habits engendered by a civilization that through the enjoyment and abuse of wine had deteriorated into an orgiastic people to whom nothing was sacred. In telling the story, the writer stigmatizes the distasteful practices of these pagans.[58]

Being enslaved by their vices, the Canaanites were to be enslaved by others. This subjugation, effected through divine intervention, is just: the moral abandon of Ham ran its course in his descendants.

It is not possible to take the oracle as an etiology, answering the questions as to why the Canaanites had sunk so low, or why they were enslaved by others.[59] At no time in the history of Israel was there a complete subjugation of Canaan. Many cities were conquered, and at times Canaanites were enslaved, but Israel failed to accomplish her task. These Canaanites survived until the final colony at Carthage was destroyed in 146 B.C. by the Romans. So there was really no time in the history of Israel to fit a retrospective view demanded by an etiology.

Rather, the oracle states a futuristic view in broad, general terms. It is a sweeping oracle announcing in part and imprecating in part the fate of the families descending from these individuals. It is broad enough to include massive migrations of people in the second millennium as well as individual wars and later subjugations.

The intended realization, according to the design of the writer, would be the period of the conquest. Israel was called to conquer the Canaanites. At the same time as the Israelite wars against the Canaanites (down through the battle of Taanach), waves of Sea Peoples began to sweep through the land against the Hittites, Canaanites, and Egyptians. Neiman states, "The Greeks and the Israelites, willy-nilly, were allies against the Canaanites and the Hittites during the great world conflict which came down through the historical memory of many peoples by many different names."[60]

In their invasions these people from the north sought to annex the coastland territory and make homes for themselves. Israel felt herself in the strongest moral contrast to the Canaanites (as Shem had felt to Ham). Any help from the Japhethites would be welcomed. Such a spirit of tolerance toward the Gentiles would not have been possible in the later period of Israel's history. Thus the curse oracle would have originated at a time *before the Conquest*, when the Canaanites were still formidable enemies.

In all probability the event and its oracle were recorded to remind the Israelites of the nature and origin of the Canaanites, to warn them about such abominations, and to justify their subjugation and dispossession through holy warfare. Israel received the blessing, but Canaan received the curse.

CHAPTER 2

Saul and the Changing Will of God

J. Barton Payne

As affirmed by both creed and catechism, God is a Personal Spirit, infinite, eternal, and unchangeable in His being and attributes.[1] His divine Personality may then be appreciated as consisting of intellect, sensibility, and will. In reference to the third of these, "will" may be understood as that within God which puts into effect all that the two previous aspects of His Personality have designed.[2] Yet such divine will has become a subject of no little confusion, because of the various meanings with which the word can be employed. By "the will of God" one may designate His sovereignty: His kingly decision, efficaciously executed among the children of men, and thus free from all modification or change. But by His "will" we may also designate His preferences—His moral desires, as revealed to free men—or His subsequent responses to such men, whether of blessing or of penalty; and these latter obviously do change, in accord with the just deserts of those involved, indeed, because of the very unchangeability of His attributes! This article thus seeks to define, to apply, and to illustrate these distinctions as they appear in one of the problem passages of God's Word, namely, 1 Samuel 8–15, on Saul's rise to kingship over Israel.

Was it God's will for Israel to have a king? The inspired words of Scripture seem to point in two ways. On the one hand the prophet Samuel said, "Behold, the Lord has set a king over you" (1 Sam. 12:13; cf. 9:16; 10:1); but on the other, and only a few verses later, He reprimanded His people as follows: "Your wickedness is great . . . by asking for yourselves a king" (12:17). Liberal writers conclude that 1 Samuel must be composed of conflicting sources, and they speak of "the diametrically opposed attitude toward the monarchy in the two accounts of its origin."[3] Evangelicals, however, object not simply because such an approach discredits the validity of God's Word, but because its "easy way out" neglects some of Scripture's deeper teachings about the

26

complexity of God's will, both as it affected Saul and as it affects believers today.

Most fundamentally, the Bible states that the Lord "works all things after the counsel of His will" (Eph. 1:11). Man cannot change what God has determined (Eccl. 3:14; Jer. 5:22; Dan. 4:35).

This reality may be identified as the sovereign will of God or, as it is often styled in systematic theologies, His decretive will.[4] One rejoices, moreover, in the assurance it gives a believer. Jesus Himself explained how it applies to His flock: "They shall never perish. . . . My Father, who has given them me, is greater than all; and no one is able to snatch them out of the Father's hand" (John 10:28–29; Rom. 8:38–39). So too, Scripture speaks of God's eternal plan to send the Savior, whose "goings forth are from long ago, from the days of eternity," it identifies Him as the one who is "to be ruler in Israel" (Mic. 5:2). This means that a kingdom in Israel must also have been a part of God's changeless decree; in fact, prophecies dating back to Moses say that "a scepter shall rise from Israel" (Num. 24:17; cf. Gen. 49:10; Deut. 17:14), indicating that it *was* God's will for them to have a king.

Yet at the same time the Bible speaks of other categories within the will of God and of matters the Lord would like to see done but which may not actually come to pass. Such a divine desire appears in 2 Peter 3:9, which states that the Lord is "not wishing for any to perish but for all to come to repentance"; yet because of the power of choice that God has granted to men some do refuse to come (John 3:19–20; in contrast to nature, which must obey Him, Luke 8:25). When God's wish for men becomes concretely revealed in the form of precepts—which men may yet choose to violate— they are designated as the preceptive will of God. Moses, for example, in the passages just cited, laid down the need of recognizing God's kingship in the future kingdom of Israel (Num. 23:21; Gen. 49:18; Deut. 17:15–19); and he set before his people the option of choosing good or evil, with corresponding results, namely, of life or death (Deut. 30:15). Not that God would change His decree—the historical outcome was already settled (cf. 31:16– 21), though often one does not know what it is (29:29)—but that Israel, on the basis of its own responses, would experience appropriate judgments from God, whether of added blessings or of curses (30:16–18). Moses concluded by exhorting, "So choose life" (v. 19), even as Jesus now says, "Come to Me and . . . rest" (Matt. 11:28).

In the days of Samuel, Israel could have submitted to God's kingship; but they did not (1 Sam. 8:8). They chose rather to conform to the standards of their pagan neighbors (v. 5). One can only speculate about the added blessings, about that "perfect will of God," which Israel might have experienced had they remained faithful—God might have set up David, "the scepter . . . from Judah" (Gen. 49:10), without those tragically intervening events with which all are familiar. But one does know that it *was not* God's will for Israel to have a king in the way they were asking for it. Still, God's resultant precept, what His "permissive will" came to be, was to direct Samuel to anoint Saul as king out of the tribe of Benjamin (1 Sam. 8:22; 9:17). Three important distinctions are to be observed. (1) God changed His preceptive will, but only because people had changed (cf. 8:3–5). In fact, it was because God's standard of righteousness had not changed that His precept *had* to change (Gal. 6:7). (2) God performed the very act that people wanted; but while their motive was wrong and in this act they became guilty, God's motive was right and in the very same act He did not become guilty. In fact, He used this man Saul to punish the people (1 Sam. 8:18), so that while they got what they asked for, they also got what they deserved! (3) God was grieved over the nation's apostasy (v. 7); and their act called forth His divine love. In spite of the sin-inspired situation of Saul, and in fact through it, God ministered a number of deliverances (9:16; 10:9, 24; 11:13). Saul had thus been a part of God's decree from the first, and God used the wrath of men to praise Him (Ps. 76:10). History's supreme parallel is stated in Peter's Pentecost sermon to the Jews: "Jesus . . . [being] delivered up by the predetermined plan and foreknowledge of God, you nailed to a cross by the hands of godless men. . . . And God raised Him up again, putting an end to the agony of death" (Acts 2:22–24); and because He lives, believers shall live also.

Israel was thus given another opportunity to submit to God, though at this point the personal career of Saul and the national reaction of Israel exhibited differing patterns of response. Despite Samuel's warnings to both king and people about the results of continued disobedience (1 Sam. 12:15, 25), Saul decided not to carry out God's commands (15:11) and even lied about it (v. 13). God again felt grief and regret (v. 11)[5] but nevertheless He revealed a new precept: Samuel, who had once been instructed to anoint Saul, was now to tell him, "Because you have rejected the word of the Lord, He has also rejected you from being king" (v. 23). The change in God's will for the king is expressly attributed to Saul's own change. Furthermore, since this time the decision was God's, who is right, there could be no regret: "The Glory of Israel will not lie or change His mind; for He is not a man, that He should change His mind" (v. 29). So too in eternal matters, there can be no escape from condemnation for those who will not accept Christ's sacrificial ransom but who choose to face the judicial will of God, being yet in their sins (Mark 10:45; John 3:18).

When children of Israel were confronted by the reality of their apostasy and by the perseverance of the grace of God, who would not forsake His people (1 Sam. 12:22), they did confess their falsehood and did repent, greatly fearing the Lord and Samuel (v. 18). This is indeed why God had determined all things in the first place (Eccl. 3:14). Such a response of trust was honored by God, whose will was then to forgive and to reassure them (1 Sam. 12:20). This in turn produced what was right; for Samuel counseled them, "Only . . . serve Him in truth with all your heart; for consider what great things He has done for you" (v. 24). In a sense their subsequent life under Saul constituted but "God's second best"; yet this need not always be the case. Scripture describes the gospel truths of our redemption as "things into which angels long to look" (1 Peter 1:12), but this complex aspect of God's will seems to lie beyond them; for, after all, angels do not know the joy salvation brings.

CHAPTER 3

A Fresh Look at the Imprecatory Psalms

J. Carl Laney

Included in the Psalter are various psalms containing appeals for God to pour out His wrath on the psalmist's enemies. These psalms are commonly classified "imprecatory psalms" for the imprecation forms a chief element in the psalm. These psalms have been problematic for Bible teachers and preachers because of the difficulty in reconciling them with Christian thought. Barnes comments on this problem.

> . . . perhaps there is no part of the Bible that gives more perplexity and pain to its readers than this; perhaps nothing that constitutes a more plausible objection to the belief that the psalms are the productions of inspired men than the spirit of revenge which they sometimes seem to breathe and the spirit of cherished malice and implacableness which the writers seem to manifest.[1]

The purposes of this chapter are to define an "imprecation," identify the imprecatory psalms, pinpoint the problem that interpreters have with such psalms, recount proposed solutions to the difficulty, and present a suggested solution to this problem.

The Definition of Imprecation

An "imprecation" is an invocation of judgment, calamity, or curse uttered against one's enemies, or the enemies of God. The morning prayer of Moses was an imprecation that the enemies of Yahweh, who were Moses' enemies as well, would be scattered and flee from His presence (Num. 10:35). The Song of Deborah and Barak concludes with an imprecation that Yahweh's enemies might perish (Judg. 5:31). Jeremiah the prophet repeated imprecations against his enemies (Jer. 11:20; 15:15; 17:18; 18:21–23; 20:12). Such imprecations are not limited to the Old Testament, but are found in the New Testament as well (Rev. 6:9–10). Other portions of the New Testament are considered by some to contain

30

imprecations (Acts 13:10–11; 23:3; 1 Cor. 16:22; Gal. 1:8–9; 5:12; 2 Tim. 4:14), but while these verses contain a curse element, they do not have a specific prayer to the Lord that the judgment would be carried out.[2] Imprecations from the Psalms, however, are quoted in the New Testament (Acts 1:20; Pss. 69:25; 109:8). Crucial to the definition of an imprecation is that it (a) must be an invocation—a prayer or address to God, and (b) must contain a request that one's enemies or the enemies of Yahweh be judged and justly punished.

The Identification of the Imprecatory Psalms

While many imprecations are in the Book of Psalms,[3] it is evident that in some psalms the imprecations form the chief element. These "imprecatory psalms" have been said to contain "expressions calling for divine judgment to fall upon the Psalmist's enemy"[4] which would involve not only the enemy's personal destruction but also the overthrow of his family and the crushing of all hope for his future. Leupold states that the term "imprecatory psalms" is used to designate "those psalms in which the writer prays that God may afflict the evildoer and punish him according to his just deserts."[5] Harrison remarks that these psalms constitute "a reply to the national enemies" and a call to God "to exercise retribution."[6] In the imprecatory psalms the imprecation, instead of being a minor element, is greatly multiplied until it becomes a major element or leading feature. An imprecatory psalm, then, is one in which the imprecation is a major element or leading feature of the psalm.

Although opinion varies as to the number and identity of the imprecatory psalms, at least these nine may be included, based on the preceding definition: Psalms 7; 35; 58; 59; 69; 83; 109; 137; and 139. A reading of these psalms reveals that the imprecatory element is a leading feature of each psalm and is crucial to the psalmist's argument. All these imprecatory psalms are Davidic except for Psalm 83, which is attributed to Asaph, and Psalm 137, which is exilic.

The Problem with the Imprecatory Psalms

The basic problem with the imprecatory psalms is an ethical one. Vos asks, "How can it be right to wish or pray for the destruction or doom of others as is done in the Imprecatory Psalms? . . . Is it right for a Christian to use the Imprecatory

Psalms in the worship of God, and if so, in what sense can he make the Psalms his own?"[7] Beardslee also calls attention to the ethical problem of these psalms.

> In our private reading we can scarcely understand why they should find a place in a book otherwise so universally fitted to stimulate devotional life. In the public service of the church they are passed in silence by the preacher as having in them nothing calculated to educate and elevate the moral character of the people.[8]

The problem with the imprecatory psalms, or more correctly, the interpreter's problem with them, is how an apparent spirit of vengeance can be reconciled with the precepts of the New Testament and Jesus' command to "love your enemies, and pray for those who persecute you" (Matt. 5:44). Essentially three problems are confronted: (1) How can the presence of these imprecations in the Hebrew hymnal be explained? (2) Do they have application to the life and worship of Christians? (3) Can these heart cries for vengeance and retribution be as inspired as the other portions of the Book of Psalms which magnify and elevate God's character? Evangelicals must answer the second and third questions in the affirmative, and then begin to deal with the first question—the ethical or moral problem of the psalms of imprecation.

The Unsatisfactory Solutions

Many possible solutions to the problem of the imprecatory psalms have been formulated. A brief review and evaluation of some major suggestions is necessary before setting forth a fresh approach to dealing with the ethical problem.[9]

THE IMPRECATIONS BY DAVID'S ENEMIES

It has been suggested that the imprecations in Psalm 109:6–20 are not the utterance of David against his enemies, but are the fierce cursing of David's enemies against David himself.[10] To adhere to this solution one must insert the participle אָמַר ("saying") at the end of verse 5 so that the imprecation would appear to be sourced in the mouths of David's persecutors. Justification for this solution is based on the insertion of an implied participle in Psalm 2:2 in the Authorized Version to explain the quotation in 2:3 which obviously must be attributed to the psalmist's enemies.

However, this proposed solution is strained. The transition from verse 5 to verse 6 in Psalm 109 does not give any intimation that the words pass from David's prayer to an imprecation by his enemies, and the alleged "quotation" (vv. 6–20) is far longer than the single verse of Psalm 2. Also this solution would certainly not work in Psalms 7; 35; 58; 59; 69; 83; 137; or 139, where the imprecation is against a plurality of the psalmist's enemies. This view must therefore be rejected as an inadequate explanation.

THE EXPRESSION OF DAVID'S OWN SENTIMENTS

A second solution offered is that in these imprecations David is uttering the sentiments of his own heart and not those of the Holy Spirit. This view is taken by Kittel who considers the imprecatory psalms to have originated from mean-spirited individuals who thought only of conquest and revenge. The presence of these psalms in the Hebrew Psalter witnesses to the fact that at one time they were accredited to God.[11] The suggestion is made that if David had been a better man, he would not have uttered such perverse thoughts. This view, however, overlooks the biblical record of David's character as a man who did not indulge in a spirit of personal revenge (1 Sam. 24:1–7; 26:5). Also the New Testament reveals that David wrote the psalms under the personal and direct inspiration of the Holy Spirit ("who by the Holy Spirit, through the mouth of our father David Thy servant, didst say . . ." [Acts 4:25], and "men moved by the Holy Spirit spoke from God" [2 Peter 1:21]). To dissect a psalm or any portion of Scripture into inspired and uninspired sections is a fundamental error, and therefore an unacceptable solution to the problem of the imprecatory psalms.

THE INFERIOR PRINCIPLE OF SPIRITUAL LIFE IN THE OLD TESTAMENT

Still another view offered is that the inspiring principle underlying the spiritual life of the Old Testament differs from that of the New.[12] It is suggested that since David lived before the full light of the truth about spirituality, as developed in the New Testament, broad ethical teaching and practice should not be expected from him. However, while those in the present dispensation of grace do enjoy the benefits and spiritual life provided by the teachings of Jesus, the Mosaic Covenant did provide David with adequate guidelines for ethical conduct. Hatred for one's neighbors is forbidden in the Old Testament, as is vengeance (Deut. 32:35), while love is commanded (Lev. 19:17–

18). This solution to the problem of the imprecatory psalms is inadequate because it underestimates the Old Testament's provision of ethical guidelines. Christians do enjoy the benefits of progressive revelation, but that progress is not from error to truth; instead, it is a progression from incomplete revelation to a more full and complete revelation or divine disclosure.

THE IMPRECATIONS AGAINST DAVID'S SPIRITUAL FOES

It has also been suggested that the imprecatory psalms are the psalmist's *spiritual* antagonists rather than human personages. According to this view evil spiritual influences are personified as evil men. Mowinckel suggests that the imprecations in these psalms are curses uttered in the name of God who is a sure defense against the powers of darkness and is able to defy and overthrow the hosts of evil which stir themselves up against His servants.[13] This solution introduces an unfortunate subjectivity and indefiniteness to the meaning of the biblical language. How is one to determine when to make the transition from a literal to a spiritual interpretation of a particular passage? Also if the psalmist's enemies are evil principles and forces of darkness, it is strange that their families should be mentioned in Psalm 109. Many of the psalms were written in a time of oppression from enemies like Doeg the Edomite (Ps. 52:1; 1 Sam. 21:7) and Shimei (2 Sam. 16:5–8), and it is therefore difficult to believe that David would have had nonphysical enemies in mind.

THE IMPRECATIONS ARE PROPHETIC

Another proposed solution to the problem is that the imprecatory psalms are to be understood as prophetic. The psalmist was not only a poet, but was also a prophet declaring what would happen to the ungodly. This is one of the solutions offered by Barnes, and was held by Augustine, Calvin, and Spurgeon.[14] This view throws the responsibility for the imprecation on God, and thus relieves the psalmist from the charge of speaking out of a spirit of bitterness or revenge. It is pointed out by advocates of this view that the imprecations are quoted in the New Testament (Pss. 69:25 and 109:8 in Acts 1:20; and Ps. 69:22–23 in Rom. 11:9–10), and that therefore all the imprecations are prophetic. Against this view is the fact that the imperfect form of the verb is sometimes preceded by an imperative, in which case the imperfect form is translated as a jussive (Ps. 69:25–26).[15] The imprecation in such a case is not a simple declaration of what will happen, but is a wish or prayer that it may happen. In Psalm 137 the imprecation involves the third person in such a way as to show that the speaker is not simply uttering the divine will as a prophet, but is expressing his own feeling as a man. Psalm 137:8–9 is an expression of the personal satisfaction the psalmist will feel when judgment overtakes the wrongdoers.

THE HUMANITY OF THE PSALMIST

A recent view of Psalm 137 is that it simply expresses the full humanity of the psalmist who loved Zion but who hated his foes passionately. According to Bright, the psalmist is "God's wholly committed man, yet a man who is estranged from God's spirit."[16] Bright asserts that the psalm must not be read and received as God's Word for today in and of itself, but that it must be read in light of the gospel. The psalmist expresses a conclusion which is "unworthy and sub-Christian," but he records the frustration of the whole man who must be confronted by Christ. The psalmist's thoughts are not approved, but are understood to be an expression of humanity's need for Christ. While Bright deals only with Psalm 137, presumably he would also apply this principle of interpretation to the other imprecatory psalms. While this view does offer an application of these psalms to Christians, it does not adequately explain the inspiration of Psalm 137 and the reason for its inclusion in the Psalter. This view appears to deny the divine authorship of the imprecatory psalms in an arbitrary attempt to distinguish between the expression of humanity and the expression of the Spirit. Such a dichotomy fails to grasp the unity of the divine and human authors of Scripture (cf. Acts 4:25).

Steps Toward a Satisfactory Solution

Having investigated several unsatisfactory solutions to the ethical problem of the imprecatory psalms, several factors toward a satisfactory solution may now be considered.

THE PURPOSES OF THE IMPRECATIONS

An awareness of the ethical and revelational purposes of the imprecatory judgments will enable one to understand better the imprecatory psalms. Six purposes are evident.

1. One major purpose of the judgments against evildoers is to establish the righteous. As God judges the wicked, He

is also invoked to establish the righteous (Ps. 7:8–9). A concern for righteousness and the righteous is foundational to the imprecation found in Psalm 7:6–11.

2. A second purpose of the imprecatory judgments is that God may be praised when the psalmist is delivered (Pss. 7:17; 35:18, 28). Closely related to this is the anticipation of rejoicing when the psalmist sees the vindication taking place (58:10).

3. A third purpose in requesting judgment against the wicked is that men will see the reward of the righteous and recognize that it is God who judges the earth (58:11). Both the righteous and the wicked will know that God is concerned with justice and that He executes judgment on the earth.

4. The imprecatory judgments are also designed to demonstrate to everyone that God is sovereign. David prayed that his enemies would be destroyed so that men from the ends of the earth may know that God rules in Jacob (59:13).

5. A fifth purpose of the imprecatory judgments is to prevent the wicked from enjoying the same blessings as the righteous. David prays that those who persist in wickedness may be blotted out of the book of life (the register of the living), that is, may be judged by physical death (69:28).

6. A sixth purpose of the imprecatory judgments is to cause the wicked to seek the Lord. Asaph prays that God would judge and humiliate His enemies so that they would seek His name and acknowledge Him as the sovereign God (83:16–18).

These purposes of the imprecations give a divine perspective to the seemingly human cries for judgment. It would appear that the high ethical and revelational purposes of the imprecatory psalms clear them of the charge of being sourced in the bitter spirit of a bloodthirsty, carnal man.

THE COVENANTAL BASIS FOR A CURSE ON ISRAEL'S ENEMIES

The fundamental ground on which one may justify the imprecations in the Psalms is the covenantal basis for a curse on

Israel's enemies. The Abrahamic Covenant (Gen. 12:1–3) promised blessing on those who bless Abraham's posterity, and cursing (אָרַר) on those who curse (קָלַל) Abraham's posterity. Because of the unconditional nature of the covenant, its promises and provisions remain in force throughout Israel's existence as a nation. Balaam is an example of one who received judgment for cursing Israel (Num. 22–24; 31:16). Actually Balaam was unable to curse Israel, and he fell under God's judgment because of his attack on Israel by undermining the spiritual life of the nation (31:8). All the Midianites except for the little ones and the virgin girls were slain because of their part in the attack against the spiritual life of Israel (31:1–18). Truly those who had cursed were cursed!

On the basis of the unconditional Abrahamic Covenant, David had a perfect right, as the representative of the nation, to pray that God would effect what He had promised—cursing on those who cursed or attacked Israel. David's enemies were a great threat to the well-being of Israel! The cries for judgment in the imprecatory psalms are appeals for Yahweh to carry out His judgment against those who would curse the nation—judgment in accord with the provisions of the Abrahamic Covenant.

THE ATTITUDE OF THE IMPRECATOR

The attitude of the psalmist is a key consideration in seeking to interpret and appreciate the imprecatory psalms. While the psalmist might appear to be a bloodthirsty and vindictive avenger, a closer examination demonstrates that this is not the case. Four significant points must be taken into consideration.

1. It is significant that David never prayed that he may be permitted to take vengeance on his enemies, but always that God would become his avenger. David's prayer was always that Yahweh would rise against his adversaries (Pss. 7:6; 35:1; 58:6; 59:5) and overthrow, smite, and destroy as the psalmist's own Avenger. The power and right to avenge belonged to God (Deut. 32:35), and David, realizing that a crisis had come, simply requested that God use judgmental retribution for His own glory and for the deliverance of His servant.

2. It is also important to distinguish between "vindication" and "vindictiveness." The psalmist's passion was for justice, and the imprecatory psalms are not sourced in per-

sonal vindictiveness or bitter malice that seeks revenge. David was capable of generosity under personal attack (2 Sam. 16:11; 19:16–23), yet no ruler was more deeply stirred to anger by unscrupulous actions, even when they appeared to favor his cause. What David pleaded for in his imprecations was that justice be done and that right be vindicated. He simply asked for the judgmental intervention which any victim of injustice deserved. David's concern was for vindication—justice—a concern which also the New Testament upholds (e.g., Luke 18:1–8).

3. David's concept of kingship sheds considerable light on the attitude of the imprecator. The king of Israel was God's chosen man (Deut. 17:15), sitting on an earthly throne as God's representative. David had great respect for the anointed king and refused to stretch forth his hand against Yahweh's anointed (1 Sam. 24:10; 26:11). To have done so would have been not only treason but also utter sacrilege and disregard for the theocratic office. When the office of king was conferred on David, he then regarded himself and everything that concerned him in light of his official relationship to God and the theocratic government. As the representative of God to the people, an attack on the king—the theocratic official—differed in no way from an attack on Yahweh! David saw attacks against him as attacks on the name of Yahweh. He thus prayed for the destruction of the wicked, not out of personal revenge, but out of his zeal for God and His kingdom.

4. It is also helpful to see that the imprecations in the Book of Psalms reflect an Old Testament saint's abhorrence of sin and evil. Those against whom the imprecations were directed were not the private enemies of David, but those who opposed God and His cause. Divine judgment was called down on those who were the very incarnation of wickedness. David's heart was sensitive to sin (Pss. 51:3, 9; 139:23–24), and out of his abhorrence for sin and evil he appealed to God for justice and the execution of judgment on the wicked.

Conclusion

The imprecatory psalms present to the Bible student the problem of reconciling the apparent spirit of vengeance with the precepts of the New Testament and the teachings of Jesus. The key to solving this ethical problem is to understand that the imprecations are grounded in the Abrahamic Covenant (Gen. 12:1–3), in which God promised to curse those who cursed Abraham's descendants. The psalmist, then, merely appealed for God to fulfill His covenant promise to Israel. It is also helpful to note that the imprecations were motivated by a desire to promote righteousness (Ps. 7:6–11), to demonstrate God's sovereignty (58:11; 59:13), to cause the wicked to seek the Lord (83:16–18), and to provide an opportunity for the righteous to praise God (7:17; 35:18, 28). Therefore out of zeal for God and abhorrence of sin the psalmist called on God to punish the wicked and to vindicate His righteousness.

In light of the fact that the Abrahamic Covenant reflects God's promise to Abraham and his descendants, it would be inappropriate for a Church-Age believer to call down God's judgment on the wicked. One can appreciate the Old Testament setting of the imprecatory psalms and teach and preach from them. However, like the ceremonial dietary laws of the Old Testament, the imprecations in the Psalms should not be applied to Church-Age saints. This is clear from Paul's exhortation in Romans 12:14, "Bless those who persecute you; bless and curse not." Paul admonished the Romans, "Never take your own revenge, beloved, but leave room for the wrath of God, for it is written, 'Vengeance is Mine, I will repay, says the Lord'" (12:19). Paul's words in 2 Timothy 4:14 indicate that he practiced what he preached. Rather than calling down divine wrath on Alexander the coppersmith, Paul simply stated, "The Lord will repay him according to his deeds." And John made it clear that God in the future will judge the wicked for their sin (Rev. 20:11–15).

CHAPTER 4

Structure, Style, and the Prophetic Message: An Analysis of Isaiah 5:8–30

Robert B. Chisholm, Jr.

I n her final, unforgettable adventure in Wonderland, Alice appeared as a witness at the trial of an unfortunate knave accused of stealing the queen's tarts. After listening to the White Rabbit present some cryptic, nonsensical verses as evidence against the defendant, Alice in exasperation challenged the jurors, "If any one of them can explain it, I'll give him sixpence. I don't believe there's an atom of meaning in it." In moments of absolute honesty every would-be interpreter of the Old Testament prophets, when confronted by their all-too-often impenetrable messages, has uttered words similar to those of Alice.

Why are these prophetic messages so difficult to comprehend? Often the reason is the major barrier the interpreter faces, the immense distance (chronological, geographical, cultural, and linguistic) that separates him from the prophetic author. Due to modern advances in textual criticism, philology, and archaeology, however, one is often able to cross the expanse. Yet even when this long, arduous journey is successfully completed, problems sometimes remain. Frequently the prophetic message defies attempts to discern its organizing principle(s) and summarize its theological theme(s). On occasion the prophet's words seem to be a disorganized collection of unrelated themes. To make matters worse, the prophets did not always express their ideas in straightforward, propositional statements. In fact their highly poetic, impassioned style frustrates efforts to theologize their messages.

Fortunately the situation is not as bleak as it seems. As the recent trend toward literary study of the Bible gains impetus,[1] significant breakthroughs in the understanding of Scripture are taking place. In particular, studies in the prophets are revealing that the prophetic messages are organized in a highly artistic manner. The force of the messages and their theological themes are linked to and at times veiled within their structure and style. As more is learned about the literary structures and rhetorical devices employed by the prophets, understanding of and appreciation for their profound messages grow. Even in texts whose organization and meaning have been reasonably clear for some time, this new emphasis is bringing greater precision and sophistication to interpretation.

The Method

Many scholars call this study of structure and style rhetorical criticism. However, proponents of this approach have yet to achieve unanimity in defining the discipline and outlining its method.[2] For some, rhetorical criticism is a rather loosely defined, all-encompassing analysis of a text's structure(s) and stylistic devices.[3] Others propose a more restricted definition and apply the categories of classical rhetoric to the biblical text.[4] Despite these differences in approach, it is possible to arrive at a basic working definition of biblical rhetorical criticism. Understanding "rhetoric" as "the art of speaking or writing effectively" one may define rhetorical criticism as "the study of a speaker's/author's communicative technique." Rhetorical criticism studies the dynamics of the author's/speaker's relationship to his audience via his message. It examines how the author/speaker has organized (structure) and expressed (style) his message in order to achieve maximum effectiveness in light of his purpose.

Some might object to applying the term "rhetoric" to the biblical message for at least two reasons. First, the word frequently has negative connotations in today's culture. "Rhetoric" makes one think of campaign speeches and political demagoguery. Second, "rhetoric" is usually associated with oral presentations. Since the Bible is a collection of *writings* in book form, the term "rhetoric" seems inapplicable.

Both of these objections are invalid. While the term does have a specialized meaning that conveys a negative idea, it can also carry the more general, neutral sense defined above. Also the term may be applied legitimately to written texts.[5] Even more importantly, one must recognize that the Bible, in the context in which it originated, was primarily intended to be read aloud.

Before the invention of printing, it was impossible for copies of texts to be widely distributed. Consequently public readings of texts were the normal means of dissemination. One presupposes that texts would be composed with this form of communication in mind. This built-in oral orientation should leave no doubt that the biblical texts are valid objects of rhetorical analysis.[6]

Biblical rhetorical criticism has built on the foundation of form criticism. Despite the great value of form criticism,[7] especially in its identification of typical structural patterns in biblical texts, it has proven inadequate. Many have become dissatisfied with its inflexibility, overemphasis on the typical, and tendency to fragmentize texts.[8] Rhetorical criticism moves "beyond" form criticism in that it gives attention to a text's individuality and unique structural elements and focuses on the unity of the text in its present form. Its concern for stylistic devices takes it far beyond the scope of form criticism.

This brief study employs rhetorical criticism in analyzing Isaiah 5:8–30.[9] The purposes are (a) to illustrate the types of observations a rhetorical approach might include and (b) to demonstrate the benefits of such an approach to the interpretive-theological process. The study is intended to be illustrative and provocative, not exhaustive or methodologically definitive. A thorough rhetorical study of the passage would need to include an application of classical categories and a detailed treatment of figures of speech, both of which are beyond the scope of this study.

Isaiah 5:8–30: Audience and Purpose

The rhetorical situation or context of Isaiah 5:8–30 must first be determined. Several factors complicate this task. While the broad outlines of Isaiah's time are known, it is impossible to date this particular message precisely. The internal evidence of the prophecy indicates that Isaiah's purpose was to convince the sinful people of Judah that divine judgment was both necessary and certain. There appears to be no intent to motivate repentance. The prophet's role was to condemn sin and announce divine vengeance. An examination of Isaiah's commission at the time of his call (Isa. 6:9–13) supports this conclusion.

One cannot limit the scope of Isaiah's message, however, to the sinful audience in the prophecy or to the context in which it was initially proclaimed. A righteous remnant also became recipients of the message (cf. Isa. 3:10; 6:13b). For them the message was a reminder of the Lord's demand for covenant fidelity and a motivation to continued faithfulness (cf. 8:11–17). The prophecy's heavy emphasis on divine justice possibly even encouraged this group. If evildoers were punished in an appropriate manner, then the righteous could expect an appropriate reward from the divine Judge (cf. 3:10–11). The remnant would have interpreted the coming judgment as the first stage in the divine program of renewal and restoration (cf. 1:21–31).

Once the prophecy is viewed in the larger context of chapters 1–12, the major theme of which is restoration through judgment, this positive emphasis is apparent as well. In this canonical context Isaiah 5:8–30 became a warning to all who heard or read it that only the faithful will participate in the Golden Age to come.[10]

The Structure of Isaiah 5:8–30

FORM CRITICISM

One is immediately struck by the sixfold use of הוֹי (translated "woe" in the NIV and NASB) in verses 8–22. Its repetition suggests its function as a structural device. Most commentators, following this lead, have divided verses 8–24 into six individual units, each introduced by הוֹי.[11] Form critics, who have isolated the הוֹי (or "woe") oracle as a distinct prophetic speech form with a specific *Sitz im Leben*, usually support this arrangement.[12]

From a form-critical standpoint this outline is acceptable but inadequate. A more basic formal pattern, the judgment speech, into which the הוֹי pattern fits, is discernible. Westermann has shown that the prophetic הוֹי oracle is a subcategory or variant of the judgment speech.[13] The basic components of the judgment speech are an accusation and an announcement of judgment.[14] In the הוֹי type, the vocative of address following the interjection often contains, at least in part, the accusation. As will be seen, הוֹי itself suggests impending doom, but often a more developed announcement will appear.

At first glance verses 8–30 fit incompletely into the judgment speech pattern. Only the first, second, and sixth woe oracles follow the accusation-announcement scheme.[15] The pattern appears to break down in verses 18–21. Woes 3–5 (vv. 18–21) are only accusatory; in each case no announcement of judgment intervenes before the following הוֹי oracle. Form critics explain this inconsistency in various ways. For example, Clements maintains that the expected announcements have fallen out in the course of transmission.[16] Kaiser, on the other hand, regards the announcements attached to the other woes as later additions.[17]

Once certain rhetorical features are recognized in verses 18–30, the apparent breakdown in the judgment speech pattern can be explained without resorting to such explanations. If one combines woes 3–6 (vv. 18–23), they constitute a lengthy accusation, to which verses 24–30 (v. 24b being an exception) form the concluding announcement. The clustering of woes with no intervening announcements has the rhetorical effect of heightening the accusatory tone of the section. The sequence of four הוֹי pronouncements delivered in rapid succession leaves one overwhelmed by and thoroughly convinced of the people's guilt. Thus rhetorical design led the author to depart from the usual formal pattern involving הוֹי. Nevertheless the typical judgment speech pattern was preserved.

This heightening or intensifying effect actually characterizes the entire passage as illustrated by the following form-critical outline of verses 8–30:

Section	Woe(s)	Accusation	Announcement
I	1	v. 8	vv. 9–10
II	2	vv. 11–12	vv. 13–17
III	3–6	vv. 18–23, 24b	vv. 24a, 25–30

The accusations increase in length from 2 lines of Hebrew text in I (following the arrangement in the *Biblia Hebraica Stuttgartensia*) to 4 (in II) to 10 (III). Likewise, the announcements of judgment increase in length from 3 lines (I) to 7 (II) to 15 (III). Consequently the three major sections as a whole increase from 5 lines (I) to 11 (II) to 25 (III). Through this snowballing effect the reader/listener becomes increasingly impressed by two facts: The people are indeed guilty, and their judgment is certainly impending.

"BEYOND" FORM CRITICISM

The form-critical approach above, even though supplemented by rhetorical considerations, fails to reflect all the structural artistry of Isaiah 5:8–30. A more thorough rhetorical analysis yields the following outline, which fits into the form-critical framework presented above, but also reflects a chiastic pattern within the larger unit:[18]

(I)   A   Accusation: social injustice (v. 8)
       *   Announcement of judgment (vv. 9–10)
(II)   B   Accusation: carousing (vv. 11–12a)
                   C   Accusation: failure to recognize the Lord's
                        work (v. 12b)
       *   Announcement of judgment (vv. 13–17)
(III)   C'   Accusation: failure to recognize the Lord's
                        work (vv. 18–21)
             B'   Accusation: carousing (v. 22)
       A'   Accusation: social injustice (v. 23)
       *   Announcement of judgment (vv. 24–30)

This outline reflects the chiastic arrangement of the individual elements in the three accusatory sections.[19] Two related examples of social injustice are condemned in verses 8 and 23. The condemnation of accumulation of properties (v. 8) is not a general criticism of real estate endeavor. Rather, economic exploitation (cf. Mic. 2:1–2), though under the guise of pseudolegality, is in view. As Kaiser states, greedy landowners were "taking advantage of the distress of small farmers and craftsmen which may have been caused by sickness, crop-failure, inflation, or excessive taxation." He explains, "Such people would be offered a loan; and if they were unable to pay it back at a later date, their movable possessions would be pawned, their children would be taken in payment and thus be made slaves, and finally their house and land would be seized."[20] This self-seeking and cruel practice reduced a large segment of the population to a level of inescapable poverty and represented a blatant practical denial of the covenantal principle that the Lord alone owns the land (cf. Lev. 25:23).[21] The legal corruption described in Isaiah 5:23 was one of the means whereby these wealthy individuals accomplished their purposes.[22]

Verses 11–12a and 22 contain accusations against those who lived only to carouse. From sunrise to sunset their time was spent in revelry. This group included the wealthy upper crust referred to in verse 8. They had both the time and the means to sustain such a lifestyle (cf. Amos 4:1; 6:1–7).

Insensivity to the Lord's purposes is condemned in Isaiah 5:12b, 18–21. The references to the Lord's "work" in verses 12 and 19 (מַעֲשֵׂה—probably the impending judgment He had threatened through His prophet; cf. 10:12; 28:21–22)—tie the two sections together. The arrogant (5:21) perverters of all proper ethical standards (vv. 18, 20) failed to recognize the Lord's approaching "work" (v. 12b). In fact, in mockery they urged Him to bring it to pass quickly (v. 19).

A closer examination of the substructure of verses 11–17 reveals two more chiastic patterns. In verses 11–12 carousing and insensitivity to the Lord's work are condemned, respectively. In the announcement of judgment in verse 13 these are taken up in reverse order. Insensitivity would be punished by exile (v. 13a) and the carousers would die, appropriately, of hunger and thirst (v. 13b).[23] The chiasmus can be outlined as follows:

A Carousing condemned (vv. 11–12a)
   B Insensitivity condemned (v. 12b)
   B' Insensitivity punished (v. 13a)
A' Carousing punished (v. 13b)

The judgment announcement in verse 13 is expanded in verses 14–17.[24] The carousers, besides dying of hunger and thirst, would themselves become the main course at another banquet—Sheol's.[25] Death, personified as a devouring enemy, was about to open its mouth wide and swallow up the revelers (v. 14).[26] At that time proud men would be abased (v. 15) as the Lord exalted Himself (v. 16). Thematically verses 15–16 present two sides of the same coin, a fact highlighted by the repetition of the root גבה (cf. גְּבֹהִים in v. 15 and וַיִּגְבַּה in v. 16). The "eating" motif, used in verse 14, reappears in verse 17. Following the disappearance of the carousers, only sheep[27] would be left to graze on the ruins of the wealthy.[28] Once more a chiastic arrangement is apparent:

A Sheol *eats* the sinners (v. 14)
   B The self-*exalting* sinners are humbled (v. 15)
   B' God *exalts* Himself (v. 16)
A' Sheep *eat* on the ruins of the sinners' dwellings (v. 17)

The placement of verses 15–16 in the middle of this chiasmus is significant. The theme expressed in these verses is the dominant one for verses 8–30, namely, that the sovereign Lord was about to exalt Himself through His just judgment of arrogant rebels against His covenant. The announcement of judgment (vv. 13–17), which provides the context for verses 15–16, is the second of three in verses 8–30 and is therefore central to the overall structure of the passage. Thus the central place of verses 15–16 in the structure of this particular announcement highlights their thematic centrality in the passage. This is an example of form contributing in a significant way to the force and emphasis of the prophetic message.

The structure and function of verses 24–30 require special attention, Verse 24a contains an announcement of judgment (cf. the introductory לָכֵן) complementing the accusation of verses 18–23. However, in verse 24b there is a movement back to accusation (cf. the introductory כִּי). One gets the impression that verse 24b is designed to summarize and conclude the preceding message by clearly identifying the essence of Israel's sin (breach of covenant). Consequently verses 25–30 seem to be a rather awkward appendix or addition. Indeed many commentators regard verses 25–30 as a misplaced intrusion that really belongs with 9:8–21.[29] However, the matter is not that simple. Once again rhetorical considerations prove to be instructive.

The expansion of the announcement of judgment in 5:25–30 has an important rhetorical function in the development of the message. It was simply impossible for Isaiah to terminate his message with a reference to Judah's sin (v. 24b). Throughout the preceding context the movement has been from sin to judgment. The prophet emphasized that Judah's sin demanded and would receive appropriate punishment. A return to the reason for judgment (v. 24b) also required a return to the announcement of that judgment. The nature of the accusation in verse 24b, by which the essence of Judah's sin is exposed, demands an announcement of judgment that is commensurate with the transgression. The detailed and terrifying picture drawn in verses 25–30 satisfies this demand.

Also the brief announcement of verse 24a fails to bring to an appropriate conclusion the developing intensity that the prophet has created, especially through his heaping of the woes in verses 18–23. Something more is needed, a fact to which the text itself testifies in verse 25b. The expansion of the judgment announcement in verses 25–30 brings the developing pattern of the preceding verses to a powerful culmination. These final verses demonstrate beyond all doubt that justice would indeed be carried out in a most tangible way on the violators of the covenant.

Stylistic Devices in Isaiah 5:8–30

IRONY AND POETIC JUSTICE

The prophet employed several stylistic devices that contribute to the effectiveness of his message. Particularly prominent is his use of irony to express the theme of poetic justice.

Irony is present in each of the accusation-announcement cycles. Verses 9–10 describe the judgment about to come on the rich landowners of verse 8. Appropriately those who added "house to house" would see those same houses destroyed and left uninhabited. The fields they accumulated would yield only a fraction of their potential.[30] According to verse 13, the carousers described in verses 11–12 would die, ironically, of hunger and thirst. Even more appropriately, they were to become the main course at Sheol's banquet (v. 14), with only sheep being left to inhabit the banqueting halls (now in ruins) the carousers once frequented (v. 17). Verses 26–30 describe in vivid detail how the "warriors" of verse 22 (note גִּבּוֹרִים and אַנְשֵׁי־חַיִל), whose skill was solely in the area of mixing drinks, would be overwhelmed by true warriors, armed with all the destructive implements of warfare.

In this third cycle (vv. 18–30) word repetition contributes powerfully to the theme of poetic justice. In verse 19 the proud rebels challenge the Lord to hasten His work (cf. יְמַהֵר). They mockingly called for the plan of the Lord to come (cf. וְתָבוֹאָה). According to verses 24–30 this work of judgment would indeed come hurriedly, in the form of the mighty Assyrian army. Appropriately the same roots employed in verse 19 are used in verse 26 to describe the Assyrians' swift approach (cf. יָבוֹא מְהֵרָה קַל). The proud rebels would get just what they scoffingly requested.[31]

Another example of wordplay involves the use of חֹשֶׁךְ, "darkness," and אוֹר, "light," in verses 20 and 30. In the former verse the rebels' perversion of moral and ethical standards is compared to turning darkness into light and light into darkness. Darkness and light correspond to evil and good mentioned in the preceding line. According to verse 30 the "darkness" produced by the clouds of judgment would sweep over the sinners' land, blotting out the "light" (cf. esp. וְאוֹר חָשַׁךְ). While חֹשֶׁךְ and אוֹר are used in different senses in verses 20 and 30, the repetition of the words is essential to the overriding theme of the judgment announcement, namely, that the coming judgment would be appropriate for the crime committed. Those who had brought "darkness" to the moral/ethical realm would find their sphere of sinful activity "darkened" by God's judgment.

הוֹי AND AN APPROACHING FUNERAL

By addressing the Judean sinners with הוֹי, the prophet compared them, by implication, to a dead man. While the background of the woe oracle has been debated by form critics, it is likely that if originated in the funeral lament.[32] In several passages הוֹי introduces a mourning cry. For example the old prophet lamented the death of the Judean man of God with the words הוֹי אָחִי, "Oh, my brother" (1 Kings 13:30).[33] Thus when the prophets prefaced their judgment speeches with הוֹי, they were suggesting that the sinners' demise was so certain that their death could be lamented proleptically.[34] Rhetorically this would have been a powerful device.[35] The prophet was figuratively acting out their funeral before their very eyes, reminding them in the process of the reasons for and manner of their death.

A WORD PICTURE OF THE ASSYRIAN ARMY

A vivid, detailed description, or word picture,[36] of the invading Assyrian army (vv. 26–30) brings this prophecy to a powerful, terrifying climax. The fact that the campaign originated with the Lord (v. 26a; cf. 7:18–20) spells doom for Judah. The foreignness of the enemy (5:26a) creates an ominous atmosphere,[37] especially in light of the covenant curse of Deuteronomy 28:49, to which the prophet may have been alluding.[38] The army's approach is swift and unswerving (Isa. 5:26b–27). Its seemingly superhuman warriors (v. 27a) never rest (v. 27b). They are prepared for battle and equipped with the best of weapons (v. 28a). The Assyrians' horses gallop along without injury, while their chariots race toward their objective (v. 28b).[39] The invaders are comparable to a vicious, roaring lion that allows its prey no escape (v. 29). The deafening Assyrian roar is accomplished by the descent of the dark clouds of judgment (v. 30).

This preview of the forthcoming Assyrian invasion is immensely effective from a rhetorical standpoint. Invincible armies, roaring uncaged lions (cf. Amos 3:8), and ominous storm clouds are inherently fear-provoking. Also Isaiah's audience was certainly familiar with Assyria's military might, if not by firsthand experience, then by oral accounts of earlier or contemporary campaigns against neighboring states.[40]

The language used in Isaiah 5:29–30 resembles that employed by Assyrian kings contemporary with Isaiah to describe their military prowess and accomplishments. The comparison to lions was quite common. For example Sargon described his valor as follows, "In the anger of my heart I mustered the masses of Assur's troops and, raging like a lion, I set my face to conquer those lands."[41] The references to roaring (vv. 29–30) may allude to the king's powerful battle cry, a motif that appears as well in Assyrian battle accounts. Sennacherib recalled, "I raised my voice, rumbling like a storm. Like Adad I roared."[42] On the other hand, Clements suggests that the roaring metaphor "makes allusion to the general noise and din of an army."[43] Sargon described a siege as follows: "Over that city I made the loud noise of my army resound like Adad, and the inhabitants . . . his people, the old men and old women, went up on the roofs of their houses and wept bitterly."[44] The darkness motif (v. 30b) may allude to the invading forces sweeping over the land. Sargon described an invasion in similar terms: "As with a dense cloud of the night, I covered that province, and all of its great cities."[45]

Of what significance are these points of contact between Isaiah's description and that of the Assyrians? Since the motifs are conventional in nature and widespread, in both biblical and other ancient Near Eastern literature, the similarity may be purely coincidental. In this case, both Isaiah and the authors of the Assyrian annals drew on a common stock of conventional ancient Near Eastern warrior imagery. However, it is possible that Isaiah was familiar with Assyrian propaganda and purposely described the Assyrian army in Assyrian terms.[46] If the Judean populace, at least to some extent, was also aware of this propaganda, the rhetorical effect of Isaiah's description would have been greatly enhanced.

Conclusion

A form critical and rhetorical approach to the structure of Isaiah 5:8–30 enables one to move beyond a simplistic outline of the text (based on the succession of "woes") and reveals several overlapping structures that testify to the author's literary and rhetorical artistry. The overall structure of the message contributes to its rhetorical force and highlights its central theme (cf. vv. 15–16). Several literary devices enhance the power of the message and emphasize its themes. Especially noteworthy is the use of irony and word repetition to express the theme of poetic justice. In this way one gains greater insight into the character of the coming judgment and of the Judge Himself.

CHAPTER 5

The Virgin Birth in the Old Testament and Isaiah 7:14

Charles Lee Feinberg

No student of the Old Testament need apologize for a treatment of Isaiah 7:14 in relation to the doctrine of the virgin birth of the Lord Jesus Christ. From earliest times to the present the discussions that have centered about this theme have been interesting, varied, and at times even heated. Lindblom characterizes Isaiah 7:14 as "the endlessly discussed passage of the Immanuel sign."[1] Rawlinson maintains:

> Few prophecies have been the subject of so much controversy, or called forth such a variety of exegesis, as this prophecy of Immanuel. Rosenmueller gives a list of twenty-eight authors who have written dissertations on it, and himself adds a twenty-ninth. Yet the subject is far from being exhausted.[2]

Barnes emphasizes the obscurity of the passage: "Who this virgin was, and what is the precise meaning of this prediction, has given, perhaps, more perplexity to commentators than almost any other portion of the Bible."[3] Again, he insists, "Perhaps there is no prophecy in the Old Testament on which more has been written, and which has produced more perplexity among commentators than this. And after all, it still remains, in many respects, very obscure."[4] Skinner seeks in a general way to pinpoint the source of the difficulties. He states,

> Probably no single passage of the Old Testament has been so variously interpreted or has given rise to so much controversy as the prophecy contained in these verses. The difficulties arise mainly from the fact that while the terms of the prediction are so indefinite as to admit a wide range of possibilities, we have no record of its actual fulfillment in any contemporary event.[5]

In view of these statements concerning the difficulties in the passage, one may scarcely expect unanimity among either liberals or conservatives in theology.

The logical point at which the investigation should be initiated is a careful treatment of the immediate context. In the reign of Ahaz, king of Judah,[6] a coalition was formed between Rezin, king of Syria, and Pekah, king of Israel, against Ahaz. Their avowed objective (Isa. 7:5–6) was the dethronement of Ahaz and the setting up in his place of a Syrian pretender, a vassal king, Tabeal. When the fact of the confederacy was made known to the royal house, the consternation was great indeed. The text states it under a strong figure (v.2). But God had not been consulted in the matter, and He made known that the plottings of Judah's enemies would be frustrated. Moreover, in just 65 years the northern kingdom of Ephraim would be no more. In that dark hour it required faith to lay hold of this pronouncement of Isaiah, and he warned that if God's word through him were not believed, there would be no establishment of the king and his people. Then God, out of His boundless love and mercy to the Davidic house, wishing to confirm the strong assurances already made, invited Ahaz to ask for a sign in attestation of these predictions. Ahaz was not to feel in the least confined, for he was allowed a latitude of request from heaven above to Sheol below. Any request within these extensive areas was permissible. But Ahaz in a hypocritical display of sudden piety refused to put God to the test. This was an affront to God to disobey in so peremptory a manner. Isaiah's patience had long since been exhausted with the vacillating, faithless monarch. Would Ahaz now wear out God's patience as well?

In spite of the king's disobedience and without his cooperation, the Lord Himself promised a specific sign: a virgin with child was to bring forth a son whose name would be Immanuel. Before certain stages of growth were reached in the life of the child, both Syria and Ephraim would no longer be threatening powers to Judah. How is this passage to be understood? Is it a prediction of an ominous nature? Is it a prophecy of a salutary character? Or is it composed of both elements?[7] To determine answers to these basic questions it is necessary to treat the individual terms of the passage.

What is meant by the word אֹות ("sign")? If there were agreement here among interpreters of the prophecy, one could feel he were off to a good start. But the variety of views is disconcerting, to say the least. Brown has counted 79 occurrences of the word in the Old Testament, 44 times in the singular and 35 in the plural. He understood the usages in Isaiah 7:14 passage as relating to a sign which takes place before the promised event happens, and serves as a pledge to those to whom it is given that the event suggested by it will come to pass. We shall expect, then, to find in the sign given to Ahaz something which occurred prior to the deliverance foretold in the same passage, and became a pledge to him of that deliverance.[8]

Fitch holds that the sign was "not necessarily miraculous."[9] Gray feels that the sign has in view something that was previously foretold, but had then actually happened.[10]

But the traditional position that a miracle is demanded by the context is not without its able exponents. Barnes unequivocally maintains that the sign is "a miracle wrought in attestation of a Divine promise or message. This is its sense here."[11] Kraeling concludes that something unusual is to be looked for, "so that the ancient virgin birth interpretation was not without a good psychological basis when viewed from this angle."[12] Alexander reasons that

> it seems very improbable that after such an offer, the sign bestowed would be merely a thing of every day occurrence, or at most the application of a symbolical name. This presumption is strengthened by the solemnity with which the prophet speaks of the predicated birth, not as a unusual and natural event, but as something which excites his own astonishment, as he beholds it in prophetic vision.[13]

Those who insist that Isaiah must be speaking of an event already past or one on the contemporary scene are not giving the interjection hN:h' its proper force. Delitzsch maintains: *"hinneh* with the following participle (here participial adjective; cf. 2 Sam. 11:5) is always presentative, and the thing presented is always either a real thing, as in Genesis 16:11 and Judges 13:5; or it is an ideally present thing, as is to be taken here; for except in chapter 48:7 *hinneh* always indicates something future in Isaiah."[14] Young has posited how the Ras Shamra literature relates to the term. After pointing out similar constructions to Isaiah 7:14 in Genesis 16:11; 17:19; and Judges 13:5, 7, he states:

> At present it is sufficient to remark that the phrase introduced by hinneh is employed in the Scriptures to announce a birth of unusual importance. It is therefore of particular interest to note that this formula has been found upon one of the texts recently excavated at Ras Shamra.[15]

The storm center of the text is, of course, the word עַלְמָה. Reams have been written on it and, doubtless, reams will be written on it in the future. What is the exact translation of this important and pivotal word? Is there an element of ambiguity in it, or has the vagueness been imported into the discussion by interpreters? Here the exegete has a splendid opportunity to go slowly and plow deeply. To be accurate in one's conclusions all the evidence available must be weighed properly. It is important to note that the noun has the definite article. For many this phenomenon is without significance, but Lindblom affirms, "The most natural explanation is that a definite woman is in view."[16] Hengstenberg is even stronger when he declares, "In harmony with *hinneh*, the article in *ha'almah* might be explained from the circumstance that the Virgin is present to the inward perception of the Prophet— equivalent to 'the virgin there.'"[17] The prophet's use of the definite article points to a specific person.

But what is the precise meaning of עַלְמָה? Many scholars are noncommittal on whether the term signifies a virgin or a married woman. Rogers states his position clearly:

> First of all, it must be said that the Hebrew word *almah* may mean "virgin," but does not necessarily mean anything more than a young woman of marriageable age. Had the prophet intended specifically and precisely to say "virgin," he must have used the word *bethulah*, though even then there would be a faint shade of uncertainty.[18]

Many reputable scholars have held and do hold that the Hebrew term in this context means virgin. Gray affirms that

> *almah* means a girl, or young woman, above the age of childhood and sexual immaturity . . . a person of the age at which sexual emotion awakens and becomes potent; it asserts neither virginity nor the lack of it; it is naturally in actual usage often applied to women who were as a matter of fact certainly (Gen. 24:43; Ex. 2:8), or probably (Ca. 1:3; 6:8; Ps. 68:26), virgins.[19]

Gordon, an able Jewish Semitic scholar, presents an interesting sidelight on the problem.

> The commonly held view that "virgin" is Christian, whereas "young woman" is Jewish is not quite true. The fact is that the Septuagint, which is the Jewish translation made in pre-Christian Alexandria, takes *'almah* to mean "virgin" here. Accordingly, the New Testament follows Jewish interpretation in Isaiah 7:14. Little purpose would be served in repeating the learned expositions that Hebraists have already contributed in their attempt to clarify the point at issue. It all boils down to this: the distinctive Hebrew word for "virgin" is *betulah*, whereas *'almah* means a young woman who may be a virgin, but is not necessarily so. The aim of this note is rather to call attention to a source that has not yet been brought into the discussion. From Ugarit of around 1400 B.C. comes a text celebrating the marriage of the male and female lunar deities. It is there

predicted that the goddess will bear a son. . . . The terminology is remarkably close to that in Isaiah 7:14. However, the Ugaritic statement that the bride will bear a son is fortunately given in parallelistic form; in 77:5 she is called by the exact etymological counterpart of Hebrew betulah "virgin" for Isaiah 7:14 rests on the older Jewish interpretation, which in turn is not borne out for *precisely this annunciation formula* by a text that is not only pre-Isainic but is pre-Mosaic in the form that we now have it on a clay tablet.[20]

The position espoused here has been ably set forth by many but not more cogently than by Machen.

The question, we think, cannot be settled merely by a consideration of the meaning of the Hebrew word *'almah*. It has been urged, indeed, on the one hand that the Hebrew language has a perfectly unmistakable word for "virgin," *bethulah*, and that if "virgin" had been meant that word would have been used. But as a matter of fact there is no place among the seven occurrences of *'almah* in the Old Testament where the word is clearly used of a woman who was not a virgin. It may readily be admitted that *'almah* does not actually indicate virginity, as does *bethulah*; it means rather "a young woman of marriageable age." But on the other hand one may well doubt, in view of the usage, whether it was a natural word to use of anyone who was not in point of fact a virgin.[21]

The reference is undoubtedly to the virgin Mary, a fact clearly attested by Matthew 1. Those who cannot interpret עַלְמָה as a virgin present a variety of views as to the identity of the young woman. Some assert it was the consort of Ahaz, any contemporary young woman, Isaiah's wife, one of Ahaz' harem, or a princess of the court of Ahaz. Manifestly these do not meet the requirements of the context for a miraculous occurrence.

If there is divergence of thought on the identity of the mother of the child, there is no less agreement on the child himself. One position is that the child is an unknown one born in that day to confirm the prophecy of Isaiah. Others hold that the son was the son of Isaiah. Still others maintain that the child was Hezekiah, not realizing or overlooking the chronological difficulty here. A number of expositors contend for a double or multiple fulfillment, one in Isaiah's day and one in the life of Christ Himself. Alexander states a valid refutation of this view.

It seems to be a feeling common to learned and unlearned readers, that although a double sense is not impossible, and must in certain cases be assumed, it is unreasonable to assume it when any other explanation is admissible. The improbability in this case is increased by the want of similarity between the two events, supposed to be predicted in the very same words, the one miraculous, the other not only natural, but common, and of everyday occurrence.[22]

Against the view that verses 14–16 relate wholly and entirely to the virgin birth of the Lord Jesus Christ, the position maintained here, has been leveled the charge that it gives the prophecy no relevance to the day in which it was uttered. This is a serious matter, for the prophet must speak to his own generation as well as to future ones. To many, a fulfillment centuries later would be worthless to Ahaz and his contemporaries in their distress. But the exact opposite is true. Ahaz and his courtiers were fearful of the extinction of the Davidic dynasty and the displacement of the king by a Syrian pretender. However, the longer the time needed to fulfill the promise to the Davidic house, the longer that dynasty would be in existence to witness the realization of the prediction. It is well stated by Alexander: "The assurance that Christ was to be born in Judah, of its royal family, might be a sign to Ahaz, that the kingdom should not perish in his day; and so far was the remoteness of the sign in this case from making it absurd or inappropriate, the further off it was, the stronger the promise of continuance of Judah, which it guaranteed."[23] The conclusion, then, is inescapable that "there is no ground, grammatical, historical, or logical, for doubt as to the main point, that the Church in all ages has been right in regarding this passage as a signal and explicit prediction of the miraculous conception and nativity of Jesus Christ."[24]

CHAPTER 6

Modern Rationalism and the Book of Daniel

Gleason L. Archer, Jr.

An Early Proposal for a Late-Date Daniel

One very curious feature about the modern late-date theory of the Book of Daniel is that it was first proposed in ancient times. The Neoplatonic philosopher Porphyry back in the third century A.D. devoted a considerable portion of his polemic *Against the Christians* to a rationalist explanation of the Book of Daniel. He reasoned that the detailed and accurate predictions in the book point to its having been forged by some unknown author who lived in the days of the Maccabean patriots. According to Jerome, Porphyry argued that "he who wrote the book under the name of Daniel lied for the sake of reviving their hope"[1]—that is, the hope of the Jewish rebels who longed to throw off the yoke of Antiochus Epiphanes. The underlying assumption for Porphyry was the absolute impossibility of predictive prophecy. He rejected the idea that a personal God by special revelation could have foretold to a sixth-century Daniel what was going to happen through the centuries to come.

It is beyond dispute that this same antisupernatural presupposition has been adopted as a basic premise by the negative school of higher criticism ever since the appearance of Leonhard Bertholdt's commentary on Daniel in the year 1806.[2] This work followed the same deistic, skeptical viewpoint as that employed by J. G. Eichhorn in his source-criticism of the Pentateuch[3] and Johann Doederlein in his theory of sixth-century B.C. authorship for Isaiah 40–66, published in 1789.[4] All three writers assumed that apparently "prophecy" could only have resulted from forgery after the fulfillments had already taken place. Pentateuchal predictions of the Babylonian captivity and of the return of the Jewish exiles to Jerusalem in the 530s could not have been truly foreseen as early as the 15th century (or 13th century) B.C. Neither could the author of Isaiah 40–66 ("Deutero-Isaiah") have foretold the Babylonian exile and the subsequent restoration unless he actually wrote at a time when the approaching fall of Babylon to the forces of King Cyrus of Persia was already evident to a keen human observer (ca. 540 B.C.).

Revealed prediction by a supernatural God was completely out of the question so far as these rationalists were concerned. All apparently successful prediction had to be explained as *vaticinium ex eventu* ("prophecy after the event"). According to this view, no attention should be given to the arguments of Bible-believing scholars, no matter how learned they might be, for genuine predictive prophecy was a sheer impossibility. Ever since 1806 the rationalist school of biblical criticism has been content to restrict their reading to the works of one another. They have felt no need to work out any serious refutation of evidence advanced by conservative scholarship. They only mention the writings of such authors in order to scoff them away. A few experts, such as H. H. Rowley in his 1935 discussion of Darius the Mede,[5] have attempted to buttress the case for historical inaccuracy in the Book of Daniel by scholarly refutation of conservative claims. But even his well-constructed arguments have been rendered untenable and obsolete by subsequent archaeological discovery and careful analysis of the cuneiform evidence.

So far as 20th-century liberal scholarship is concerned, little or nothing has happened since 1806—or indeed, since the third century A.D. The same old threadbare arguments, the long-refuted "proof texts," the circular reasoning of doctrinaire rationalism, have persisted up to the present time. Even in most Roman Catholic circles it is now commonplace to speak of Daniel as a Maccabean pseudepigraph. They too seem to ignore completely the rising tide of historical and linguistic data which render that view completely indefensible, and are content to parrot the discredited arguments of Porphyry and Bertholdt as if they had never been refuted.

Produced under the auspices of a leading publishing house, Raymond Hammer's *The Book of Daniel*,[6] might be expected to show some awareness of recent discovery and scholarly discussion. But the amazing fact is that this British scholar completely ignores the writings of many leading conservative scholars.[7] He handles his material as if no evangelical scholar had ever composed a refutation of the Maccabean-date hypothesis. Yet it must be said to his credit that he at least takes the trouble to lay out the standard twentieth century arguments for this position, rather than simply assuming its validity without question, as most other recent liberal scholars tend to do.

Refutation of Arguments for a Late-Date Daniel

Hammer has proposed at least nine proofs for a late and spurious authorship of the Book of Daniel. These will now be examined.

THE MASORETIC DIVISIONS

Hammer states that in the Masoretic text, the vowel-pointed text of the Hebrew Bible handed down from the medieval period, the Book of Daniel is included in the third division (the so-called "Kethubim" or "Hagiographa") rather than in the second division (the "Nebi'im" or "Prophets"). He comments, "This suggests that the book was not known by 200 B.C. about the time when the collection of prophetic writings was assembled."[8]

It should be observed that this argument has no validity whatever, in view of the fact that the eminent Jewish historian, Flavius Josephus (ca. A.D. 100) clearly indicates that in his day the Book of Daniel was included among the Prophets, rather than with the third division of the Hebrew canon. Josephus observed that the Hebrew Scriptures contain 22 books (in contrast to the Masoretic text, which numbers them as 39), of which five contain the Torah (i.e., the Pentateuch), four "comprise hymns to God and practical precepts to men" (i.e., Job, Psalms, Proverbs, Ecclesiastes), and 13 are books of the Prophets.[9] The only possible inference to draw from this category is that Daniel, as late as the first century A.D., was included among the Prophets, not among the Kethubim.[10] The New Testament refers to the Hebrew Scriptures as consisting of the Law and the Prophets, with only the Book of Psalms belonging to a third division (Luke 24:44). Obviously at that time Daniel was considered one of the Prophets, and Jesus undoubtedly referred to him as such in His discussion with the disciples on the road to Emmaus. After all, His self-designation as "the Son of man" was evidently adopted from Daniel 7:13, and so He must have discussed Daniel among the prophets who foretold His coming. It can only be concluded that the later assignments of Daniel to the third division of the canon is totally irrelevant to the question of when the book was written.

ECCLESIASTICUS AND DANIEL

Hammer also points out that the apocryphal Book of Ecclesiasticus, written around 180 B.C., fails to mention Daniel by name, although many of the other prophets are referred to in this work. From this he infers that Daniel could not have been written by 180. But it should also be noted that Ecclesiasticus makes no attempt to list all the important readers in Israel's history; even so outstanding a hero as Ezra fails to receive a single mention in his text. Yet it is universally admitted that Ezra was the chief architect of the spiritual reconstruction of Jewry after the Babylonian Exile.

DANIEL AND DAN'EL

Hammer insists that no Old Testament contemporary of the sixth-century Daniel makes any reference to him, and this is a very strange omission if Daniel was indeed as important an official as the book makes him out to be. As for Ezekiel 14:14 ("even though these three men, Noah, Daniel, and Job, were in its midst, by their own righteousness they could only deliver themselves, declares the Lord God"), Hammer asserts that this cannot refer to the contemporary Daniel living in Babylon. It must refer to some patriarchal hero, since Job was thought to date from the time of Moses or earlier, and Noah of course lived in the time of the Flood. Therefore the Daniel referred to in Ezekiel must have been the ancient hero named Dan'el, whose life story is narrated in the Ugaritic legend of Aqhat (dating from about the 15th century B.C.).

There are at least two serious difficulties with this theory. The first is that several thousands of years must have elapsed between the time of Noah and the appearance of the patriarch Job. That being the case, there remains no problem whatever with the inclusion of a sixth-century Daniel as a third paragon of piety a thousand years later than Job. Thus the Lord's declaration quoted in Ezekiel 14:14, 20 and 28:3 amounts to this: Even though such godly leaders as Noah (at the dawn of history), and Job (in the time of Moses or a little before), and Daniel (from the contemporary scene in Ezekiel's own generation) should all unite in interceding for apostate Judah, God could not hear their prayers on behalf of that rebellious nation.

The second difficulty with identifying the Daniel of Ezekiel 14 with the Dan'el of the Ugaritic epic is found in the character and spiritual condition of Dan'el himself. When the legend of Aqhat is studied in its full context, which relates the story of Dan'el, the father of young Aqhat, it is found that he is praised as being a faithful idol worshiper, principally occupied with seven-day periods of sacrifices to the various gods of the Canaanite pantheon, such as Baal and El. His relationship to Baal was especially close, and he made bold to petition him for a son, so that when Dan'el became so drunk at a wild party that he could not walk by himself, his son might assist him back to his home, to sleep off his drunken stupor. Later on, after the promised son (Aqhat) is born, and is later killed at the behest of the spiteful goddess Anath, Dan'el lifts up his voice in a terrible curse against the vulture (Samal) which had taken his son's life. He prevails on Baal to break the wings of all the vultures that fly overhead, so that he can slit open their stomachs and see whether any of them contains the remains of his dead son. At last he discovers the grisly evidence in the belly of Samal, queen of the vultures. He then kills her and puts a curse on Abelim, the city of the vultures. The next seven years he spends in weeping and wailing for his dead son, and finally contrives to have his own daughter (Paghat) assassinate the warrior Yatpan, who was also involved in Aqhat's murder seven years before.

From this portrayal of Dan'el it is quite apparent that he could never have been associated with Noah and Job as a paragon of righteousness and purity of life. Nothing could be more unlikely than that a strict and zealous monotheist like Ezekiel would have regarded with appreciation a Baal-worshiper, a polytheistic pagan given to violent rage and unremitting vengefulness, a drunken carouser who needed assistance to find his way home to his own bed. Apart from a passing mention of Dan'el's faithful fulfillment of his duties as a judge at the city gate—a requirement expected of all judges according to the Torah—there is no suggestion in the Ugaritic poem that he is any outstanding hero of the faith, eligible for inclusion with Noah and Job. It is therefore quite hopeless to maintain this identification of Ezekiel's "Daniel" with the Dan'el of Ugaritic legend.

BELSHAZZAR AND NABONIDUS

Hammer argues that the historical inaccuracies committed by the author of Daniel in regard to personalities and events of sixth-century history make it certain that the author himself lived at a much later period. The first of these relates to Belshazzar.

The relationship of Belshazzar in Daniel 5:11 is stated to be that of a "son" to Nebuchadnezzar, whereas it is known, Hammer argues, that actually Belshazzar was the son of Nabonidus.[11] But Hammer seems completely unaware of the fact that Dougherty dealt with this question in a thorough and satisfying manner in 1929. Since Dougherty was professor of Assyrioiogy at Yale University, it seems incredible that Hammer could have totally ignored his scholarship, but he never makes mention of him. Yet the Yale scholar shows that Nabonidus was in all probability married to Nitocris, the daughter of Nebuchadnezzar, at least as early as 585 B.C.[12] It hardly needs to be added that a grandfather in Hebrew usage is often referred to as a "father" (אָב and Aram. אַבָּא) as, for example, in Genesis 28:13 and 32:10. Indeed, there is no other term for "grandfather" besides this in the Old Testament.

Hammer asserts that despite the fact that Belshazzar is referred to as "king" (Aram. מַלְכָּא) Daniel 5:1–30, he served only as regent, never as king. But in renewing this long-refuted argument, Hammer seems to be unaware that cuneiform temple receipts from Sippar attest that Belshazzar presented sheep and oxen there as "an offering of the king."[13] While it is true that no cuneiform record refers to Belshazzar by the explicit term *sharru* ("king"), it is clear that during the latter years of Nabonidus's reign, while the latter made his headquarters at Teima in Arabia, Belshazzar ruled as his viceroy, with all the authority of king. That this fact was well known to the author of Daniel is clearly implied by the fact that in Daniel 5:7, 16 the viceroy could promise to the successful interpreter of the handwriting on the wall only the honor of *third* ruler (תַּלְתִּי) in the kingdom. Obviously Belshazzar himself was only the second ruler.

DARIUS AND CYRUS

Hammer objects that Darius the Mede is given the credit for the capture of Babylon, instead of Cyrus the Persian, and that he is described in 5:31 and 6:28 as the king of Babylon. Hammer alludes to the Persian records as referring to Gubaru as the first governor of Babylonia after the Persian conquest, but he never mentions the discussions of Robert D. Wilson and John C. Whitcomb which support the view that "Darius" was a royal title bestowed on Gubaru.[14]

No cuneiform record states the nationality of Gubaru as Persian; this assertion is found only in the Greek historians Herodotus and Xenophon, who are demonstrably inaccurate regarding the capture of Babylon in 539. They confused the elderly general, Ugbaru of Gutium (who performed this feat by stratagem and who died a few months afterward) with Gubaru, the ruler who governed Babylon after the death of Ugbaru and continued in office at least until the fifth year of Cambyses (525 B.C.).[15] Aalders endorses this interpretation of the data, pointing out that Gubaru-Darius probably did not carry the title of king beyond a few months, or possibly a year.[16] Cyrus himself, having completed his military operations elsewhere, was then able to make a proper triumphal entrance into Babylon and formally receive the crown and title of king over all the Babylonian domains. Gubaru remained on as his deputy, however, even after that event. Daniel therefore refers to no later year of Darius's reign than his first (9:1), and thereafter dates his public service (1:21) and his visions (10:1) by the regnal years of "Cyrus, king of Persia." Hammer takes no notice of the dictum of Albright: "It seems to me highly probable that Gobryas did actually assume the royal dignity along with the name 'Darius,' perhaps all old Iranian title, while Cyrus was absent on a European campaign."[17]

THE TERM *CHALDEANS*

Hammer also condemns as unhistorical the appearance of the term "Chaldeans" (בַּשְׂדִּים), "Kasdim" (in Dan. 2:2 and elsewhere), as referring to a class of astrologers, even though it could never have been used in this way during the sixth century B.C. He seems to be completely unaware of the learned discussion of Wilson, who points out that in Daniel 5:30 the author uses the term *Chaldeans* in the ethnic sense when he calls Belshazzar "king of the Chaldeans."[18] This ethnic use of the term is utterly irreconcilable with the Maccabean-date hypothesis, for it demonstrates that whoever wrote Daniel was perfectly aware of the fact that Belshazzar ruled over the Chaldean *nation*. This is impossible to explain away if the author of the book lived in the second century B.C. and therefore supposed that the term *Chaldeans* referred only to a class of astrologer-priests. Since the author shows in 5:30 that he knows this also as an ethnic term, it is impossible to accuse him of garbling tradition over a period of four intervening centuries. Some other explanation must be found for the other usage of *Chaldeans* as referring to a class of astrologers.

Wilson shows that this second use of *Chaldeans* may have derived from a completely different origin, and that it happened to come out as a homonym, sounding just like the name of the Chaldean nation. In other words, it may have come from an old Sumerian title, *Gal.du* ("master builder"), which later became altered to the pronunciation *Kas.du* (the singular of *Kasdim*) through a sound-shift well known in the development of the Babylonian language.[19] This would be somewhat similar to the confusion in English between the ethnic term *Armenian* and the religious term *Arminian*.

PREDICTIVE PROPHECY

Hammer maintains that Daniel shows consistent accuracy only in connection with later history, the history of the Seleucid and Ptolemaic empires during the Greek period, from the time of Alexander the Great (ca. 330 B.C.) to the reign of Antiochus Epiphanes (175–164 B.C.). He implies that the mention of only four kings during the Persian period (whereas there were actually 11 in all) suggests a rather vague acquaintance with the Achaemenid era (539–334 B.C.).[20] But, Hammer argues, the detailed accuracy of the struggle between Syria and Egypt as set forth in Daniel 11 indicates an author living in the time of Epiphanes himself. He seems to focus particular attention on the three years or so (168–165 B.C.) during which the Jerusalem temple lay in a desecrated condition, devoted to heathen worship by the decree of the tyrannical Antiochus.

Several serious objections present themselves to this line of argument. In the first place, there is an important segment of Daniel 11 which did *not* find fulfillment by the time of Antiochus Epiphanes. Daniel 11:40 states, "And *at the end time* the king of the South will collide with him, and the king of the North will storm against him with chariots, with horsemen, and with many ships. . . ." The details that follow do not correspond with the known events of the reign of Antiochus, and the circumstances of the death of this latter-day "king of the North" are completely at variance with the demise of Antiochus himself in 164. Daniel 11:4 indicates that the future tyrant will camp in the Holy Land and there he will come to his end, "with none to help him." But Antiochus IV died of illness or poison in Tabae, Persia, after an unsuccessful raid on a wealthy temple in Elymais (1 Macc. 6), more than a thousand miles away from Palestine. It would seem to be a biased and perverse handling of evidence to maintain that Daniel 11 must have been composed in the 160s because of its accurate prediction of events occurring at that time, and yet that 11:40–45 was written at the same period even though it does *not* predict events which then took place. Plainly the author of Daniel undertook some prediction even though the fulfillment had not yet occurred. But if this is so, it serves to discredit the whole premise that the work was nothing but a pious fraud.

Furthermore a very important section of the prophetic scheme in Daniel had not taken place by the 160s, but only began to find fulfillment a hundred years later. These are the various passages predictive of the Roman Empire, which took control of the Near East and of Palestine in the year A.D. 63, when Pompey took possession of Syria and Israel in the name of the Roman Republic. If the author of Daniel had successfully predicted the Roman conquest back in the heyday of the Seleucid Empire, when Antiochus had temporarily conquered even the land of Egypt and was riding at the crest of his power, then he was certainly capable of genuine predictive prophecy. And if he received divine revelation enabling him to predict such earth-shaking events a hundred years in advance, it necessarily follows that he could have predicted all the earlier events that are recorded in Daniel as prophecies of the future. In other words the basic premise of Porphyry and his modern successors has been completely overturned.

The defenders of the Maccabean-date hypothesis are well aware of this danger to their theory, and so from the time of Porphyry on, they have endeavored to show that the fourth empire of Daniel's prophetic scheme was not the Roman Empire, but the Greek kingdom established by Alexander the Great. To make the Grecian Empire the fourth, it is necessary to show that the author of Daniel mistakenly believed what was historically untrue: that it was not Cyrus the Great, king of Persia, who overthrew Babylon in 539 B.C., but rather it was a certain Darius the Mede (who actually never existed), who established a Median Empire separate from and independent of Cyrus and the Persians.

The historical fact, of course, was that Cyrus defeated Astyages, the last king of Media, around 550 B.C., and merged the Medes and Persians into a single Medo-Persian Empire, before attacking Babylon in 539. But it is argued that somehow the befuddled and confused author of Daniel, living as he did three and one-half centuries later, conceived the notion that the Medes conquered Babylon before the Persians conquered them, and that the name of their king—Darius—was derived from garbled tradition relating to Darius the Great, who reigned from 522 B.C. to 485 B.C. In other words according to Hammer the tradition that Darius was a Mede was derived from a Darius who was actually a Persian, and that he reigned just before Cyrus the Great (whereas Darius the Persian was the third ruler after Cyrus), and that he was only assumed to be 62 years of age (Dan. 5:31), even though the historical Darius could not have been much over 22 at the time he assassinated Pseudo-Smerdis.

Proponents of this view take no notice of the fact, moreover, that Daniel 9:1 states that Darius the Mede was *made* king (הָמְלַךְ) over the Chaldeans—a term that strongly suggests that some higher authority put him in power. The earlier statement in Daniel 5:31 (Heb. 6: 1) that Darius *received* (קַבֵּל) the kingdom clearly points in the same direction, for a conqueror does not *receive* authority (as from a higher sovereign who entrusts it to him) but he wins it by force and claims it as his own by right of conquest. Any open-minded study of the text of the Book of Daniel can only lead to the deduction that the aged Darius was entrusted by his superior Cyrus with temporary authority over the newly conquered territory of the Chaldean Empire. Quite evidently Cyrus found it expedient to turn Babylon over to a trusted lieutenant while he took care of more urgent business along his northern frontier possibly to crush an invasion from the troublesome Scythians. Since the record in Daniel refers only to the first year of Darius's reign (9:1) and does not indicate that he had any more than a single year in office as king of Babylon, it is a fair inference that his regime could not have lasted more than two years at the most. All subsequent dates are reckoned as part of Cyrus's reign (e.g., 10:1 refers to a revelation received by Daniel "in the third year of Cyrus king of Persia"). The unavoidable conclusion is that Darius the Mede was a very brief episode indeed. It is therefore incredible that the author of Daniel, whoever he was and whenever he wrote, could have regarded a one-year or a two-year "Median" regime as on a par with the Chaldean Empire (which lasted from 612 to 539) and the Persian (539–332) and the Greek (332–165 at least). The whole notion of an earlier Median Empire, independent of Persia, is incapable of rational defense in the light of such evidence as this.

It could also be pointed out that the symbolism of the four successive kingdoms in Daniel's prophetic series points unmistakably to the identity of the second empire as the federated Medo-Persian government, rather than Media alone. Thus the second beast described in Daniel 7:5 is a bear which was raised up on one side and was devouring the meat of three ribs. There is no ascertainable correspondence here with anything known concerning the Median Empire overthrown by Cyrus in 550, but the second beast perfectly fits the specific characteristics of the Medo-Persian domain. The bear raised up on one side depicted the Persian side of the federation which dominated the Median side. The three ribs refer to the three major conquests of Lydia, Babylonia, and Egypt, which marked the expansion of the combined forces of Media and Persia united under Cyrus's command, and under the leadership of his son Cambyses, who conquered Egypt soon after his father's death.

The third beast (7:6) is a four-winged leopard with four heads, which suggests a very rapid conquest of the Middle East by a new power, which soon broke up into four divisions. This corresponds with nothing in the Persian Empire (to which it would have to correspond, according to the late-date theory), but fits in perfectly with the Alexandrian Empire, which broke up into four independent kingdoms not too long after Alexander's death in 323. The fourth beast (7:7)—the fearsome predator with the ten horns, more powerful and ruthless than all its predecessors—clearly finds perfect correspondence with Rome rather than with the Greek Empire and its quadripartite division. The 10 horns obviously correspond with the 10 toes of the dream-image of Daniel 2 which likewise fits only with the Roman Empire (the two legs of iron), which divided into the Eastern Roman Empire and the Western Roman Empire in the time of Diocletian and after the death of Theodosius the Great in A.D. 395. This bipartite division accords with the two legs of the image, and the end-time phase of the 10 toes is perfectly paralleled by the 10 horns of the beast in Daniel 7:7.

Still another item of evidence makes the identification of the second empire with Media completely untenable. In the dramatic episode of the handwriting on the wall of Belshazzar's banquet-hall (Dan. 5:25–28) Daniel is quoted as explaining the third word of the inscription, פַּרְסִין, in following fashion: "Your kingdom has been divided (פְּרִיסַת) and given over to the Medes and *Persians* (פָּרֵס)." Here is a wordplay involving three units: (a) פַּרְסִין ("division" or "half-shekel"), (b) פְּרִיסַת from the verb פְּרַס ("divide"), and (c) or פָּרֵס ("Persian" or "Persia"). In other words according to the author of Daniel, the first empire, the Chaldean, was given over directly to the Persians, who with the Medes constituted the second empire. The wordplay is not with the "Medes" (as it would have to have been had there been an earlier, independent Median Empire) but expressly with the "Persians." If then one is to pay any attention to the testimony of the text itself, it must be conceded that Daniel regarded the second empire as Medo-Persian, with the Persians predominating over the Medes, rather than as Median alone. This being the case, the third empire has to be the Greek Empire, and the fourth power can only be that of Rome. Again, one is faced with conclusive internal evidence from the text that the author of Daniel predicted the overthrow of the Greek Empire by the Roman at least one hundred years (even on the assumption of the Maccabean date) before it took place. Thus it turns out that the entire effort to explain the predictive elements in Daniel as prophecy after the event ends up in failure.

Another rather obvious factor should be pointed out. The Hellenistic age was marked by widespread literacy. Although multitudes of Greek authors have been lost by the vicissitudes of time, there can be no doubt that the general public during the two and one-half centuries between Alexander and Pompey were well read. Homer, Hesiod, Pindar, the Attic tragedians and masters of comedy were studied and admired all over the Near East. The same was true of the historians Herodotus, Thucydides, and Xenophon. Greek culture had so thoroughly penetrated Jerusalem itself that a large and influential pro-Hellenic party had risen to prominence. But in Herodotus' and Xenophon's account of the rise of the Persian Empire it is perfectly clear that the conquest of Media by Cyrus the Great took place at least 10 years before the fall of Babylon. Neither author contains the slightest intimation that the Chaldean Empire was overthrown by a Median power before the rise of Persia. It is therefore evident that if any author living in the 160s had attempted to foist such a perversion of historical fact on a second-century Greek-reading, Greek-speaking public like the Jews of Jerusalem, he would have been derided as a mere simpleton, and would have found credence with no one. The alleged confusion must therefore be relegated to the imagination of the modern higher critic, and to that alone.

GREEK AND ARAMAIC

Turning to the linguistic evidence, Hammer argues that the appearance of Greek words in the Aramaic portion of Daniel (i.e.,

2:4b–7:28) demonstrates that the work must have been composed in the Greek period, that is, in the time of Antiochus Epiphanes. Regrettably enough, he seems quite unaware of how damaging to the late-date hypothesis this evidence of the Greek loan-words turns out to be. Numerous discussions by such able scholars as Wilson, Young, Harrison, Yamauchi, and others[21] have conclusively established that the linguistic evidence renders a date as late as the second century B.C. completely impossible. A full appreciation of this type of data requires technical training in the various languages of the ancient Near East, but a few comments by way of summary may prove helpful.

These discussions all point out that there are only three well-attested loan-words from Greek in the Aramaic of Daniel and that they all occur in one verse (3:5) in connection with a list of the musical instruments included in the royal philharmonic orchestra: קִיתְרוֹס, פְּסַנְתֵּרִין and סוּמְפֹּנְיָה. It is known that foreign names of imported musical instruments often find currency in the language of the purchasers as soon as they are purchased, and that Greek traders had been selling their wares on the Near Eastern markets from the Mycenean age and onward. The Greek poet Alcaeus of Lesbos (living around 600 B.C.) mentions (in one of his surviving fragments) that his brother Antimenidas had served in the Babylonian army. There is no difficulty, therefore, in reconciling the appearance of three Greek instruments in the Aramaic of Nebuchadnezzar's time, to say nothing of the reign of Cyrus the Persian. But insuperable difficulties are encountered in attempting to explain how it was possible in the 160 years between Alexander's conquest of the Near East and the reign of Antiochus Epiphanes that not a single Greek term pertaining to administration or government had been adopted into the Aramaic of the early second century. Since 15 Persian loan-words (largely pertaining to government functions and administrative titles) to be found in Daniel's Aramaic, it is perfectly evident that Aramaic, the lingua franca of the Babylonian capital, readily adopted foreign terms of this sort. But the fact that no such Greek terms are to be found in Daniel demonstrates beyond all reasonable doubt that this work was composed in the Persian period rather than after Greek had become the language of government in the Near East.

It should be added in this connection that the discovery of Aramaic documents in the Qumran caves, some of which were composed in the second century B.C. (like the "Genesis

Apocryphon" of Cave One) furnish a clear sample of Palestinian Aramaic from the period of the Maccabees. Elsewhere the present author has demonstrated that the Apocryphon shows a characteristic Western Aramaic word order, which tends to place the verb at the beginning of the clause.[22] Daniel, however, tends to defer the verb to a later position in the clause (somewhat like the word order in Akkadian). This feature was acknowledged by Kutscher, who concluded: "With regard to Biblical Aramaic, which in word order and other traits is of the Eastern type (i.e., freer and more flexible in word order) and has scarcely any Western characteristics at all, it is plausible to conclude that it originated in the East."[23]

Now this is a very damaging admission, for if Daniel was composed by a Jewish patriot in Judea during the early second century B.C., it could not possibly have been composed in an eastern type of Aramaic. It would necessarily have conformed to the western Aramaic word order and style exemplified by the Apocryphon. Furthermore a marked contrast is evident between the Aramaic chapters of Daniel and the Aramaic text of the Genesis Apocryphon in every significant category of linguistic comparison.[24] In each of these categories (morphology, grammar, syntax, and vocabulary) the Apocryphon (an admittedly second-century composition) stands out as centuries later than the language of Daniel. The same is true when the Hebrew of the Qumran sectarian documents (such as "The Rule of the Congregation" and "The War of the Sons of Light against the Sons of Darkness") is compared with the Hebrew portion of Daniel (i.e., 1:1–2:4a; 8:1–12:13).[25] In light of the linguistic evidence, therefore, it is no longer possible to speak of the Book of Daniel as a second-century B.C. composition; otherwise there is no validity at all for the science of linguistics.

DANIEL'S 70 WEEKS

It is interesting to observe how Hammer handles the prophecy of the 70 weeks found in Daniel 9:24–27. The terminus a quo for the 70 weeks is clearly stated in 9:25 to be "from the issuing of a decree to restore and build Jerusalem." But Hammer assumes that it commences at the year 587 B.C., when Jerusalem was captured and destroyed by the Chaldeans. From this point he reckons the "seven weeks" mentioned in verse 25 as running from 586 to 538 (the date of the issuing of Cyrus's decree of restoration for the captivity of Judah). Then he computes the 62 "weeks" or 434 years as extending from 538 to 171, when the high priest Onias III was murdered. (This reckoning incurs a slight difficulty, however; the interval between 538 and 171 is only 367 years, or 67 years short of 434!) Then Hammer construes the 70th week of 9:27 as running from 171 to 164 (when Antiochus died). After these suggestions he states that "the second period of 434 years is much greater than the actual years—only 367 years—but the precise length of the Persian period was not known to the later Jewish writers."[26]

In reply to this remarkable assertion of the misinformation of "late Jewish writers" certain observations should be made regarding the general level of public awareness concerning chronology. As stated earlier, the people of the Near East during the Hellenistic period were thoroughly acquainted with the classical Greek authors. Accurate information concerning the Persian period was certainly available to the public from both Herodotus and the Athenian historiographer, Xenophon. It is scarcely conceivable that any Jewish writer at any age would ever have been so naive as to suppose that he could draw a figure out of his imagination and convince his keen-minded compatriots that 434 was equivalent to 367. It should be remembered that all secular documents and animals throughout this period were dated from 312 B.C., the year when Seleucus I asserted his independence as ruler over the Seleucid Empire. All the world knew that this followed within 10 or 15 years after the death of Alexander the Great (in 323 B.C.), and that Alexander overthrew the Persian Empire in a mere 10 or 12 years before his death. What schoolboy in the domains of Antiochus Epiphanes could possibly have been unaware of the true date of the fall of the Persian Empire, when he had to date all his school papers in the Seleucid era? (For example the year 168 B.C. would have been the year 145 from the coronation of Seleucus I in 312 B.C.) No literate citizen of the Maccabean period could have been confused about the true date when Alexander conquered the Middle East. Even the coins that were daily handled by the public through the Near East bore this regnal date. Thus there is no possibility that any Jewish citizen who ever handled money could have been confused about this matter!

If the true terminus a quo for the decree of rebuilding the walls of Jerusalem is understood to be the date of Ezra's return to Jerusalem in 457, clothed with authority from King Artaxerxes (cf. Ezra 7:6 and 9:9), then the interval of 49 plus 434 years (i.e.,

483 years in all), comes out to A.D. 27 for the appearance of "Messiah the Prince." If Christ were crucified in A.D. 30 (as is usually believed) and if His ministry lasted three or three and one-half years, this means that A.D. 27 was indeed the commencement of His earthly ministry (the date of A.D. 27 is suggested rather than A.D. 26, since a year is gained in the transition from 1 B.C. to A.D. 1). This computation of 483 years from 457 B.C. to A.D. 27 is based on the solar year, and is the view of the present writer. Other evangelical writers, however, prefer the date of 444 B.C. as the terminus a quo of the 69 weeks. This is based on Artaxerxes' decree in his 20th year in which he authorized Nehemiah to rebuild the walls (Neh. 2:2). The terminus ad quem thus becomes A.D. 33, the date of Christ's triumphal entry (and subsequent crucifixion). This view is based on the "prophetic year" (also the lunar year) of 360 days, authority for which is based on Revelation 11:2–3.[27]

Whether the beginning of the 69 weeks is 457 B.C. or 444 B.C., the important point to emphasize here is that the 483-year prophecy comes out to the very year. This is explicable only on the ground of special revelation from God Himself, and demonstrates the complete trustworthiness and divine inspiration of the Book of Daniel.

The 70th week explicitly said in Daniel 9:26 not to commence until the end time, a time of wars and desolation. Not until 9:27 is the final week referred to, and this clearly relates to the last seven years before the battle of Armageddon, during which the "prince who is to come" will make a covenant with the Jewish believers that will purport to endure for seven years, but which he treacherously will abrogate when only half of that period has elapsed. He will then set up the "abomination of desolation," probably an image of some sort symbolizing his own divine kingship (Matt. 24:15 and 2 Thess. 2:3–4). In view of the perfect congruity of this prediction of 483 years with the time of Christ's ministry, it seems quite conclusive that Daniel 9:24–27 is a supernatural disclosure of God's plan for the future. Thus one need not resort to a theory of misinformation or confusion on the part of a "late Jewish writer" in order to account for this prophecy of the 70 weeks. On the contrary that prophecy with its accurate fulfillment turns out to be one of the compelling arguments for the authenticity of Daniel.

For Hammer, however, "The book of Daniel is not to be treated as a piece of writing through whose magical guidelines we can predict the future."[28] Thus after Hammer has winnowed away all the genuinely predictive validity of Daniel and by implication has convicted Christ and the apostles of error when they applied Daniel 7:13 to Christ Himself as the Son of Man, Hammer endeavors to salvage some sort of uplifting hope from this supposedly pious pseudepigraph, and glean some spiritual principle from it all—on a purely voluntaristic basis. But what he fails to see is that such voluntarism can only result in divesting Scripture of all objective authority as an authentic revelation from God. It becomes a record of man's futile search after God, like all the writings of the other world religions—full of conjectures and yearning hopes, but containing no trustworthy answers from the Creator and Lord of the universe.

Yet the fact remains that the internal and external evidence for the genuineness and the divine authority of the Book of Daniel are of such a compelling nature as to demand a verdict of approval and acceptance on the part of any unbiased jury. The attempt to explain away the numerous and detailed fulfillments of prophecy ends up in a complete failure, since no second-century B.C. author could possibly have foreknown the complete overthrow of the Greek Empire by the Roman Republic and the permanent establishment of its power by Pompey in 63 B.C., over a century later than the date assigned to the hypothetical Maccabean pseudepigraph. Nor could the author of such a pious fraud have foreknown the exact year of the commencement of Christ's ministry as predicted in Daniel 9:25. Nor can the manifestly later type of Aramaic and Hebrew exhibited by genuinely second-century documents from the Qumran be reconciled with a second-century date of a composition reflecting a stage of language in each case centuries earlier than the time of Antiochus Epiphanes. It is therefore safe to say that no Bible scholar can today make a defensible claim to intellectual respectability and still maintain the theory of a Maccabean time of composition for this remarkable book, from which Christ derived His most characteristic title for Himself, "the Son of Man."

CHAPTER 7

The Temple Vision of Ezekiel

Merrill F. Unger

T he final nine chapters of the prophecy of Ezekiel, while forming a grand climax to the prophet's message, presents problems and difficulties that place them among the most perplexing portions of the entire prophetic Word. The most prominent feature of this much-disputed passage is the temple Ezekiel saw in vision. For this reason it is sometimes called "The Temple Vision." What is to be done with the temple? Where is it to be placed? How is it to be interpreted? These and similar questions have disturbed Bible students and occupied their researches ever since Ezekiel published his vision.

Much of the literature on the subject is a veritable labyrinth of confusion. The reader is left in a maze, either groping for a mere ethereal and imaginary temple that was never supposed to have any substantial existence at all, or else being presented with an actual sanctuary set in an environment that clashes at every turn with the plans and specifications outlined by the prophet.

One thing seems clear. The premillennial plan of prophetic interpretation alone can supply the key to open an otherwise fast-closed door. What is depreciatingly referred to by some as "literalistic chiliasm" alone can offer the clue to resolve an otherwise unsolvable puzzle. To assert this, however, must not be construed as tantamount to saying that the premillennial plan does not have its difficulties and problems. It does. But to insist that these difficulties and problems are fewer in number and of a far less serious character, ought to be frankly allowed by anyone facing the facts without bias or prejudice. To reject the premillennial plan because of a few perplexities and to embrace a nonpremillennial explanation which entails many more, and of a more serious nature, is to "jump out of the frying pan into the fire," as the saying goes. This, though, is apparently what the great majority of commentators on this portion choose to do. It is therefore necessary to examine inadequate views.

Inadequate Views

THE PROPHECY OF EZEKIEL'S TEMPLE WAS MERELY TO
PRESERVE THE MEMORY OF SOLOMON'S TEMPLE SO
THAT IT COULD BE RESTORED AS NEARLY AS
POSSIBLE

In this view the prophet's account is merely a prosaic delineation of what he had himself seen at Jerusalem in the Solomonic temple, so as to preserve for the returning remnant some semblance of that house. Such is the concept that Villalpandus tries vainly to prove by a huge apparatus of learning. He is followed by Grotius, Calmet, Secker, and in part by the elder Lowth, Adam Clarke, Bottcher, Thenius, and others. A superficial examination, however, demonstrates that such an assignment of position to Ezekiel's temple involves flat contradictions, and completely fails to satisfactorily account for the notable differences between the Solomonic temple and the restored temple, in relationship to Ezekiel's. It is manifestly a strained and twisted view, the result of adopting an unworkable eschatological hypothesis.

THE PROPHECY OF EZEKIEL'S TEMPLE PORTRAYED
WHAT SHOULD HAVE BEEN PUT INTO EFFECT ON THE
RETURN FROM THE BABYLONIAN CAPTIVITY

The pattern exhibited to the prophet presented for the first time what *should have been* after the return from the Captivity. The neglect of the returned remnant accounts for the temple not being rebuilt. God gave them the ideal. They fell short of it. This is the explanation offered by Eichhorn, Dathe, and Herder. It, of course, escapes many difficulties involved, but is a weak makeshift to avoid facing the problems presented. No such fulfillment could have possibly taken place at the restoration from Babylon, because the 12 tribes were not restored then to occupy the land as tribes. The temple could not have been built unless certain topographical changes were first divinely brought about, and unless the land of Palestine has been glorified. No Shekinah glory filled the second temple. No river such as Ezekiel's was realized. The seer's vision includes these and other features manifestly impossible of accomplishment at that time, even if the remnant had so understood the vision and made an aggressive attempt to carry it out as outlined.

There are others who hold substantially the same position, but modify it somewhat to lay great stress on the idealistic purpose of the vision. They claim there were features in the description that were never intended to receive a literal accomplishment, yet it is maintained that the prophet did not fail to present a perfect design of what was desirable and proper for the people to set as a goal. This concept is expressed well in the words of Whitelaw: "The temple is, in truth, an ideal construction never intended to be literally realized by returned exiles or any other body of people. Visionary in origin, the ideas embodied, and not the actual construction, are the main things to the prophet's mind."[1]

This modification of the view proceeds on the basis of the abandonment of the strictly prophetic character of the vision. It reduces its announcements to a vague and well-meaning anticipation of some future good. It does little credit to inspiration and attaches slight importance to the prophet's message. It is to be rejected by those who reverently handle Scripture as the infallible Word of God.

THE PROPHECY OF EZEKIEL'S TEMPLE SETS FORTH THE KINGDOM OF GOD IN ITS FINAL PERFECT FORM

This is the opinion advanced by Keil who connects the whole scene with the eternal state of bliss as pictured in Revelation 21 and 22. That this is unwarrantable, and even impossible, is attested by the obvious contrasts between the two pictures. Ezekiel's temple is a literal structure, whereas in the New Jerusalem there is no temple at all (Rev. 21:22). Ezekiel's river flows from the threshold of the temple eastward (Ezek. 47:1), whereas the river seen by John proceeds not out of a temple at all, but out of the "throne of God and of the Lamb" (Rev. 22:1). In Ezekiel's vision there is the presence of sin (45:20). In the eternal state there is "no more curse" (Rev. 22:3). In Ezekiel the temple and the city are distinctly separated (Ezek. 48:8, 15). In the Revelation there is no temple at all. Keil cannot shield his view from these obvious discrepancies by the weak makeshift of saying that Ezekiel's picture "could not rise to such an eminence of vision" as John's.[2]

If things that are obviously in contrast and saliently differ are arbitrarily made to refer to one and the same thing, how can the true meaning of the Word of God ever be ascertained? The Word must be construed as saying what it means, and meaning what it says. In rejecting the literal premillennial interpretation of this portion, as well as weak traditional nonpremillennial views, Keil is hard pressed to offer an adequate explanation that bears any semblance of adherence of scriptural facts and statements.

THE PROPHECY OF EZEKIEL'S TEMPLE SYMBOLICALLY DESCRIBES THE CHRISTIAN CHURCH IN ITS EARTHLY GLORY AND BLESSING

Aptly this is called the Christian-spiritual interpretation. It is the weakest of all and yet, strange to say, it is the most popular of all. It is but an added proof of the havoc wrought by the indiscriminate allegorizing and spiritualizing of Old Testament prophecies. It tries to mix the unmixable. It commits the serious blunder of not making a difference between things that differ. It gives no actual exposition of the text. It abounds with fanciful applications. It leaves the greater part of the vision an unanswerable puzzle. One word preeminently characterizes it—vagueness. This appears in the statements of its definition by Fairbairn: "The whole representation was not intended to find either in Jewish or Christian times an express and formal realization, but as a grand, complicated symbol of the good God had in reserve for His church especially under the coming dispensation of the gospel."[3]

Thus according to this position Ezekiel's temple becomes merely an evanescent, unsubstantial picture that evaporates into thin air. Without any actual proposed existence, it is a mere figment of the imagination.

When it is realized that this method of interpreting the vision has been the prevailing one from the time of the Fathers downward, and that the greater part held it to the exclusion of every other, especially the great Reformers, Luther and Calvin, and their successors, Cappellius, Cocceius, Pfeiffer, and the majority of modern theologians, is it to be thought strange that prophetic interpretation in general has remained through the centuries "a grand complicated symbol"? The greatest scholarship but wastes its talents and dissipates its energies in trying to solve a puzzle if the secret to its solution is rejected, or in trying to open a door if the right key is passed by. The fact that some writers combine the Christian-spiritual with one or more of the other nonpremillennial views does not decrease the resulting confusion.

The Result of Inadequate Views

It becomes at once apparent that no fitting place is accorded Ezekiel's temple by any of the nonpremillennial theories of interpretation, or by any combination of them. Such systems are simply at a loss over what to do with the prophet's sanctuary. To give it a past literal fulfillment is to come into direct conflict with the well-attested facts of history regarding the Solomonic, the Restoration, or the Herodian temples. To give it a historical-idealistic realization is to resort to the poor makeshift of insisting that God required the small band of less than 50,000 from Babylon to do what for manifest and obvious reasons it was utterly impossible for them to do. To assign it a purely idealistic turn, as if it were never supposed to be actually realized, is to allow scant importance to the prophet's message, and do little credit to inspiration. To connect it with the eternal state, as Keil does, is to clash with plainly revealed scriptural facts. To spiritualize it and try to make it fit the Christian church is not only to deny it all actual existence, but to plunge the whole subject into fancifulness and vagueness according to the mere caprice of the interpreter.

Only one conclusion is possible. Nonpremillennial views just do not supply any appropriate place for Ezekiel's temple. This great section of the Old Testament prophecy must remain wrapped in darkness and confusion, unless some plan of prophetic interpretation is provided to give a fitting and suitable future fulfillment to all that is written in this vision. To this problem attention must now be turned.

That there is a prophetic plan of interpretation, which alone gives fitting and appropriate place for Ezekiel's temple, and that this is the premillennial position, shall now be the subject of scriptural proof.

The Adequate View

This maintains that all that is written by the prophet concerning the temple relates exclusively to the future, and that all will be fulfilled precisely as written. Stated more specifically, it is that *Ezekiel's temple is a literal future sanctuary to be constructed in Palestine as outlined during the millennium.*

The words of the prophet are taken in their natural grammatical and literal sense. Nothing is spiritualized or idealized that is not so indicated by the Scriptures. The scene is not made to refer to the church, which, as a mystery hidden in God, was veiled from the Old Testament prophets (Eph. 3:1–10). The simple unvarnished meaning of the details given are taken as saying what they mean, and meaning what they say.

But are there not difficulties with this position? The answer is yes, there are. However, it may truly be said that they are far less in number, and are far less serious in nature than those presented by any of the other views. It may be added that they are by no means unanswerable, or so insuperable as to warrant the abandonment of the whole premillennial system, as some would imagine. On the contrary, the view opens up an otherwise closely shut subject, and floods with light what is otherwise very dark. More than that, in the light of essential dispensational distinctions the difficulties largely disappear when God's purpose for Israel, on the one hand, is comprehended, in distinction to His plan for the church, on the other hand.

Perhaps the reason so many reject the literal-futuristic view in spite of its manifest superiority over any other, and its undeniable excellencies, is because the difficulties and problems it presents are accounted insurmountable, and hence fatal to its tenability. If there were not warrant from the internal evidence of Scripture itself for dispensational distinctions, this rejection would be legitimate, and the difficulties unresolvable. But in the light of such indispensable and thoroughly warranted time distinctions demanded by the Scriptures themselves, the difficulties lose their force, and the rejection of the view is accordingly unsustained and inexcusable.

THE TIME OF THE CONSTRUCTION OF EZEKIEL'S TEMPLE

The construction of the edifice cannot take place until after the second coming of Christ, who in His glorious advent will effect necessary physical changes in Palestine. The whole central portion of the land will be converted into a "very great valley" or "plain" from Geba, about six miles northeast of Jerusalem, to Rimmon (En-rimmon), identified with Umm er Ramamin, some 30 miles south of Jerusalem (Zech. 14:4, 10). The holy oblation, or land devoted to Jehovah, in the middle of which is located the sanctuary (Ezek. 48:8, 10), may comprise this very portion. It is therefore clear that Ezekiel's temple cannot be built until after the glorious second advent of Christ. Standing on the Mount of Olives, He will bring about the radical change in the topography of the land essential to the exalted location and unique construction of the millennial seat of worship.

The millennial temple Ezekiel saw in his vision must not be confused with the tribulation temple. A temple will be built in

Daniel's 70th week (Dan. 9:27; Matt. 24:15; 2 Thess. 2:4; Rev. 11:1–2). It will doubtless be built shortly after the rapture of the church. Whenever it is built, it will be in existence by the time of the middle of the week. It may be that some existing structure, such as the Dome of the Rock, might be converted into a temple for the restoration of Judaism (Hos. 3:4–5). This worship will not be in the divine favor, and will end in the abomination of desolation (Matt. 24:15). The temple will certainly be destroyed by the violent earthquakes and cataclysmic judgments of the great tribulation. It will give way to Ezekiel's magnificent edifice to be erected at the commencement of the messianic-Davidic kingdom according to the detailed specifications given God's prophet over 2,500 years ago. The whole religious, social, and governmental life of the kingdom age will radiate from the temple as the grand focal point.

THE LOCATION OF EZEKIEL'S TEMPLE

In a general way the sanctuary may be said to be located in the heart of Palestine, which will be the religious and governmental center of the millennial earth.

The temple's relationship to the restored 12 tribes. The millennial temple will have seven tribes to the north of it—Dan, Asher, Naphtali, Manasseh, Ephraim, Reuben, and Judah (Ezek. 48:1–7), and five tribes to the south of it—Benjamin, Simeon, Issachar, Zebulun, and Gad (48:23–29). Ezekiel gave in careful order from north to south the relationship of the various divisions of the land with special regard to the temple and the holy oblation.

The extreme northern border of Dan extends from the entrance of Hamath, some 160 miles north of Jerusalem, to the southern border of Gad, some 80 miles south of Jerusalem (48:1, 28). Each of the seven tribes to the north of the temple is given a parallel portion of equal width, with the Mediterranean Sea as a western boundary, and the Jordan River, the Lake of Galilee, and a line skirting just east of ancient Damascus northward to Hamath as an eastern boundary (47:15–18). Each of the five tribes to the south is given a parallel strip of the same width with the Mediterranean Sea and the River of Egypt as a western frontier, and the Dead Sea and the Arabah as an eastern boundary (48:18–19).

The temple's relationship to the "holy portion." The location of the temple is unique. It is "in the middle of" this "holy portion," as the portion of the land especially dedicated to the Lord is called (45:1; 48:8, 10, 21). It is a tract of land forming a large square

25,000 reeds long and 25,000 reeds wide. It is divided into three principal parts: a portion for the priests, 25,000 reeds by 10,000 reeds (45:4; 48:10–12), a portion for the Levites, 25,000 reeds by 10,000 reeds (45:5; 48:13–14), and a place for the city, 25,000 reeds by 5,000 reeds (45:6; 48:15–19).

The so-called "prince's portion" is pictured as being on the east and west of this great square, stretching to the eastern and western boundaries of the land (45:7; 48:21).

An important question is whether the figures given in 45:1–8 and chapter 48 are to be construed as cubits or reeds ("measuring rods"). Neither in 45:1–8 nor in chapter 48 is this stated, except with one instance in 45:2, where the cubit is named. That the reed is meant in the other unnamed measurements, and not the cubit, is concluded on the basis of the following.

The cubit being mentioned in the one instance may imply that the other measurements are different.

The space of 500 reeds by 500 reeds measured for the sanctuary plot in 42:15–20 seems identical with the measurements of the external bounds of the temple given in 42:2, and hence the denomination is to be construed as the reed. The 50 cubits surrounding the sanctuary plot is to separate between the holy and the profane and to prevent the priests' houses being built against the temple wall, thus defiling the holy sanctuary precincts.

That the unit of measurement must be the reed is the only reasonable conclusion for the size of the millennial city of Jerusalem (48:15, 17). Its space is specified as 5,000 by 5,000, including the suburbs. If these are cubits the city would be a small insignificant place, a mere village 1.136 miles square. Adopting the reed, which is six cubits (40:5; 43:13), the city becomes appropriate in dimensions to millennial glory, being 6.81 miles square, covering at least 47 square miles.

That the measurement must be the reed appears further from the fact that Levi, one of the tribes, has its complete inheritance as part of the heave-offering (10,000 by 25,000). If the cubit were meant, he would have a mere 15 square miles, while the other tribes would have from 800 to 1,000 square miles.

Evidently, therefore, the reed is intended in these specifications for the holy portion. But how long is a reed? This is given as being "six" cubits, "a cubit and a handbreadth" (40:5). "The cubit is a cubit and handbreadth" (43:13). So the question is, How long is the cubit specified by Ezekiel?

Archaeological research has established the fact that three cubits were employed in ancient Babylonia.[4] Each was confined to its own department of work. The smallest of 10.8 inches or three palms (handbreadths) was used in gold work. The second of four palms or 14.4 inches was applied to buildings, and the third of five handbreadths or 18 inches was utilized in land spaces. The shortest cubit of three handbreadths, or palms (a palm is 3.6 inches), equaling 10.8 inches is the basic fundamental unit. There can be no doubt that Ezekiel was thoroughly familiar with this system of measurement, either from his acquaintance with it in Palestine or from his long residence in Babylonia. As the prophet was very specific in stating that the unit of measurement in his vision is a "cubit and a handbreadth" (40:5; 43:13), he no doubt meant the smallest cubit of three handbreadths as the basic measure, plus one handbreadth, or what is equivalent to the middle cubit of 14.4 inches. On this calculation the reed would be 7.2 feet. The holy portion would be spacious square, 34 miles each way, containing about 1,160 square miles. This area would be the center of all the interests of the divine government and worship as set up in the millennial earth.

The temple itself would be located in the middle of this square (and not in the city of Jerusalem), on a mountain, which will be miraculously made ready for that purpose when the temple is to be erected. This shall be "the mountain of the house of the Lord," established "as the chief of the mountains" and "raised above the hills," into which all nations shall flow (Mic. 4:1; cf. Isa. 2:4; Ezek. 37:26). "My dwelling place also will be with ['over' or 'above'] them" (Ezek. 37:27). The prophet saw the magnificent structure on a grand elevation commanding a superb view of all the surrounding country.

On the basis of this calculation the "holy portion" will fall within the prescribed boundaries of the land, with the Dead Sea and the Jordan River on the east and Mediterranean Sea on the west. It also makes allowance on both the east and west sides for the possession of the prince. This is the view of Grant, who says, "To adopt the middle cubit solves this difficulty [of boundaries], and enables us to keep within the requirements of the text."[4]

If Ezekiel referred to the Egyptian royal cubit of 20.63 inches, the holy portion would extend beyond the limits of the land. If he meant the short Egyptian cubit of 17.68 inches, the heave-offering would fall just within the bounds of the land, but would leave no portion for the prince.

Larkin uses the large cubit of approximately 18 inches and a handbreadth, thereby arriving at a reed of 10.5 feet, and a holy portion of some 50 miles square. He locates the sanctuary, and hence the center of the holy portion, on the site of ancient Shiloh, where the tabernacle was set up by Joshua (Josh. 18:1) and where it remained until the death of Eli. This arrangement would place the millennial city of Jerusalem on the south side of the oblation, in approximately its present location, with the temple some 18 or 20 miles to the north of it. This view would provide a highway running north of the city and connecting it with the sanctuary (Isa. 35:8). This view shoves the whole sacred offering much farther to the north, so that the southern extremity of it skirts the northern extremities of the Dead Sea.

The main objection to this view is that it ignores the eastern boundaries of the land as given in Ezekiel 47:18. The holy portion would extend beyond the Jordan River and the Dead Sea. To answer this difficulty the eastern and western boundaries, as promised to Abraham, from the River of Egypt to the River Euphrates (Gen. 15:18) are adopted. The inheritance, moreover, of each tribe and the prince's portion are likewise extended to Mesopotamia.[6] This interpretation would indeed give a much larger area, extending far beyond the limits of Palestine proper. If "Abraham's descendants" (literally, "seed") means the descendants of Jacob through Isaac ("In Isaac shall thy seed be called," Rom. 9:7, KJV), then there might be some ground for such an extension of the bounds.

Commentators usually locate the holy portion immediately north of the Dead Sea and customarily use the larger cubit, permitting it to extend beyond the Jordan River. Grant prefers not only the use of the smaller cubit but also the location of the offering between the Mediterranean Sea and the Dead Sea. This is done on the basis of Zechariah's prophecy (14:10), which pictures the land as a great plain from Geba, six miles north of Jerusalem, to Rimmon 30 miles south of Jerusalem. Calculating the land on the basis of the smaller cubit fits these boundaries remarkably. An additional indication that the holy portion seems to be located here is the easterly direction of the stream which flows from under the threshold of the millennial temple (Ezek. 47:1–2, 8). This flows eastward into the Arabah and into the Dead Sea. Grant maintains that in the location usually assigned the holy portion, and hence the temple, this stream flowing east "would enter the river Jordan, not the Sea."

The temple's relationship to the city of Jerusalem. Zechariah describes "living waters," which are certainly to be connected with the temple stream (Ezek. 47:1–12) "out of Jerusalem, half of them toward the eastern [Dead] sea and the other half toward the western [Mediterranean] sea" (Zech. 14:8). Larkin attempts to meet this detail by locating the city on the south side of the holy portion, so that the temple stream flowing eastward turns southward to the city, in the midst of which it divides into two streams, one flowing into the Mediterranean Sea and the other flowing into the Dead Sea.[7]

Grant places the city to the north of the holy portion and makes no attempt to meet this detail of the inspired picture. The natural order would seem to indicate that the city and its portion are located on the south side of the holy portion. The order of the tribes in Ezekiel 48 is uniformly from north to south. However, when the holy portion is described, the priests' portion is mentioned before the Levites' (Ezek. 45:4–5). This continuity is broken perhaps because the sanctuary is located in the priests' portion, and the order of the presentation of the temple has been from within out. Accordingly, that order seems to be observed with the holy portion itself. Next in order is the Levites' portion, and farthest from the sanctuary, but within the sacred portion, is the city. This would argue for the city on the south side of the portion, bordering on the portion of the tribe of Benjamin rather than contiguous to the tribe of Judah.

The city with its suburbs will be adjacent to the priests' portion (Ezek. 45:6), and will be from six to nine miles square, according to the size of the cubit used. It will have 12 gates, named for the 12 tribes of Israel—a gate each for Reuben, Judah, and Levi toward the north; a gate each for Joseph, Benjamin, and Dan toward the east; a gate each for Simeon, Issachar, and Zebulun toward the south; and a gate each for Gad, Asher, and Naphtali toward the west (48:30–34). It is noteworthy that during the millennium the temple will not be located in the city or its suburbs, as in the past. And yet Jerusalem will be so characterized by God's presence as to be called in that day "Yahweh Shammah" ("The Lord is there," 48:35).

Some expositors wrongly claim that Ezekiel's description of Jerusalem with its gates is but an Old Testament portrayal of the same Jerusalem John beheld in his visions on the Island of Patmos (Rev. 21:2). This cannot be the case, for Ezekiel saw the earthly city as it will exist during the millennium, whereas John saw the eternal city prepared for the new heavens and the new earth. According to Ezekiel a millennial temple will be built in the center of the land of Israel, but in Revelation the prophet wrote, "I saw no temple in it" (Rev. 21:22). No wall or foundation is mentioned for the millennial Jerusalem, whereas the wall of the heavenly Jerusalem will have 12 foundations, and in them the names of the 12 apostles. The size and the shape of the two cities are in contrast. Ezekiel's city has but two dimensions, length and breadth, but John's city will also have height, evidently being in the shape of a cube. However, Ezekiel's earthly city will not attain the glory and the magnificence of John's heavenly city. It will give way to the eternal Jerusalem.

CHAPTER 8

The Use of Hosea 11:1 in Matthew 2:15: An Alternative Solution

Tracy L. Howard

T he use of the Old Testament in the New continues to be a subject of great debate. One of the thornier problems is the use of Hosea 11:1 ("Out of Egypt I called My son") In Matthew 2:15. The difficulty of this problem is evidenced by the numerous solutions offered by evangelicals, some of which have serious ramifications in both hermeneutics and theology. The purpose of this chapter is to evaluate the various attempts to solve the problem. After proposing a solution, both the hermeneutical and theological implications will be set forth. However, it is necessary first to state clearly the problem that exists in the quotation by Matthew.

The Problem

The problem of Matthew's use of Hosea 11:1 is articulated by Ellis, who writes, "To many Christian readers, to say nothing of Jewish readers, the New Testament interpretation of the Old appears to be exceedingly arbitrary. For example, Hosea 11:1 ('Out of Egypt I called my son') refers to Israel's experience of the Exodus; how can Matthew 2:15 apply it to Jesus' sojourn in Egypt?"[1] As Ellis correctly points out, Hosea 11:1–2 describes the history of the nation of Israel at the time of the Exodus as well as the succeeding events. In verse 1 the Lord declared, "When Israel was a youth I loved him, and out of Egypt I called My son." This verse looks back to the beginning of the nation, at which time the Lord manifested His electing love in bringing her out of bondage in Egypt.[2] He compared His relationship to Israel with that of a parent to a son. The word בֵּל ("son") expresses the endearment the Lord has toward His people; this complements the biblical figures of the Lord as Shepherd, Husband, and Redeemer of His people.[3]

It is important to observe that the reference in Hosea 11:1 is to the nation Israel and her historical Exodus. No exegetical evidence exists that a concept of Messiah (either explicitly or implicitly) is in this passage. That Hosea's focus was on the nation and not Messiah is also demonstrated from verse 2, in which he described the events after the Exodus. Instead of obeying the Lord and reciprocating His love, the nation acted like a disobedient son and went after other gods. Hosea 11:2b states that Israel "kept sacrificing to the Baals and burning incense to idols."[4] As in verse 1, the nation is in view and in this case the prophet described her disobedience to the Lord. Any reference, therefore, to Messiah is inconceivable contextually.

However, when Matthew quoted Hosea 11: 1, he said it was "fulfilled" (ἵνα πληρωθῇ) by events that transpired in the life of the Messiah (specifically, Jesus' departure into Egypt to escape the slaughter by Herod).[5] Herein lies the problem. Matthew wrote that the two events are connected in such a close fashion that the latter "fulfilled" the former. The question that must be addressed is this: How and on what basis could Matthew make the connection between two events that on the surface appear so disparate?

Various Solutions to the Problem[6]

PREDICTIVE PROPHECY

Some commentators regard Matthew 2:15 as a direct fulfillment of Hosea 11:1. This interpretation explains the phrase ἵνα πληρωθῇ as meaning a fulfillment of predictive prophecy Such an understanding is coupled with a translation of קָרָאתִי in Hosea 11:1 as "I *will* have called (My Son)," that is, as a future perfect. This would mean that Hosea 11:1 is a reference *solely* to Christ and not to Israel at all.[8]

This interpretation faces at least two problems. First, πληρόω can convey the nuance of "to complete" or "to establish" without any reference to predictive fulfillment.[9] Delling notes that this nuance of "complete" is possible because "God fulfills His Word by fully actualizing it."[10] In other words this concept views an event in process which God ultimately brings to completion. Metzger comments on this idea as it applies to Jesus in Matthew 2:15: "More precisely the characteristically Christian view of the continuing activity of God in the historical events comprising the life, death, and resurrection of Jesus of Nazareth, fulfilling and completing the divine revelation recorded in the Old Testament is reflected even in the choice of formulas introducing quotations of Scripture in the New Testament."[11]

Thus Matthew viewed Hosea 11:1 as being confirmed or fulfilled by another event that was much like it and that came to pass at a later time.[12] So it is unnecessary to see Matthew 2:15 as a predictive fulfillment simply because πληρόω is used.

Second, to take קָרָאתִי in Hosea 11:1 as a future perfect is tenuous contextually. On the one hand the previous verb וָאֹהֲבֵהוּ is a "definite past" preterite that looks back to God's election of Israel at the Exodus. On the other hand verse 2 picks up the theme of the nation's rejection of the Lord to follow Baal, also a past reference. Nothing could be further from the context of Hosea 11:1 than a prediction of the Messiah. Thus to interpret the second colon of verse 1 as a predictive prophecy is unwarranted.

SENSUS PLENIOR

William LaSor has argued that the use of Hosea 11:1 in Matthew 2:15 is an appropriate example of *sensus plenior.*[13] The principle of *sensus plenior*, advocated primarily by Roman Catholic scholars,[14] has been debated frequently. However, in recent years it has also been the subject of discussion by evangelicals, particularly with the renewed study of the use of the Old Testament in the New.[15]

The subject has been treated most fully by Catholic scholar Raymond E. Brown. He defines *sensus plenior* as follows: "The *sensus plenior* is that additional, deeper meaning intended by God but not clearly intended by the human author, which is seen to exist in the words of a Biblical text (or group of texts, or even a whole book) when they are studied in light of further revelation or development in the understanding of revelation."[16]

The principle of *sensus plenior*, however, is not without its problems. First, this view presents questionable implications with regard to inspiration. The principle of *sensus plenior* makes the inspired writer a secondary element in the process, while God is viewed as supplying directly to the interpreter many additional meanings not intended in the original context. This would suggest a process of inspiration that closely parallels "mechanical dictation."[17]

Second, a problem that is perhaps the most critical for the modern exegete is that of *objectivity* in the interpretive endeavor. If God is supplying meanings unknown to the human author, how would an interpreter ever understand all the divine implications given in the text other than the written expression? One cannot go beyond that and attempt to discover a "fuller sense" unknown to the human author. To do so immediately thrusts one from objectivity into total subjectivism. Kaiser remarks, "When extrinsic implications are read into the biblical text, with a note of divine authentication, then we have introduced an uncontrollable element of subjectivity if not indeed eisegesis."[18]

Third, some have advocated the "fuller sense," particularly in the Matthean fulfillment texts, because of the use of πληρόω ("to fulfill").[19] However, as with the position of "predictive prophecy" this view also fails to consider that πληρόω does not have to mean "predictive fulfillment" or "fuller sense" but can convey the nuance of "to complete." Hence the use of πληρόω in Matthew 2:15 does not necessarily validate the principle of *sensus plenior*.

To suggest a genuine example of the *sensus plenior*, criteria would have to be established to control and ensure objectivity in the interpretation. Three are suggested. First, the *sensus plenior* would have to be given by further revelation in the New Testament. Second, the *sensus plenior* would have to be a sense of which the human author was at least vaguely aware, that is, a messianic tendency.[20] Third, the "fuller sense" would have to be grounded in a historical-grammatical interpretation of the Old Testament text. In other words it would not be something arbitrary or unrelated to the meaning of the Old Testament passage.[21] There would have to be some continuity between the Old and New Testament texts. Yet even with these criteria, it seems that many instances labeled as *sensus plenior* would better fit under another category. Hosea 11:1 in Matthew 2:15 seems to be one of these instances.

One might argue that the Hosea quotation in Matthew 2:15 satisfies the first requirement, namely, that Matthew explicitly stated that the calling of Jesus out of Egypt fulfilled (ἵνα πληρωθῇ) the historical Exodus described in Hosea 11:1. However, a nuance of "fuller sense" or even "fulfillment" for πληρόω is debatable. Regarding the second and third requirements, it is difficult to conceive that Hosea had any messianic tendencies in his description of the Exodus. It is evident from what follows in verse 2 that the nation went after the Baals in spite of the Lord's love in calling her from Egypt. Thus Israel and not Messiah is certainly what the prophet referred to. For this reason, it is improbable that someone using the historical-grammatical hermeneutic could derive a prophetic implication from a historical proposition as found in Hosea 11:1. The difficulty in seeing any clear connection between Matthew 2:15 and Hosea 11:1 is admitted even by LaSor, who writes regarding both Isaiah 7:14 and Hosea 11:1:

> In neither case is there any indication that the author had some distant future event in mind, hence it is most difficult to conclude that the authors were speaking of Jesus Christ or even an unnamed Messiah. . . . Yet both of these passages are cited as fulfilled in Jesus Christ.[22]

For reasons cited, *sensus plenior* must be rejected as a valid solution to the problem of the use of Hosea 11:1 in Matthew 2:15.

MIDRASH-PESHER

In 1954 Krister Stendahl published *The School of St. Matthew and Its Use of the Old Testament*, in which he attempted to articulate a theory of the origin of the Gospel of Matthew. One of the key features of Stendahl's work is his understanding of the exegetical procedure of what he calls the "Matthean school" in its use of the Old Testament. He labels this procedure "midrash-pesher," arguing that such an exegetical technique closely resembles the exegetical procedure of the Qumran sect, particularly in the Dead Sea Scrolls (Qumran) commentary on Habakkuk (1QpH5).[23] He includes Matthew's use of Hosea 11:1 in this category.

Several problems are evident with Stendahl's hypothesis. First, the formal features between the quotations in the Qumran commentary on Habakkuk and Matthew are not similar. The formal quotations in Matthew are of the so-called "fulfillment" type ($\text{ἵνα } \pi\lambda\eta\rho\omega\theta\tilde{\eta}$), of which Matthew 2:15 is an example. However, this type of introductory formula is singularly absent from the Qumran texts.[24]

Second, the reason for this absence of $\pi\lambda\eta\rho\acute{o}\omega$ is that the hermeneutical features are quite different from what is found in the Matthean use of the Old Testament. The Qumran community saw itself as being in the "last days" to which all prophecy pointed. As a result of this perspective the Qumran community completely disregarded the original context when exegeting prophetic passages. The community felt that the original intention of the particular citation was for the community. Such exegesis can be seen in the community's attempt to equate the Chaldeans in the Dead Sea Scrolls with the Kittim, or Romans.[25] Admittedly some New Testament authors, as well as those of Qumran, introduced quotations that were understood as reapplying Old Testament texts eschatologically to the contemporary situation. This certainly could be said for Matthew 2:15, as will be noted later. However in Qumran, application became virtually equivalent with interpretation in which there was little if any regard for the original context of the Old Testament citation. Matthew's Old Testament quotations (particularly Matt. 2:15), on the other hand, exhibit a different character because of the clear connection with the historical intent of the Old Testament context.

Third, there is a significant difference between Matthew's technique of recording a story about Jesus (and accompanying it with Old Testament citations fulfilled therein) and the "pesher" technique of Qumran in which the method is a line-by-line analysis of the Old Testament.[26] Davies comments on the considerable stylistic difference between the use of fulfillment texts in Matthew and the "pesher" use at Qumran:

> In the former [Matthew], the 'historical' event seems to determine the incidence and nature of the quotation, which serves as a closure to a pericope, that is, the scriptural quotation subserves the event. In the latter [Qumran], the opposite is the case: the scriptural text is normative for the event, not a commentary upon this, but its ground.[27]

The same point could be made for any attempt to compare the Matthean quotations and contemporary midrash.[28] So in Matthew 2:15, Matthew was not giving a midrashic homily on the Hosea text but rather was supporting his record with the Old Testament quotation.

Fourth, an identification of a Matthean hermeneutic with that of the Qumran community raises serious questions regarding inspiration.[29] The reason is that frequently the Qumran community distorted the original intent of the Old Testament passage they were quoting.[30] In essence this implies that the Old Testament writer was at times misinformed and thus communicated error that the community then correctly interpreted.

Though Stendahl's thesis has been influential, the criticisms cited provide a sufficient basis for rejecting his "midrash-pesher" category as applicable for the formal quotations of Matthew. Since Matthew 2:15 falls into this category, Stendahl's hypothesis is inadequate as a solution to the problem of Matthew's use of Hosea 11:1.[31]

TYPOLOGICAL

This solution maintains that the events in the life of the nation as described in Hosea 11:1–2 "typified" the life of Messiah in Matthew 2:13–15. Exactly what this means can vary because the word "type" is used loosely.[32] Traditionally typology has been defined by centering on the idea of prefiguration. For example Fritsch says that a type is "an institution, historical event or person, ordained by God, which effectively *prefigures* some truth connected with Christianity."[33] According to this position, the events described in Matthew 2:13–15 were prefigured in Hosea 11:1–2.[34] However, the prefigurative view of typology has questionable implications.

Applying the concept of prefiguration to Hosea 11:1 presupposes a meaning latent in the text of which the human author was unaware. This concept is similar to the principle of *sensus plenior* discussed earlier. Brown is aware of the similarity. He recognizes that typology (as traditionally defined) and *sensus plenior* both contain meaning that exceeds human awareness. The only distinction for Brown is that the "one [*sensus plenior*] primarily deals with words; the other [type] deals with things."[35] The traditional position of typology is subject to many of the criticisms leveled at *sensus plenior* particularly in reference to Matthew's use of Hosea 11:1. There is no evidence that a messianic antitype was latent in the discussion of Hosea 11:1. Hosea's reference to the disobedient son Israel is incongruous with a prefiguring of the obedient Son, the Messiah. Thus another definition of typology must be sought if it is to be considered as a possible solution to the problem.

A REFINEMENT: ANALOGICAL CORRESPONDENCE

An excellent definition of typology is proposed by Woolcombe:

> Typology, considered as a method of exegesis, may be defined as the establishment of historical connections between certain events, persons or things in the Old Testament and similar events, persons or things in the New Testament. Considered as a method of writing, it may be defined as the description of an event, person or thing in the New Testament in terms borrowed from the description of its prototypal counterpart in the Old Testament.[36]

This definition reflects the concept of historical correspondence rather than that of prefiguration. According to this definition the New Testament writer looked back and drew correspondences or analogies with events described in the Old Testament.[37] The typological connection is retrospective rather than prospective.[38] Furthermore from the standpoint of exegesis this approach considerably reduces the element of subjectivity that the traditional prefigurement view of typology introduces. With this in mind it is now possible to posit a plausible explanation of the use of Hosea 11:1 in Matthew 2:15; the solution to the problem will be called "analogical correspondence" rather than "typological."

As previously discussed, Hosea 11:1–2 describes the history of the nation since her Exodus from Egypt and her subsequent disobedience to the Lord. Matthew looked back and saw an analogical correspondence between the history of the nation Israel and the history of the Messiah. There are specific points of similarity that Matthew used in his analogy between the events of Hosea 11:1–2 and Matthew 2:13–15. First, one sees a clear Exodus pattern in Matthew's connection with Hosea 11:1–2. This Exodus analogy contains a reference both to the nation's past and to its future. Matthew's primary connection with the nation's past was geographical. He showed that even as the nation was taken into Egypt and brought out, so also the Messiah was taken into Egypt and brought out. Coupled with this is a possible persecution parallel. Even as the nation was persecuted by Pharaoh at the time of the first Exodus from Egypt, so also the Messiah was persecuted by Herod at the time of His "exodus" (cf. Matt. 2:13).

Matthew also drew a connection with the nation's future. It is quite possible that Matthew looked beyond Hosea 11:1 to the entire chapter and included Hosea 11:10–11 in his Exodus analogy. This writer would argue that Hosea 11:1 is quoted by Matthew as a touchstone for other events in the chapter. In other words Matthew was interested in more than one isolated text; he was interested in the context. The likelihood of this suggestion is supported by Albright and Mann:

> "Proof texts," with the ensuing barren controversies they have engendered down the years, would consequently have puzzled any New Testament writer. Not only would the whole context of a cited passage have to be searched—if indeed a gospel author wished to discover what we call a "verse"—*but the whole context would usually be known by heart.*[39]

Hosea 11:10–11 describes an eschatological "exodus" from Egypt. The exodus would be a starting over for the nation. This would occur at the inauguration of the "age to come." Hence if Matthew had in mind all of Hosea 11 and was attempting to present parallels between the life of the nation and the life of Jesus, it is plausible that Matthew saw Messiah as the One who will lead this new exodus for Israel and hence inaugurate the new age. In light of this, one might suggest not only a parallel between Herod and Pharaoh but also a parallel between Jesus and Moses.[40]

Second, one also can observe a "son" pattern in Matthew's connection with Hosea 11:1–2, it is evident from Matthew's reference to Hosea 11:1 that he wanted to emphasize the concept of sonship instead of using the Septuagint reading, which contains the phrase τὰ τέχνα αὐτοῦ ("His children"), he rendered the Masoretic text literally and hence used τὸν υἱόν μου ("My Son"). The Lord called the nation of Israel His son, whom Pharaoh was told to release so that they could go and worship the Lord (Ex. 4:22–23). However, Hosea 11:2 reveals the sad result that instead of worshiping the Lord the nation committed the sin of idolatry. Matthew then viewed Jesus as the *obedient* Son, who would inaugurate the new "exodus," in contrast to the *disobedient* son Israel, who after the first Exodus miserably failed to keep the covenant. All that Israel should have done, Jesus did by exhibiting obedience instead of disobedience.[41] Consequently after Jesus' "exodus" from Egypt and His baptism by John, God could say, "This is My beloved Son, in whom I am well pleased" (Matt. 3:17).

Having evaluated the different options, the most satisfactory answer to the problem of Matthew's use of Hosea 11:1 is "analogical correspondence," in which Matthew saw an analogy between the events of the nation described in Hosea 11:1–2 and the events of Messiah's life in Matthew 2:13–15. As Matthew drew these correspondences he saw Jesus as the One who *actualizes* and *completes* all that God intended for the nation.[42]

Hermeneutical Implications

Matthew's use of Hosea 11:1 would seem to be an example of conclusions at which the modern exegete would have difficulty arriving. Thus one might be inclined to agree with Longenecker, who concluded that the exegetical technique of the apostles is not a pattern for contemporary exegesis.[43] However, Longenecker seems to have confused "inspired conclusions" with "method." From this study of Matthew's use of Hosea 11:1, the exegetical technique used in Matthew 2:15 still serves as a guide to a historical-grammatical exegetical procedure. Matthew did not use the Hosea 11:1 quotation as a springboard for a totally unrelated exposition or homily (as in "midrash"), nor did he exegete the quotation as being applicable solely to Jesus at the expense of Hosea's original meaning (as in "midrash-pesher"). Neither did Matthew ascribe a meaning to the Hosea passage of which the prophet was unaware (as in *sensus plenior*). Instead Matthew drew specific "analogical correspondences" between certain events in Israel's history and certain events in Jesus' life. This requires a historical-grammatical understanding of the Hosea passage for the "analogical correspondence" to make sense; in fact nothing suggests that Matthew understood Hosea 11:1 in any way other than according to its historical-grammatical context. For this reason, it is totally unacceptable to regard the use of Hosea 11:1 in Matthew 2:15 as an example of "arbitrary" exegesis on the part of the New Testament writers.

Theological Implications

BIBLIOLOGY

All the positions discussed in this article are subscribed to by the evangelical community in some form as possible options in solving the problem of Matthew's use of Hosea 11:1. However, some of them pose serious implications for inspiration. As has been noted, *sensus plenior* can misrepresent the process of inspiration, since it must allow for some aspect of "mechanical dictation." In this view the Prophet Hosea, instead of being an active agent, was a passive instrument through whom and to whom God communicated "unknown" meanings; in this case, the meanings would be messianic.

The view of "midrash-pesher" likewise runs into problems with an evangelical understanding of inspiration. The midrash-pesher technique of the Qumran community frequently disregarded or distorted the original intent of the Old Testament text it was citing for the sake of making a "relevant" application to the community. If this exegetical procedure is the explanation of the problem at hand, then Matthew is seen as perhaps distorting or even misunderstanding the meaning of Hosea 11:1. This kind of implication points up the importance of differentiating between "midrashic tendency" and the pure midrash-pesher hermeneutic. This writer certainly agrees that Matthew, like those at Qumran, applied the meaning of the Old Testament to the contemporary situation. However, Matthew did not do so at the expense of the Old Testament text's meaning as did the writers at Qumran.

Therefore one must posit a solution that maintains the integrity of the meaning of the Old Testament quotation. The principle of "analogical correspondence" does full justice to the context of the Old Testament quotation. This solution easily explains the hermeneutical problems involved in Matthew's use of Hosea 11:1 while at the same time upholding inspiration. By using this principle, meanings unknown to Hosea are not extrapolated from the passage. Furthermore, it presents Matthew as having interpreted the events of Hosea 11 as the prophet presented them in the historical-grammatical context.

CHRISTOLOGY

Clearly Matthew presented Jesus as the King of Israel. However, the present study has yielded further insights into other Christological motifs that Matthew understood regarding Jesus' identity. For example Matthew portrayed Jesus as the One who *completes* all that Israel as a nation was designed to perform. Jesus recapitulated in a positive sense the history of the nation. He is the obedient Son in whom God delights. For that reason Matthew saw Him as the One who would inaugurate a new exodus for the nation Israel.

ESCHATOLOGY

If Matthew viewed Jesus as the One who would inaugurate a new exodus, then it is likely that he also thought of Jesus as the One who would introduce the new age. Though there is a sense in which this is "realized" today by those who are united to Him by faith, this period finds its ultimate fulfillment and consummation in the future. The promise of Hosea 11:10–11 looks at the time when the nation Israel will be restored from dispersion and will experience blessing in the land in the millennium. Jesus is the Messiah who will lead the nation through the new exodus into that new age with all its wonderful provisions.

Conclusion

Frequently evangelicals have espoused positions on the use of the Old Testament in the New without realizing the implications that stem from such positions. This chapter has attempted to tackle one passage that has caused not a few interpreters to question the Matthean hermeneutic. The conclusion drawn in this study is that the Hosea 11:1 quotation by Matthew is not an example of arbitrary exegesis on the part of a New Testament writer. On the contrary Matthew looked back and carefully drew analogies between the events of the nation's history and the historical incidents in the life of Jesus. The solution proposed in this chapter—the principle of analogical correspondence—maintains the contextual integrity of both Hosea 11:1 and Matthew 2:15.

CHAPTER 9

The Meaning of Cross-Bearing

Michael P. Green

T he issue of cross-bearing is relevant to all Christians who are sincere in their devotion to their Lord, for He Himself said, "If anyone wishes to come after Me, let him deny himself, and take up his cross, and follow Me" (Mark 8:34b). But what is involved in taking up one's cross? Is it literal or figurative, active or passive, once-for-all or ongoing, required for all believers or optional for only the more mature? What are its prerequisites and what are its consequences? In light of the many and diverse interpretations proposed to explain this phrase and because of the stress laid on this concept by various groups of Christians, especially those suffering or undergoing persecution and because of its relationship to personal discipleship, it is important that the meaning of cross-bearing be clearly understood by the church.

Various Interpretations of Cross-Bearing

An overview of the many proposed interpretations of cross-bearing evidences the confusion that exists over what Jesus actually meant. The following views of Mark 8:34b—more than a dozen of them—are grouped on the basis of their starting points. Often differing starting points yield views with similar interpretations.[1]

LITERAL VIEWS (MARTYRDOM)

The fully literal view. Proponents of this view argue that since Jesus' cross was unquestionably literal, so the cross for His followers should be.[2]

The theoretical-literal view. This view recognizes that not every believer will be crucified, or even martyred. Thus it substitutes "willingness," "readiness," or "preparedness" for martyrdom (in place of actual martyrdom).[3]

FIGURATIVE VIEWS

The vast majority of Bible students hold that cross-bearing is to be understood figuratively rather than literally. They approach the subject from one of four starting points: (1) the image of crucifixion, (2) the text, (3) a religious tradition, and (4) theology. *Those starting with the image of crucifixion.* (a) The self-denial view. This interpretation is usually stated as "a vivid metaphor for self-denial"[4] or "the total death of the self-life."[5] (b) The suffering view. By far the most commonly offered interpretation of the disciple's cross is the view that it is a figure for suffering, pain, persecution, shame, humiliation, or rejection."

Those starting with the text. (a) The lexical-meaning-of-σταυρός-as-palisade view. This view sees the key to interpreting cross-bearing in the lexical meaning of σταυρός as "a stake" or "a palisade." Thus cross-bearing is understood to be "a call to follow Jesus as the commander who has prepared a new life for His men behind the bulwark set up by Him."[7] (b) The proverbial-expression view. According to this view, based on Plutarch (*Moralia* 554A), to carry one's cross is merely a proverb. Johnson, who holds this view, offers no interpretation of the phrase.[8] (c) The lifelong cross-bearing view. Carrying one's cross "suggests a beginning of discipleship which then becomes a lasting state: the disciple of Christ is a cross-bearer, and he remains this his whole life."[9] Cross-bearing is thus a lifelong process culminating in one's death.

Those starting with a religious tradition. (a) Those starting with Jewish tradition. Three views on the meaning of cross-bearing look to Jewish tradition for their starting point. One is the Zealot-expression view. This view sees the statement on cross-bearing as an adaptation by Jesus of an expression used by Zealots. Cross-bearing is thought to be "a profane popular expression,"[10] "which perhaps arose among the Zealots and was then applied to the discipleship of Jesus."[11] Another view pertaining to Jewish tradition is the cultic-marking view. Based on the precedence of signs or markings for possession, protection, and confession, this view explains cross-bearing as a mark or seal of possession. Cross-bearing is understood to mean "marking the forehead with a Tau; it is confession that one belongs to Jesus."[12] Another variation is the Abrahamic-parallel view. This is developed from the *Midrash Rabbah* on Genesis 56:3, which reads, "and Abraham took the wood of the burnt-offering (22:6)—like one who carries his stake on his shoulder." A footnote to this comment reads that the stake he carried is the one "on which he was executed."[13]

(b) Those starting with Christian tradition. One view from this vantage point is the yoke-equivalent view. Bonhoeffer has written, "The yoke and the burden of Christ are His cross."[14] This view argues that after the death of Jesus the saying in Matthew 11:29a, "Take My yoke upon you," became the basis for "Let him . . . take up his cross" in Matthew 16:24; Mark 8:34; and Luke 9:23.[15] Another approach is the Pauline theology-equivalent view, in which statements in the Gospels about cross-bearing are understood to be the Synoptic equivalent of Paul's theology of the cross and dying to self.[16]

Those starting with theology. Four views have their starting point in theology. (a) One is the requirement-for-salvation view. In his invaluable work *The Training of the Twelve*, Bruce says, "It is as if above the door of the school in which the mystery of redemption was to be taught, He had inscribed the legend: Let no man who is unwilling to deny himself, and take up his cross, enter here."[17] Weber states, "In the face of the coming judgment there is, however, one way to salvation—to follow Christ." This is done when a disciple takes "seriously Jesus' word about taking up his cross (Luke 9:23)."[18]

(b) Another view may be called the proclamation-of-salvation view. This view finds a basis for understanding the cross-bearing sayings in the proclamation of the gospel. Morris, who holds to the suffering view, sees in the Christian's sufferings "the means of setting forward the purpose Christ achieved in His atoning death" which is "the taking of the gospel to those for whom it is intended," and this "is to tread the path of the cross."[19]

(c) Another view is the pacifist-kingdom view. Griffiths relates the saying to the "Messianic purpose" with Israel, which will "in its final acme . . . be realized in a spiritual destiny." In the "new house of Israel," the "new ἐκκλησία θεοῦ" the "Messianic aim of freedom from Rome's oppression" is not to be obtained by "armed rebellion" but by "the way of voluntary suffering."[20] This view could also be classified as a variant of the suffering view, but its eschatological orientation warrants seeing this as a separate view.

(d) Still another view is what may be called the body-of-Christ view. Morris, who supports several other views, has suggested that the cross-bearing concept contains "the thought that in some sense Christ and His people are one."[21]

A Proposed View: Submission

It is this writer's position that the phrase "take up his cross" is a figure of speech derived from the Roman custom requiring a man convicted of rebellion against Rome's sovereign rule to carry the cross-beam (*patibulum*) to his place of execution. Thus the proper starting point is the historical basis for the phrase. This starting point, as will be shown, leads to an interpretation that cross-bearing means to submit to the authority or rule one formerly rebelled against, or to obey God's will.

CONTEXTUAL EVIDENCE

All three Synoptic Gospels refer to taking up one's cross. Matthew 16:24; Mark 8:34; and Luke 9:23 place it after Peter's confession that Jesus is the Messiah and after Jesus' first intimation of His coming Passion. Matthew 10:38 and Luke 14:27 place it in a series of statements concerning discipleship.

A full development of the contextual argument for each of the five occurrences of the cross-bearing sayings would require more space than is possible here. However, a few thoughts can be presented for consideration. In Matthew 16:24 and Mark 8:34 the cross-bearing statement follows Peter's rebuke of Jesus concerning His messianic role as One who must suffer many things. Then Peter was himself rebuked by Jesus (a) for not following ("Get behind Me," an echo of Jesus' response to Satan in the temptation, Matt. 4:10), (b) for being an agent of Satan, and (c) for setting his mind on or expounding man's interests, not God's. Jesus had explained what God's will is, and anyone who would dissuade Him from obeying God's will must be rebuked. For Jesus, obedience to God's plan for Him to be the suffering Messiah was imperative. Peter therefore needed to see that Jesus must always submit to the Father's will,[22] and so must those who would follow Christ.[23] Thus the issue of submission to God or obedience was the occasion for the teaching on cross-bearing in these two passages.

Though parallel to Matthew 16 and Mark 8, Luke 9 omits Jesus' rebuke of Peter. However, in verse 23 Luke recorded a significant variation: "take up his cross daily." This indicates that salvation is not in view here and also that the order of denying oneself, taking up one's cross, and following Christ is a logical order and not a chronological order.[24]

The two other occurrences of the cross-bearing sayings are in Matthew 10:38 and Luke 14:27. In both verses the Passion context is absent. In Matthew 10 Jesus gave instructions to the Twelve before they were sent out to the lost sheep of Israel. In Luke 14

Jesus urged the multitudes to count the cost of being His disciples.
Both chapters include a series of short exhortations to obedience
and submission to God and His Son.

Jesus' call to cross-bearing in Mark 8:34 was given to the
multitudes (τόν ὄχλον, "the crowd"). This indicates that these
conditions for following Jesus apply to all, not just to a special
class of believers. Jesus called them to "come after Me" (ὀπίσω
μου ἐλθεῖν). The words "come after" have a Hebrew background
meaning "to follow, to be obedient to."[25] The word translated
"follow" means "to follow someone as a disciple."[26] The person
who follows Jesus (as His disciple) must meet several requirements.

First, a disciple is to "deny himself." Was Jesus asking a
disciple to "give up his personality"? No, because God has given
each person a unique personality. Yet this idea is suggested by
Bauer, Arndt, and Gingrich.[27] What is so inherent in "self" that it
(rather than sin or greed or false gods) should be denied? The
answer is simple; "self" is in rebellion against the King. One
cannot follow Christ if he is in rebellion to Him.

To deny self is to begin to deal with one's inherent sin nature,
which results in his being hostile to God and His will (cf. Mark
7:15).[28] Self is what caused Peter to set his mind on man's interests
rather than God's (Mark 8:33). That same spirit of rebellion
caused the elders, chief priests, and scribes to reject the King
(Mark 8:31). One cannot follow Jesus if he is going the opposite
way. But to deny oneself is incomplete. At best it leaves one in a
neutral state, whereas "following" is active and positive. This
calls for a second requirement.

Second, a disciple is to "take up his cross." This is the
positive action needed after one has denied "himself." It is the
active submission of the disciple, who formerly had been a
rebel, to the authority of the King. To deny oneself is to cease
rebelling against the King's rule and to take up one's cross is to
submit to His rule. A disciple's cross, then, is not Jesus' cross,
nor is it crucifixion. This distinction is crucial for a proper
interpretation.[29]

In summary, the contexts of the cross-bearing statements in the
Synoptic Gospels lead one to expect the figure to mean obedience
or submission. The phrases "come after," "follow Me," and "deny
himself" all direct the reader to expect a command to obey and
submit.

THEOLOGICAL EVIDENCE

Theologically Jesus' work on the cross was associated with obedience or submission. This has direct implications for disciples' cross-bearing.

Morris wrote, "it is integral to the very nature of [Jesus'] sacrifice that it was . . . wrought in obedience.[30] Morgan has observed that "the cross was the supreme demonstration of Christ's absolute conformity to the will of God."[31] According to Murray, the atoning work of Christ is set forth in the Scriptures under four categories: sacrifice, propitiation, reconciliation, and redemption. But he includes them all under obedience.

> But we may properly ask it there is not some more inclusive rubric under which these more specific categories may be comprehended. The Scripture regards the work of Christ as one of obedience and uses this term, or the concept that it designates, with sufficient frequency to warrant the conclusion that obedience is generic and therefore embracive enough to be viewed as the unifying factor or integrating principle.[32]

In another place Murray provides a very insightful summary of the role of obedience in Christ's atoning work as seen in the Old Testament.

> No passage in Scripture provides more instruction on our topic than Isaiah 52:13–53:12. It is in the capacity as Servant that the person in view is introduced and it is in the same capacity He executes His expiatory function (Isa. 52:13, 15; 53:11). The title "Servant" derives its meaning from the fact that He is the Lord's Servant, not the Servant of men (cf. Isa. 42:1, 19; 52:13). He is the Father's Servant and this implies subjection to and fulfillment of the Father's will. *Servant* defines His commitment, and *obedience* the execution.[33]

According to the New Testament Christ's atoning work is not to be thought of simply in terms of suffering, pain, grief, or even death, but in terms of a servant's obedience. It is not this author's desire to minimize the terrible agony of the Savior's sufferings nor their soteriological importance, but rather to point out, as do the Scriptures, that their underlying value is found in their being the outworking of His obedience.

In Gethsemane Jesus prayed, "My Farther, if it is possible, let this cup pass from Me; yet not as I will, but as Thou wilt" (Matt. 26:39), and "My Father if this cannot pass away unless I drink it, Thy will be done" (Matt. 26:42; cf. Mark 14:36; Luke 22:42). Jesus wrestled that night with His willingness to do the Father's will. He clearly saw the events before Him as requiring submission to the Father's will. In a similar way John 17 could be analyzed to demonstrate the theme of submission to the Father's will. "In obedience to God's will He accomplished the work of redemption."[34]

Paul also stated that Christ's atoning work should be understood in terms of obedience. "For as through one man's disobedience the many were made sinners, even so through the obedience of the One the many will be made righteous" (Rom. 5:19). Paul did not write that a person is made righteous because Christ *suffered*, but rather that one is made righteous because He *obeyed*. Philippians 2:6–11 is a classic passage on the nature of Jesus' incarnation.[35] Verse 8 is the climax, in which Paul explained the real work of Christ as "becoming obedient." In extent His obedience was "to the point of death," and in manner it was "even death on a cross." For Paul the central issue in Christ's death was that it was an act of obedience; all else flows from this.

The writer of the Epistle to the Hebrews, referring to the prayer of Christ at Gethsemane, wrote, "although He was a Son, He learned obedience from the things which He suffered" (Heb. 5:8). Westcott has commented that "sufferings in this sense may be said to teach obedience as they confirm it and call it out actively."[36] Thus the New Testament provides abundant evidence that Murray is correct when he says that the entire atoning work of Christ can be understood best under the rubric of "obedience." Calvin wrote that "our Lord had no need to undertake the bearing of the cross except to attest and prove His obedience to the Father."[37]

By advancing the interpretation of cross-bearing as obedience/submission, and thereby excluding suffering from its meaning, some readers might be led to assume that this view excludes suffering from the believer's life as inevitable. On the contrary, this author believes that, assuming a believer lives long enough, every believer will somehow suffer, in view of his identification with Christ. Mark 4:17 seems to indicate this, as do Mark 13:9, 13. In addition, one could note Romans 8:17–25, 35–39, as well as 1 Peter 2:20–25; 3:14–4:2; and 4:12–13.

In summary, even if an interpreter desired to explain the figure of the disciples' cross-bearing on the basis of a parallel to the Savior's cross, rather than as a figure from Roman custom, he should still conclude that the figure represents obedience or submission to God's will. While this author emphasizes that the believer's cross is not Christ's, there is a strong and clear evidence from theology that for Christ the cross was in its essence an act of obedience or submission to the Father's will. If there is any sense in taking up His cross, it is this.

HISTORICAL EVIDENCE

The Roman penal system required a condemned man to carry his cross to the place of his execution. The phrase "take up his cross" is a reference to this practice. But why did the Romans require a condemned man to carry his cross through the city to the place of his execution?

Non-Roman references to crucifixion. Crucifixion was used by the ancient Persians, as well as by the Indians, Assyrians, Scythians, Taurians, and Celts. Later the Germani and Britanni adopted it.[38] The Numidians employed crucifixion and the Carthaginians especially used it. Hengel suggests that Rome adopted this practice from Carthage.[39] In Greece "it was never even considered for free Greeks,"[40] and in the pre-Roman Hellenistic period "crucifixion was not unknown as a punishment for state criminals."[41] Crucifixion was generally associated with crimes against the state, whereas other forms of capital punishment were used for other crimes.

Two helpful references to cross-bearing occur in Greek writings from the Roman period. Plutarch, in describing the relationship of wickedness to punishment, cites several examples, one of which is that "every criminal who goes to execution must carry his own cross on his back."[42] Though Plutarch does not here explain the significance of cross-bearing, his use of "every" (ἕχαστος) is significant because most ancient references to crucifixion do not mention cross-bearing. Thus Plutarch's reference to cross-bearing as apparently normative provides substantial evidence for assuming that the common man would be familiar with this practice.

The second Greek reference to cross-bearing is by Chariton of Aphrodisias. He lived in Asia Minor and wrote in the first or second century A.D. Sixteen escaped slaves, having been captured, were led to their execution in chains, each carrying his own cross. Chariton comments, "The executioners supplemented the necessary death penalty by other wretched practices such as were *effective as an example* to the rest" (of the slaves).[43] Hengel comments that "the whole proceedings were designed above all as a deterrent."[44] Thus cross-bearing and other practices associated with crucifixion had as their purpose not a more horrible death, as is usually assumed, but rather the fulfillment of an exemplary function. They were intended to be observed and understood.

Roman references to crucifixion. In the Roman Empire crucifixion was reserved for the most serious of capital crimes.[45] Bruce notes that crucifixion was "customary for seditious provincials."[46] Hengel concludes that it was "as a rule reserved for hardened criminals, rebellious slaves and rebels against the Roman state."[47] And "crucifixion was practiced above all on . . . groups whose development had to be suppressed by all possible means to safeguard law and order in the state."[48] Tacitus wrote that the crucifixion of slaves was to prevent rebellion, to maintain the slaves in submission to Roman rule.[49] In a province the local governor could impose the penalty of crucifixion as he willed "based on his *imperium* and the right of *coercitio* to maintain peace and order."[50] "Governors imposed this servile punishment especially on freedom fighters who tried to break away from Roman rule."[51] The imposition of crucifixion on those "who rose up against the empire"[52] and resisted its authority[53] "was seen as a disciplinary measure for the maintenance of existing authority, intended more as a deterrent than as a means of retribution."[54] Crucifixion was therefore done in a public place. Hengel refers to this deterrent function as "the chief reason for its use."[55] Again and again the literature on crucifixion stresses the themes of the sovereignty of the state, its rule and power, and the nature of those crucified as "rebellious." It is in this historical context that cross-bearing occurred, and it is in this context that the purpose of cross-bearing and thus its meaning will be found.

Cross-bearing was only one part of the crucifixion process. Normally in the Roman era the process began with flogging till the criminal's blood flowed. Next the victim carried the transverse bar (*patibulum*) of his cross to the place of execution. The cross-bearing journey was through public areas, and "crucifixion took place publicly on streets or elevated places."[56] The vertical stake of the cross was a permanent fixture, installed beforehand at the execution site. "On the way to execution a tablet was hung around the offender stating the *causa poenae*, and this was affixed to the cross after execution so that all could see."[57] Once at the execution site, the offender was fastened to the beam with ropes or nails and the cross-beam and body were lifted into place on the vertical stake.[58] There were many variations of cross structures and methods of affixing the offender to the cross.[59]

Judaism and crucifixion. God placed a curse on anyone who hung on a tree (Deut. 21:23). The Jews also applied this curse to anyone crucified.[60] "In the Hellenistic Hasmonean period crucifixion was practiced as the form of death penalty applied in cases of high treason."[61] Herod, however, broke with the Hasmonean practice and in light of the excessive use of crucifixion in pacifying Judea, he abandoned it. By the time of Jesus, the death penalty and thus crucifixion was entirely a matter of Roman jurisdiction.[62] Thus the meaning of cross-bearing to a Jew of Jesus' day would be derived from the Roman use of it.[63]

Crucifixion was well known to the Jews of Jesus' time. The best known example is the crucifixion of 2,000 Jewish rebels in 4 B.C. (According to Hoehner's chronology Jesus was born in the winter of 5 or 4 B.C.,[64] thus placing this event in His lifetime.) Nazareth was a small village about four miles southeast of Sepphoris, the capital of Western Galilee.[65] After Herod's death in March/April 4 B.C. a revolt under Judas the Galilean broke out and the rebels raided the palace and armory at Sepphoris. The Roman commander Publius Quintilius, governor of Syria, put down the revolt which had spread across the countryside and crucified 2,000 of the rebels.[66] Thus there is abundant evidence that even in the countryside the common Jew would have had enough experience with Rome to know what cross-bearing meant. Hengel notes that "the cross never became the symbol of Jewish suffering."[67] The primary purpose of crucifixion was not to maximize the pain of death, though it certainly was painful. In support of this, "according to Talmudic tradition (bSanh., 43a; Str.-B., I, 1037) high-placed ladies in Jerusalem used to give an intoxicating drink to the condemned before execution in order to make them insensitive to pain."[68] If the purpose of crucifixion was to maximize suffering this could not be allowed; yet it was done with the Romans being aware of it.[69] If, however, crucifixion was to be a public example that every rebel ultimately must submit to Rome's rule, then the authorities could allow the practice.

It is this author's opinion that the historical evidence best supports a submission view of cross-bearing. In the provinces Roman rule was held together by the popular perception that any challenge to her authority was doomed. It was thus imperative that any serious challenge to Rome's rule be met not only victoriously but also turned into a public demonstration that in the end the rebel had submitted. Having condemned a man to die for his rebellion, Rome required him, as his last act, to display submission publicly to the authority against which he previously had rebelled. This was done by having him carry the instrument of his judgment through the city to a public place while wearing a sign which said that he had been a rebel. But as all could see, he was now submissive. To "take up his cross" was thus a figure of speech easily understood by anyone in the Roman Empire to mean "to submit to the authority against which one had previously rebelled."

Conclusion

The requirement that a disciple "take up his cross" means "to submit to the rule against which he was formerly in rebellion." Evidence for this meaning of "obedience" or "submission" was developed from the biblical passages and their contexts, theology, and history. To "deny self" means to cease rebelling against the King and His rule—to cease being hostile to God, to stop being disobedient. To "take up his cross" means to submit actively to the King and His reign—to obey God and do His will. The one who does this is thus following Jesus.

CHAPTER 10

The Significance of the First Sign in John's Gospel

Stanley D. Toussaint

The miracle of Christ's turning water to wine, recorded in John 2:1-11, tells much about the Lord. It indicates, for instance, that the Lord hallowed marriage and family life. The well-known words of the Book of Common Prayer refer to marriage as a "holy estate" which "Christ adorned and beautified with His presence and first miracle that He wrought in Cana of Galilee. . . ." This miracle also manifests the fact that Christ approved of festivities. More than once this aspect of the Lord's ministry is seen and misunderstood (Matt. 9:14; 11:19; Luke 15:2). This miracle is commonly viewed as a sign which reveals the Lord Jesus as the Creator. In this miracle He "created" wine—the whole process of growth, bearing fruit, harvest, and production of wine is compressed into a minuscule fragment of time.

While those facts are true, do any or all of them reveal the *real* significance of the miracle?

Of course there are many attendant difficulties and problems that must be answered. Did Jesus make actual wine? Why did Jesus speak to His mother as He did? Why is this the first miracle? Interestingly all these attendant questions are answered when the basic problem is solved: What is the significance of this first miracle?

The fact that John called attention to this miracle as being first is enough to indicate its primacy among the wonders Christ performed. That he should describe it as a sign also indicates its importance and consequence. The word σημεῖον looks at a miracle as proof of a point or as a means of teaching something. The crucial thing is not the miracle, as genuine and important as it is, but the lesson to be learned from the miracle. The fact that John used only σημεῖον in his Gospel to refer to Christ's miracles does not detract from the purpose of the miracles to teach something about the Lord Jesus Christ. In fact, it enhances this truth.

The Situation

The situation is described in John 2:1–2. The time was the third day. It is obvious John was emphasizing the first week of Christ's ministry. Just as the last days were crucial, so also the initial hours of the Lord's earthly work were important. The first day is referred to in John 1:35; the second is mentioned in 1:43; and the third day is seen in 2:1.

Cana was evidently a relatively unknown village because every time John referred to it he described, it as being "of Galilee" (2:1, 11; 4:46; 21:2). No other New Testament writer alludes to it. The location of Cana is not definitely known; however, all the possible sites are near Nazareth. The most probable site is nine miles to the north.

A wedding and its attendant wedding feast were the occasion for the miracle. Evidently the marriage had already been contracted; the groom had gone to the bride's home to acquire his wife; the wedding procession to the groom's house had taken place; and now the wedding festivities had begun. This celebration could last for days, possibly even a week.

The presence of the Lord's mother, the Lord Jesus, and His disciples is described in verses 1 and 2. John assumed the reader knows the basic Gospel narrative; this is attested by his referring to Mary simply as "the mother of Jesus." It is of interest to note the absence of any reference to Joseph. It may be assumed he had died before Christ began His public ministry.

The Lord Jesus must have been an intimate friend of the family. He was personally invited and so were His disciples; He was told of the embarrassing lapse in the supply of wine; the servants were put into submission to Him. Obviously Jesus was no stranger! It is interesting to observe in this connection the contrast in the verb tenses between verses 1 and 2. The verb "was" in verse 1 is imperfect, implying Mary had been there for some time. The aorist ("had been there") in verse 2 *may* imply Christ had been invited later, on His return to Nazareth from the Jordan. At any rate the presence of the disciples was certainly something of a surprise. They were invited as an afterthought only because they were with Jesus. (The verb ἐκλήθη is singular.) After all, the five disciples who were with Jesus had only been called during the preceding two days! Could it be that their presence contributed to the shortage of the wine?

The Sign

THE COUNSEL OF MARY

In connection with John 2:3–5 the question is often raised, Was the wine Jesus made actual wine? It is difficult to answer this in the negative; the text refers to actual wine for several reasons. First, the word used here is οἶνος, which simply means "wine." That this is its meaning is difficult to dispute. Second, the word μεθύω used in verse 10 means "to be drunk" (cf. Matt. 24:29; Acts 2:15; 1 Cor. 11:21; 1 Thess. 5:7; Rev. 17:2, 6).

While it is difficult to dispute the fact that the Lord made wine, two mitigating factors must be brought into the discussion. First, drunkenness was a despised sin and was severely reprobated. No passage of Scripture teaches total abstinence, but drunkenness is clearly classified as sin (Hab. 2:15; Luke 21:34; Rom. 13:13; Gal. 5:21; Eph. 5:18). To say the Lord made wine by no means indicates He condoned drunkenness. Second, wine was normally diluted. The ratio could be as high as twenty parts of water to one of wine or as low as one to one.[1] Even the apocryphal 2 Maccabees refers to this custom of diluting wine with water. The writer of this book concludes his work with these words in 2 Maccabees 15:38–39:

> And if I have written well and to the point in my story, this is what I myself desired; but if meanly and indifferently, this is all I could attain unto. For as it is distasteful to drink wine alone and in like manner again to drink water alone, while the mingling of wine with water at once gives full pleasantness to the flavor, so also the fashioning of the language delights the ears of them that read the story.

The conclusion then seems to be irrefutable: the wine at the wedding of Cana was not simply grape juice; it was wine diluted with water. The exact ratio is unknown but a low amount of water would have left the wine intoxicating (John 2:10; Eph. 5:18). At any rate, drunkenness was looked on as a sin and a grave social error. Inebriation was detested and severely censured.

When the supply of wine lapsed, the Lord's mother informed Christ of this most embarrassing situation. This was a social faux pas of the first order.[2] It could even result in a lawsuit by the bride's parents against the family of the groom!

What is the significance of Mary's informing the Lord that the supply of wine had been depleted? Certainly she was not doing this to ask the Lord and His disciples to leave. Perhaps their presence contributed to this disconcerting plight; but this explanation of her words, "They have no wine," does not fit the remainder of the narrative. In verse 5 Mary told the servants, "Whatever He says to you, do it."

It is quite clear Mary was expecting a miracle. It is true the Lord had not as yet performed any miracles, but she certainly had many evidences of His supernatural character—His conception, the events surrounding His birth and presentation in the temple (cf. Luke 2:8-38), and the incident in the temple area when He was only 12 years old. Now His appearance with the disciples whom He had called would point to the beginning of His public ministry. Mary informed the Lord of the problem so He could supernaturally solve it.

The Lord's answer recorded in verse 4 has perplexed many. "Woman, what do I have to do with you? My hour has not yet come." The vocative γύναι is a term not of reproach but of respect (cf. John 19:26–27). Liddell and Scott say the vocative was used to express respect or affection.[3] A modern equivalent would be "ma'am" or more properly "madam."

"What do I have to do with you?" is more literally translated, "What to me and to you?" It means, "What do we have in common?" Godet says, "This formula signifies that the community of feeling to which one of the interlocutors appeals is rejected by the other, at least in the particular point which is in question."[4] The Lord was saying they were no longer on common ground. Up to this time their relationship had been purely domestic; now He was entering into public ministry.

When the Lord Jesus stated, "My hour has not yet come," He used an expression that occurs several times in John's Gospel (7:30; 8:20; cf. 7:6, 8). Contrariwise, the coming of the Lord's hour is also referred to in the later sections of this Gospel (12:23, 27; 13:1; 17:1). A study of these passages indicates that it points to the process of the Lord's glorification. It describes the Lord's "hour" from His crucifixion to His coming reign on earth. Evidently Mary expected Christ to manifest Himself supernaturally in such a way as to bring about the kingdom age. This explains the Lord's response.

Mary's command to the servants indicates she still expected a miracle. She now also saw a new relationship with her Son and she recognized His authority.

THE COMMANDS OF THE LORD

The presence of six large stone waterpots each capable of holding 20 to 30 gallons of liquid set the stage for what was about to happen. The total amount of wine involved in the miracle was between 120 and 150 gallons! Normally the pots were employed for holding water in the various rites of purification. Verse 7 indicates the servants filled the empty and partially filled waterpots "to the brim." This was important because it left no room for the addition of any solutions. Furthermore, these waterpots had been used for water so there would not have been any residue of grapes in them. There was no way, humanly speaking, in which the water could have been made to taste like wine.

The word ἀρχιτρίκλινος used in verse 8 actually means "ruler of a room with three couches." This person who was the first to taste the wine had the combined responsibilities of head waiter and master of ceremonies. He was to be the objective but unwitting witness and testimony to the reality of the miracle. Of all people he would be the most qualified to judge the quality of the wine.

THE COMMENT OF THE HEAD WAITER

The remark of the head waiter in verse 10 expressed his surprise that the best wine had been withheld so long. It was normal to serve the inferior wine after the guests' tastes had been dulled. As noted earlier, the verb μεθύω simply means "to be drunk."[5] Certainly the comment of the head waiter does not mean the guests were drunk nor does it imply that Jesus condoned drunkenness. The words of the head waiter—the master of ceremonies—simply express the modus operandi at most wedding feasts. The text is only recording the words of an astonished professional. The point of the remark is the high quality of the wine; the best available had been served earlier, but the miraculous wine far surpassed it.

The Significance

John designates this miracle as the Lord's first sign. The fact that this is said to be the first does away with the apocryphal miracles recorded in the apocryphal Gospels. That it is a sign indicates there is a truth *behind* the miracle, a truth greater than the miracle itself. The *first* message by way of a miracle in John's Gospel and the Lord's ministry is this sign.

THE SIGNIFICANCE FOR ISRAEL

There is significance in the miracle first for Israel, especially the Israel of Christ's day. The wedding feast with its new wine portrays the coming of the kingdom. By this sign the Lord declared He is the Messiah of Israel who is capable of bringing the predicted kingdom into its glorious existence. A number of factors show this is the point of the miracle. (1) The kingdom is often portrayed in terms of a banquet, especially a wedding feast (Matt. 8:11; 22:1–14; Luke 13:29; 14:15–24; Rev. 19:7–9). The presence of the Lord at these marriage festivities at Cana graphically pictures the coming of the kingdom. (2) A number of references in the Old Testament picture the kingdom age in terms of wine. For instance Isaiah 25:6 joins the figures of a banquet and wine together to illustrate the joys of the future kingdom age. In Isaiah 27:2–6 the prophet described Israel as God's vineyard in the millennium. An abundance of wine was a description often used in the Old Testament of the time when Abraham's promises would be fulfilled (Gen. 49:11–12; Jer. 31:12; Hos. 2:22; 14:7; Joel 2:19, 24; 3:18; Amos 9:13–14; Zech. 9:15–17; 10:7).

This gives significance to the lapse of wine. Not only was this a gross social error; it was also a picture of the obsolescence of Judaism. The old wine had run out and Christ the Messiah was here to bring the new. As Paul put it, "the fullness of time" had come (Gal. 4:4). The Lord used the same kind of a figure in the parable of the wineskins (Matt. 9:17; Luke 5:37–38). The Apostle John beautifully prepared for this miracle in John 1:17: "For the law was given through Moses; grace and truth were realized through Jesus Christ." The miracle shows the old order had run its course; now was the time for a new one.

THE SIGNIFICANCE FOR CHRISTIANS

The significance of this miracle is not for Jews only; it is obviously for the church as well. The basic truth for Christians is found in the joy of salvation. Wine and joy are also associated. The psalmist praised God for His generous providence in giving man "wine which makes man's heart glad" (Ps. 104:15). In a classic case of personification the vine of Judges 9:13 objected, "Shall I leave my new wine, which cheers God and men, and go to wave over the trees?" Although Westcott fails to see this miracle as an illustration of God's provision of joy for the Christian he does remark, "There is a Jewish saying, 'Without wine there is no joy.' . . ."[6]

This miracle portrays not only the joy Christ brings into a person's life but also the *abundance* of joy. The Lord made between 120 and 150 gallons of wine! Not only do believers have access to a peace that passes understanding (Phil. 4:7) and grace unbounding (Rom. 5:20), but also joy unspeakable and full of glory (1 Peter 1:8). Surely the vast supply of wine portrays both the abundance of the kingdom age and the fullness of joy in the individual Christian's experience. Hymn writers have caught this aspect of the spiritual life in various phrases and clauses—"Come we that love the Lord, and let our joys be known . . ."; "He brings a poor lost sinner into His house of wine . . ."; "Rejoice, give thanks, and sing . . ."; and a myriad more.

Finally, for the Christian there is a new life in Christ. The old is passed away and in Christ the believer has a whole new life and perspective (2 Cor. 5:17).

This miracle, then, was a sign to prompt faith in Jesus as the Messiah and to provide new life through Him, just as John stated in the declaration of the purpose of his Gospel (John 20:31).

CHAPTER 11

Abiding Is Remaining in Fellowship: Another Look at John 15:1–6

Joseph C. Dillow

The beautiful and profound analogy of the vine and the branches in John 15:1–6 has encouraged believers throughout the centuries. It has also become, unfortunately, a controversial passage regarding the eternal security of the saints.

Three approaches have been taken to the passage. Some say the person who "does not bear fruit" (John 15:2a) cannot be a Christian because all true Christians bear fruit. Others say the branches "in Me" that are taken away refer to Christians who lose their salvation. In this view when a believer stops producing fruit, he forfeits justification. Others say John 15:2a and 6 refer to Christians who do not produce fruit and who will therefore experience divine judgment in time and loss of reward at the judgment seat of Christ.

The Meaning of "Every Branch in Me"

Most evangelicals agree that the branches that "bear fruit" and are pruned to bear more fruit (15:2b) are true believers. But what about the branches "in Me" (i.e., in Christ) that do not bear fruit? Some say that those who do not bear fruit are not true Christians. They claim they are saved but are not. Smith argued that "in Me" refers to people being in the kingdom in only a general sense. He notes that the future millennium and the present form of the kingdom include a mixture of true and false believers.[1] As Ryle put it, "It cannot be shown that a branch in Me must mean a believer in Me. It means nothing more than a 'professing member of my Church, a man joined to the company of my people, but not joined to me.'"[2]

Often justification for this interpretation is found by going to the analogy of the vine in Isaiah (Isa. 5:1–7; cf. Jer. 5:10a; Rom. 11:16–24). Here there were branches who were not saved.

However, this is irrelevant to John 15, for Isaiah wrote of a *covenant* people. All Jews (saved and unsaved) are in Israel, but not all professing Christians are in Christ! As will be demonstrated, it is unlikely that "in Me" can refer to an "Israel within Israel" (i.e., the truly saved within the professing company) in view of the consistent usage of "in Me" in John's writings to refer to a true saving relationship.

Laney has argued differently that those "in Me" are only professing Christians. He notes that the phrase "in Me" can be taken either adjectivally with the noun "branch" or adverbially with the verb "does not bear." If it is rendered adverbially, then the sentence could be translated, "Every branch not bearing fruit in Me He takes away." The phrase "in Me" then refers to the sphere in which fruit-bearing can occur.[3] Though this view is exegetically possible, most evangelical commentators and English translations render the phrase "in Me" as an adjective modifying "branch," so that some branches do not bear fruit. The phrase "in Me" is used 16 times in John's Gospel (6:56; 10:38; 14:10 [twice], 11, 20, 30; 15:2, 4 [twice], 5–7; 16:33; 17:21, 23). In each case it refers to fellowship with Christ.[4] It is inconsistent then to say the phrase in 15:2 refers to a person who merely professes to be saved but is not. A person "in Me" is always a true Christian. But what does "in Me" signify? The preposition ἔν is used "to designate a close personal relation."[5] It refers to a sphere within which some action occurs.[6] So to abide "in" Christ means to remain in close relationship to Him.

What kind of relationship is meant? A review of the 16 occurrences of "in Me" in the Gospel of John seems to suggest that when Jesus used this phrase, He referred to a life of fellowship, a unity of purpose, rather than organic connection. This is somewhat different from Paul's emphasis. While Paul did occasionally use the phrase "in Christ" (not "in Me") in this way, he more often used it in a forensic sense to refer to the believer's position in Christ (e.g., 2 Cor. 5:17; Eph. 1:7) or to organic membership in Christ's body (e.g., 1 Cor. 12:13). John, however, never used the phrase in that way. For him, to be "in Christ" meant to be in communion with Him.

Christ did not mean that the Father was inside Him and that He was inside the Father. He spoke instead of a relationship between Him and the Father. The "works" (miracles) the Son did enabled the people to understand the nature of the relationship between the

Son and the Father. Obviously seeing Jesus' miracles did not prove to the people that the Son is of the same essence as the Father, organically connected with Him. If that were so, then when an apostle later performed a miracle, it would show that he was also of the same essence with the Son. Instead, Jesus' miracles showed that God was with Him. They showed that what God the Father did, the Son did, and that what the Son did, the Father did. The miracles demonstrated that the Son and the Father are like-minded and speak the same things. Therefore people are to believe what the Son says because what He says is the same as what the Father says. So the "in Me" relationship speaks not of organic connection or commonality of essence, but of commonality of purpose and commitment.[7]

In John 14:30 the Lord stated that the ruler of this world has nothing "in Me," that Satan has no part with Christ, no communion of purpose with Him.[8] Jesus was not teaching that the devil has no part of His essence but that they are not like-minded. "In Me" refers not to common essence or organic connection but to fellowship.

The experience of peace in the midst of persecution comes only to believers who are obediently walking in His commandments and aligned with His purposes. "These things I have spoken to you, that in Me you may have peace" (John 16:33). John's writings and the rest of the New Testament confirm that salvation does not automatically result in an experience of peace in the midst of trials. Only when a believer is in Christ in the sense of walking in fellowship with Him does he have peace (Phil. 4:6–7).

The view that "in Me" means oneness of purpose and not organic connection is also seen in John 17:21. Here Christ prayed for the kind of oneness among the disciples that He enjoys with the Father, a oneness of love and fellowship: "that they may all be one; even as Thou, Father, art in Me, and I in Thee." If this "in Me" relationship referred to organic connection, Jesus would not have prayed for an organic connection between Him and believers because it already existed. Jesus desired that believers experience oneness of purpose because that observable unity will prove to the world that they are His disciples, models of Christian love (v. 23). If being in Christ referred only to an organic connection, it would prove nothing. But if it refers to an experiential unity of purpose and fellowship, this would have great testimonial impact.

In John 3:21 Jesus referred to the fact that His deeds had been done "in God." Bauer, Arndt, and Gingrich correctly observe that this means that His works were done in communion or fellowship with God the Father.[9] Being "in God" does not refer to an organic relationship but to a relationship of commonality of purpose. Therefore it seems that the phrase "in Me" in John does not require the sense of organic connection often found in Paul's epistles. To be "in Me" is to be in fellowship with Christ, living obediently. Therefore it is possible for a Christian not to be "in Me" in the Johannine sense. This seems evident from the command to "abide in Christ." Believers are to remain in fellowship with the Lord. If all Christians already remain "in Me," then why command them to remain in that relationship? It must be possible for them not to remain. This leads to a discussion of "abide," one of John's favorite terms.

The Meaning of "Abide"

The English word "abide" means "(1) to wait for; (2) to endure without yielding, to bear patiently, to tolerate, to withstand; (3) to remain stable or in a fixed state, to continue in a place."[10] These are also the meanings of the Greek word μένω. However, the slightly mystical connotation in English Bible translations has freighted it with overtones of faith or dependence.

Most Greek lexicons suggest that μένω simply means "to remain."[11] In the Gospel of John μένω always means "to remain, to stay, to reside, to continue, to endure" (e.g., 1:32, 38–39; 2:12).[12] For this reason the New International Version translates the word "remain." In 15:4 Jesus told His disciples, "Abide in Me," that is, "Remain in Me."

What does it mean "to remain"? When the Lord said, "He who eats My flesh and drinks My blood abides [remains] in Me" (6:56), He meant that such an individual continues in close relationship to Him. Eating His flesh and drinking His blood seem to refer to the initial act of appropriating Christ by faith with the resultant gift of regeneration (6:50–51, 54, 58). When a person believes in Christ, he comes into a close relationship with Christ. The richness of that fellowship is determined by the believer's obedience (15:10). However, even though he has believed in Christ, and presently remains in fellowship, he might at some time in the future not continue in that fellowship. Hence the command to stay in fellowship is given.

When Jesus said that the person who believes in Him remains

in fellowship with Him, He was speaking a general maxim. He knew some Christians would not continue their fellowship. The proof of this is that in John 15:4 He commanded them to continue to abide. The verb is in the imperative mood, whereas 6:56 has an indicative present participle. If it is not possible to lose fellowship with Christ, why would the Lord warn about this possible failure? A warning regarding a danger no Christians would ever face and against an action no Christian would ever commit is pointless.

There is no basis for equating "remaining" with "believing" in John 6:56, as Blum does.[13] The word "remain" cannot mean "to accept Jesus as Savior." A believer remains in Christ's love by obeying His commandments (John 15:9–10). If remaining and believing are equated, then believing means obeying commandments, a thought far removed from the truth of the gospel by faith alone. Had Jesus intended μένω ("remain") to equal πιστεύω ("believe"), He could have used πιστεύω in 6:56 and 15:4, 7, 10. Not only would a works gospel be taught, but 6:56 would be reduced to the absurd statement "he who believes in Me believes in Me."

The first condition of abiding in Christ, or being in fellowship with Him, is to have believed on Him. A number of other conditions for remaining in fellowship with Christ are mentioned in John's writings: love other believers (1 John 2:10; 4:12), walk as He walked (2:6), be strong in the faith (2:14), do the will of God (2:17), hold to the truth learned at salvation (2:24), not hate one's brother in Christ (3:15), keep His commandments (1 John 3:24; John 15:10), and publicly confess Christ (1 John 4:15).

The rewards for meeting these conditions are great. Believers will truly be the Lord's disciples (John 8:31). But more important, such a life will enable them to stand before Him with confidence when He returns (1 John 2:28).

To "remain in Him" a Christian must keep Christ's commandments. Only if believers love one another does the love of God remain in them (1 John 4:12). For the love of God to remain in them, it must have been in them to begin with. As elsewhere in John's writings, "remain" never signifies the initial event of saving faith in Christ but the enduring relationship of walking in fellowship with Him. The word "remain" implies staying in a position already obtained, not entering for the first time. If a nonbeliever should ask, "What must I do to be saved," it would be wrong to answer, "Remain in Christ." The *believer* remains in Christ (i.e., remains in fellowship with Him) by keeping His commandments.

God remains in fellowship with Christians only if they love one another (1 John 4:12). A person *becomes* a Christian, however, by faith alone. Through the experience of the Holy Spirit a believer then enjoys the fellowship of the Father (4:13). The Holy Spirit is the source (ἐκ, "out of") from which the child of God draws strength to sustain that fellowship. "And the one who keeps His commandments abides in Him, and He in him. And we know by this that He abides in us, by the Spirit which He has given us" (3:24). This same Spirit not only energizes love and obedience but also public confession of Christ (4:15). If a Christian refuses to confess Christ, his fellowship with the Savior is broken.

In summary, it is preferable to hold that the analogy of branches abiding in a vine depicts a relationship that mature and growing Christians sustain with Christ because of remaining in close relationship to Him, rather than a relationship that all Christians have because of salvation. Fellowship rather than organic union is pictured. A branch "in Me" is not a branch organically connected to Him as a literal branch is organically connected to a vine. Instead it is a branch that is deriving its sustenance from Christ, living in fellowship with Him (as a literal branch derives sustenance from a literal vine), and thus bearing fruit.[14] This is demonstrated by the fact that "in Me" means "in fellowship with Me."

The Meaning of the Fruitless Branches

Four views have been proposed on the destiny of the fruitless branches mentioned in John 15:2 and 6.

THEY ARE LIFTED UP AND ENCOURAGED

R. K. Harrison points out that the word translated "takes away" (αἴρω) is best rendered "lifts up."[15] It is used this way in at least 8 of its 24 occurrences in the Gospel of John (5:8–12; 8:59; 10:18, 24). Contrary to Laney,[16] Harrison says fallen vines were lifted "with meticulous care" and allowed to heal.[17] The writer has observed this practice in the vineyards behind his home in Austria. If that is the meaning, then a fruitless branch is lifted up to put it into a position of fruit-bearing. This does not contradict verse 6, which states that a branch that does not abide is "thrown away," literally "cast out" (βάλλω ἔξω). This would suggest that the heavenly Vinedresser first encourages the branches and lifts them in the sense of providing loving care to enable them to bear fruit. If after this encouragement, they do not remain in fellowship with Him and bear fruit, they are then cast out.

THEY LOSE SALVATION

Some teach that the taking away of the branches points to a believer's loss of salvation. However, even if verse 2 means "remove" and not "lift up," loss of salvation is not in view. The figure of the vine and the branches signifies not regeneration but fellowship. As already demonstrated, to cease to abide in Christ does not mean to cease to be organically in Him but only to fail to remain in fellowship with Him. Thus the removal here would simply refer to the removal from fellowship of the Christian who fails to obey.

THEY ARE SEPARATED FROM A SUPERFICIAL CONNECTION WITH CHRIST

A third view is that the removal refers to the separation of professing Christians from a superficial connection with Christ. This is Laney's view.[18] But a branch connected to the vine is an illustration of the believer in fellowship with Christ. If "in Me" means to be in fellowship with Christ, as Laney says,[19] then the branch connected with the vine must be a branch in fellowship with the vine, that is, a true Christian, not merely a professing one.

If the fruitless branches are only professing Christians, then what bearing did the passage have on the disciples? Laney argues that it is intended to give them instruction concerning those to whom they would minister and who would not bear fruit.[20] Yet the passage gives every indication that it was addressed in its entirety to the disciples to tell them how they could bear fruit in *their* lives. Jesus said to them, "If you [the disciples, not those to whom they would one day minister] abide in Me, and My words abide in you, ask whatever you wish, and it shall be done for you. By this is My Father glorified, that you bear much fruit, and so prove to be My disciples" (John 15:7–8). He then told them of His love for them, that He wanted them to complete His joy, and so forth (15:9–16).

Jesus wants His followers to bear fruit and in this way to "be" (aorist middle subjunctive of γίνομαι) disciples (15:8). The basic difference between εἰμί and γίνομαι is that the latter suggests a coming into being in contrast to merely being. Thus in the act of fruit-bearing, a believer comes into being as a disciple. This is difficult to translate in English but the sense is clear: when a Christian is bearing fruit, in that act of fruit-bearing he is becoming a disciple: "that you bear much fruit and . . . be My disciples" (15:8).

When Jesus said, "You are already clean because of the word which I have spoken to you" (15:3), He was not contrasting the disciples with those who are only professing Christians. Verse 2 mentions two kinds of Christians: those who are in fellowship with Him who are not yet producing fruit, and those in fellowship with Him who are bearing fruit. The former need to be lifted up by the Vinedresser so they can become fruitful, and the latter need to be pruned so they will bear more fruit. The disciples had already been "pruned" (they were "clean"—the same Greek word καθαιρέω) through Jesus' word spoken to them. The disciples were now given instruction on how they, not those to whom they would minister, could continue to bear fruit. They could continue to bear fruit if they remained in fellowship with Him (i.e., if they were abiding in Him).

In John 15:4, Jesus said, "Abide in Me and I in you. As the branch cannot bear fruit of itself, unless it abides in the vine, so neither can you, unless you abide in Me." Here Jesus was apparently warning His hearers about the danger of their removing themselves, by disobedience, from His influence and enablement. But that does not imply that the ones being warned are not believers. In fact since they are commanded to remain in that sphere of influence and enablement, it seems that they are in it already and hence are regenerate.

THEY RECEIVE DIVINE DISCIPLINE IN TIME AND LOSS OF REWARDS

The fourth view on the destiny of unfruitful branches is that they receive divine discipline in this life (possibly including physical death) and loss of rewards at the judgment seat of Christ. This is the view Chafer propounded and seems to fit the context well.[21] The consequences of the failure of a true Christian to abide in fellowship with Christ are stated in verse 6: "If anyone does not abide in Me, he is thrown away as a branch, and dries up; and they gather them, and cast them into the fire, and they are burned."

If a true Christian does not remain in fellowship with Christ, he will be thrown away (βάλλω ἔξω, "cast out," much as a branch is severed from the vine) and discarded. As argued earlier, the point of the figure of the vine and the branches is not to portray organic connection but enablement and fellowship. This casting out then is not from salvation but from fellowship. The result is that these branches, carnal Christians, are cast into the fire.

To what does the fire refer? Fire is a common symbol in the Bible for God's judgment on His people in time (e.g., Isa. 5:24; 9:19). Less frequently it is associated with the fires of hell. Believers out of fellowship with Christ are therefore cast into divine judgment in time (cf. 1 Cor. 3:15). It seems mere quibbling to say that since the fire in 1 Corinthians 3:15 is applied to believer's works and the fire in John 15:6 refers to the believer himself, therefore those two verses could not be referring to the same event.[22] Paul wrote that the believer is the building and that the building is built up with various kinds of building materials and that the fire is applied to the building. The apostle obviously saw an intimate connection between the believer and his work. To apply the fire of judgment to the believer is the same as applying it to his work. Indeed the believer's works are simply a metonymy for the believer himself.[23]

Conclusion

According to John 15, when a believer is not bearing fruit because of sin or spiritual immaturity, the Lord lovingly lifts him up so he can bear fruit. The believer who is in fellowship with Christ and who is bearing fruit is pruned so he can bear more fruit. The analogy of the vine and the branches signifies not organic connection with Christ but fellowship with Him. The believer who does not remain in fellowship because of disobedience is cast out in judgment and withers spiritually, and faces severe divine discipline in time and loss of reward at the judgment seat of Christ. Nothing in John 15:1–6 demands that it pictures loss of salvation. Nor does the passage suggest that all believers will always bear fruit. It is only believers who remain in fellowship with Christ who bear fruit.

CHAPTER 12

Paul's Use of "About 450 Years" in Acts 13:20

Eugene H. Merrill

No period of ancient Israel's history has occasioned more chronological difficulties to the modern reader of the Old Testament than that of the period covered by the Book of Judges.[1] The apparently successful untangling of the complex threads of monarchical,[2] exilic,[3] and postexilic[4] historical narratives has not been achieved for this era between Moses and David. The purpose of this study is to propose solutions that permit the historical integrity of the Old Testament text to remain intact and that resolve the tensions that seem to exist in the Old and New Testament references to the period.

The Problem

First it is necessary to define the problem. Modern scholarship is nearly unanimous in dating the division of Israel's kingdom within a decade of 931 B.C. and the reigns of Solomon and David at 971–931 and 1011–971 respectively.[5] In Solomon's fourth year he commenced the construction of the great temple, an event so momentous it was tied in by the historian to the chronological origins of the nation, that is, the Exodus from Egypt. He stated that the Exodus was 480 years earlier than the laying of the temple foundations. The fourth year of Solomon was 966 so the Exodus was 1446 B.C.

It is clear from the accounts of the judges that the first of these illustrious figures was Othniel, the nephew of Joshua's contemporary, Caleb. Othniel delivered Israel from Cushanrishathaim of Aram-naharaim within a few years after Joshua's death, surely no earlier than around 1350 B.C.[6] The last of the judges was probably Samson, the date of whose death is around 1085.[7] The period of the judges, then, was 265 years at the most.

125

The problem emerges only when one considers two other factors, one in the Old Testament and one in the New Testament. These must be briefly stated.

THE INTERNAL CHRONOLOGY OF JUDGES–1 SAMUEL

The story of Israel in the time of the judges is one of chaotic anarchy described in terms of cyclical recurrence—sin, supplication, salvation, service, sin, etc. With apparent chronological precision the historiographer records the length of foreign oppression, the tenure of the judges whom the Lord raised up to save His people, the period of rest which followed, and other data.[8] As one begins to add the figures up, however, he soon discovers that they total far more than the 265 years suggested above. The following chart presents the available information.

Chronological Data of Israel's Judges

Reference	Oppression Period	Judge's Period	Rest Period
3:7–11	8 years		40 years
3:12–30	18 years		80 years
4:1–5:31	20 years		40 years
6:1–8:28	7 years		40 years
10:1–2		23 years	
10:3–5		22 years	
10:12:7	18 years	6 years	
12:8–10		7 years	
12:11–12		10 years	
12:13–15		8 years	
13:1–15:20	40 years	20 years	
Totals	111 years	96 years	200 years

What must be observed is the fact that no figures are given at all for Shamgar, the third judge (Judg. 3:31), but that even without him there is a grand total of 407 years of oppression, judgeship, and rest—far too many years to be accommodated within the available termini a quo and ad quem. Scholars have long recognized the problem here and so have postulated concurrent oppressions, judgeships, and so forth.[9] This seems to be the case, and in fact the inspired record itself implies this in at least the period of Jephthah and Samson. Judges 10:7 states that Yahweh was angry with His people and delivered them over to the Philistines and to the Ammonites simultaneously. The narrative then goes on to describe the Ammonite scourge first, indicating that it concerned primarily the Transjordan area and was terminated by the Lord's salvation through the Gileadite, Jephthah. In the meantime the Philistines rose up against the western Israelites until they were finally overcome by Samson. The events are narrated in sequence but there are strong reasons to feel that they were contemporaneous.[10] If this be so, other oppressions, judgeships, and periods of rest may also have coincided chronologically.

THE INFORMATION OF ACTS 13:20

While one may see how the apparently conflicting data within the Book of Judges may be harmonized, Paul in his address to the synagogue at Pisidian Antioch introduced a statement about the period of the Judges that has occasioned a great deal of difficulty for students of the Old Testament and New Testament alike. While rehearsing the history of Israel to this Jewish congregation, he asserted, "And when He [God] had destroyed seven nations in the land of Canaan, He distributed their land to them by allotment. And after that He gave them judges for about four hundred and fifty years, until Samuel the prophet" (NKJV). This reading of the Majority Text seems to exacerbate the difficulties of the chronology in that it requires 450 years from the judgeship of Othniel (ca. 1350 B.C.) to the time of Samuel (ca. 1120 B.C.), a manifest impossibility since the Old Testament appears to permit no more than about 230 years.

In light of this dilemma, most scholars prefer to adopt the reading of Westcott and Hort, which, on ordinary grounds, is supported by the best manuscript and versional evidence.[11] The New International Version, for example, translates Acts 13:19–20 as follows: "He overthrew seven nations in Canaan and gave their land to his people as their inheritance. All this took about 450 years. After this, God gave them judges until the time of Samuel the prophet. "[12] The "all this"[13] refers to the events before the Conquest of Canaan as well as the Conquest itself. This is usually taken to include only the sojourn in Egypt, the wilderness wandering, and the Conquest period. This would total about five hundred years at least, a figure not likely to be "rounded off" as "about 450 years."[14] However, the problem is even more severe than this, for a careful reading of Paul's address reveals that he did not begin his history with the Egyptian sojourn but with God's choosing of the patriarchal fathers long before![15] In other words to the five hundred years must now be added the more than two hundred which spanned the period from Abram's call to the descent to Egypt. To say that Paul was referring to these seven hundred years as "about 450 years" is of course nonsense.

There are equally insurmountable problems, it seems, in following the Majority Text for there do not appear to be 450 years between the time of the end of the Conquest under Joshua and the time of Samuel.[16] If, as was proposed above, the first judge, Othniel, commenced his activity at about 1350 B.C. and Samuel was born about 1120 B.C., there are only 230 years for the period under discussion. Somehow the extra 220 years of Paul's computation must be accommodated. First, the chronological parameters of Paul's statement should be more precisely delineated. Following the reading of the Greek text preferred in this study, the apostle says that after the destruction of the seven (Canaanite) nations in the land God gave Israel judges "for about 450 years" until Samuel the prophet. The destruction, of course, was carried out under Joshua, so the point here is that the era of Conquest (the last seven years of Joshua) was followed immediately by the 450 years of judges. That era, in turn, was succeeded by the life and career of Samuel.

Information about the chronological aspects of the life of Joshua is sparse indeed, but one may inductively arrive at some tentative conclusions. After the worship of the golden calf at Horeb only three months after the Exodus (Ex. 19:1), Moses reasserted his leadership of Israel with the assistance of a "young man," Joshua (33:11). Since Joshua was involved in ministry with Moses, it may be assumed that he was at least (and probably no more than) 25 years of age, since that is the age at which the Levites undertook service at the "Tent of Meeting" (Num. 8:24).[17] A birthdate for Joshua of around 1471 would then not be out of line.

More solid information comes from Joshua 24:29, which gives Joshua's age at death as 110 years. This yields a date of around 1361. But this is not the date of the beginning of the era of the judges, for Joshua 24:31 says that "Israel served the LORD throughout the lifetime of Joshua and of the elders who outlived him and who had experienced everything the LORD had done for

Israel." These elders were, at the oldest, men who were 20 years of age in 1444 B.C. because only the youth were promised access to the land of promise after the bitter rebellion of Israel at Kadesh-barnea (Num. 14:29). If these elders averaged 110 years at death, the age of Joshua himself, that generation would have passed from the scene at about 1354. It is thus safe to say that the age of apostasy following the Conquest began not much earlier than 1350 B.C.[18]

Paul's phrase "until Samuel the prophet" must next be considered in detail. The possibilities are that he referred to (a) Samuel's birth, (b) the commencement of Samuel's public recognition as a prophet of the Lord, or (c) the end of the era of the judges, an event tantamount to the beginning of the period of Samuel. The dates of these various occurrences are all part of the same chronological complex whose resolution must now be undertaken. This involves two converging lines of evidence.

A Proposed Solution

As suggested above, David began to reign in 1011 B.C. His accession to the throne of Judah at Hebron followed immediately after the death of Saul (2 Sam. 2:4; cf. 1:1). Though the Old Testament data about the age of Saul at the beginning of his reign and the length of that reign are unclear. Paul stated in Acts 13:21 that Saul reigned for 40 years.[19] This seems to be reasonable and necessary for several reasons, not least of which is the fact that Ish-bosheth, son of Saul who briefly succeeded him at Mahanaim in Gilead, was 40 when he became ruler (2 Sam. 2:10). And yet Ish-bosheth was not even born when Saul commenced his own reign (1 Sam. 14:49).[20] Saul's reign, then, embraced the years 1051–1011 B.C. The relevance of all this to Samuel is that he was "old" when he anointed Saul king (1 Sam. 8:1; cf. 10:1). Admittedly, "old" is a subjective term and one should not use it to establish chronological exactness. However, Eli, contemporary with Samuel, was "very old" at age 98 (1 Sam. 2:22; cf. 4:15) and David was "old" at 70, so one may reasonably posit at least 70 for the age of Samuel at the time of Saul's coronation.

Given the preceding hypothesis, Samuel was born about 1120 B.C., was recognized as a prophet by no later than 1104 or so (1 Sam. 3:19–20),[21] and died after the anointing of David, sometime later than 1025 B.C. If his birth is the terminus suggested by Paul, then the judges period was about 1351–1120, or 230 years. If the terminus, on the other hand, was Samuel's recognition as a prophet by the community, the period would be 1350–1104 or 246 years. Obviously both are far too limited to qualify as "about 450 years."

One other option needs to be addressed, however, and it is this which seems most plausible. Since Paul was reciting the history of Israel by epochs and not in terms of individuals—the choice of the patriarchs to the Descent, the Descent to the Exodus, the Exodus to the Conquest, the Conquest to the judges, and the judges to Samuel—the reference to Samuel must not be so much related to his birth or even his vocation, but to that era of prophetism which he introduced. That is, Samuel stands for an age which follows that of the last of the judges. It is true, of course, that even Samuel is considered a judge (1 Sam. 7:15–17) but certainly not in the "classical" sense of the term. It is traditional to consider Samson as the last of the judges, and indeed he is the last one to be found in the Book of Judges.

This leads then to an attempt to assign dates to the life of Samson, particularly to his death, in order to determine the fixed point that marked the transition from judge to prophet.

As is well known, Samson was raised up to deliver Israel from her most inveterate foes, the Philistines. The Philistine oppression apparently commenced simultaneously with the Ammonite oppression, the latter beginning in the year 1124 B.C. (Judg. 10:7–8).[22] This means that the Philistines harassed Israel from 1124 to 1084, for its total length was 40 years (13:1). However, the oppression did not entirely end when Samson destroyed the temple of Dagon, an act that resulted in his own death (16:30–31). The Philistine menace was terminated only after their defeat by Israel's armies under Samuel at Ebenezer (1 Sam. 7:11–14). Though one cannot prove it from the text it is tempting to see this last assault of the Philistines against Israel as an act of rage and revenge following Samson's destruction of their temple. That Samson judged in the last 20-year period of the oppression may be gathered from the fact that he was not born until the 40-year oppression began (Judg. 13:5). It is unlikely that he could have undertaken his judgeship before he reached the age of 20, and he certainly died before the battle of Ebenezer.[23] A date for his death of 1086 or 1085 is therefore reasonable. But Paul could not be referring to this end date, for the 1350–1085 span would still cover only 265 years, still far short of "about 450 years."

It is clear then that Paul could not be alluding to either the period before or during the era of the judges when he spoke of "about 450 years," at least not in terms customarily employed today in chronological computation. But was he perhaps adopting a convention with which he and his first-century contemporaries were familiar? This appears to be the case as the following argument will attempt to demonstrate.

The thesis proposed here is that Paul's figure of 450 years is not to be taken as a round number for something vastly different but is instead a remarkably precise number arrived at by taking the numerical data of the Book of Judges (and 1 Samuel) at face value and with no allowance for synchronism, lapses, or other possibilities which must be entertained in a truly "scientific" approach to the problem. In other words Paul simply made a total of the figures employed in the historical narrative of Judges (and 1 Samuel) by the inspired penman. But did he use all the figures, and where did he begin and end?

The chart near the beginning of this article contains all the numbers given in Judges. The total of 111 years of oppression, 96 of judgeship, and 200 of rest (or a grand total of 407 years) is a figure, as was pointed out earlier, which is still too small and impossible to be rounded to 450. What must be observed at this point, however, is the formula "and he [or personal name] judged Israel _____ years" which invariably is used in Judges when the period of judgeship is described (Judg. 10:2–3; 12:7, 9, 11, 14; 16:31). The only other occurrence of the phrase is in 1 Samuel 4:18, which says of Eli, "and he judged Israel forty years." When these years are added to the previous total of 407, the new sum is 447 years, a figure remarkably close to 450 and naturally to be rounded as Paul does to "about 450 years."[24]

The advantage to this view is that it permits Paul to be accurate in his computation. More than this, however, it explains what is meant by "until Samuel, the prophet." The narrator in 1 Samuel makes crystal clear the transition between Eli and Samuel but never says a word about Samuel's relationship to Samson or any of the other judges of the Book of Judges. For example the record states of the sons of Eli that they "despised the offering of the Lord" (1 Sam. 2:17). Then immediately it adds, "But Samuel ministered before the Lord" (2:18). Similarly a prophet of the Lord went to Eli and informed him that his wicked sons would die violently and then related, "And I will raise up a faithful priest who shall do according to that which is in my heart and mind"

(2:35). Finally the crisis is reached when God called young Samuel and at the same time told him that Eli's judgeship would cease (3:2–18). When he learned of all this, Eli could only say, "It is the Lord; let him do what seems good to him" (3:18). The transition had been reached. The judges had ruled "for about 450 years until Samuel the prophet."

The problem that remains, perhaps, is that of finding analogies to Paul's method of computation. Can it be demonstrated that it was conventional to add numbers in sequence when in fact the periods they describe should be taken synchronously or otherwise?

In his monumental study of the chronological phenomena of the books of Kings and Chronicles, Thiele[25] has shown conclusively that the numbers used in defining the lengths of the reigns of the various kings of Israel and Judah do not always mean what they appear to mean to modern readers. A simple attempt to harmonize the figures led scholars to hopeless frustration until Thiele hypothesized that the techniques of calendrical computation were different in Old Testament Israel from what they are today. Due recognition of such factors as coregencies, interregnums, anteaccession and poastaccession dates, and differing starting points for new years now makes it possible to see that the chronologers were correct all the time; it was modern ignorance of the patterns at work which was at fault.

The same may be said of the use of large numbers, especially in the Old Testament. Careful students of the Bible and history have long been baffled by the apparently incredible figures used to describe population groups, particularly in military contexts.[26] For example Abijah of Judah is said to have fielded an army of 400,000 chosen men against Jeroboam of Israel who had 800,000. The result was the defeat of Jeroboam and the slaughter of 500,000 of his men (2 Chron. 13:3,17)! The total of the two armies is 1,200,000 men, a figure which, according to modern ratios of civilian to military populations in Israel, would presuppose a nation with a population exceeding 12 million.[27] The problem is aggravated by the fact that neither Israel nor Judah was an urban society in Old Testament times. The best solution to such numbers seems to lie in the technical meaning of אֶלֶף ("thousand") as "chieftain" or some such military leader.[28]

Finally and more directly analogous to the issue at hand is the use of numbers in the ancient Near East in what appear to be sequential lists but are in fact synchronous. The most familiar instance is in the celebrated Sumerian king list, which apparently purports to list the dynasties of the various early Sumerian city states as though one state succeeded another chronologically. What really happened, as Jacobsen has proven beyond question, is the ordering of actually synchronous dynasties in such a way that they appear to be sequential.[29] Scores of cuneiform texts of the period mention contacts between kings in the lists who, according to the expected reading of the lists, are thousands of years apart. Synchronism then must sometimes be understood where there is apparent sequence.[30]

Though other examples of this from Paul or from elsewhere in the New Testament or other first-century literature cannot be adduced as far as this writer is aware, the fact remains that chronological computation in ancient times need not conform to modern expectation. One cannot criticize Paul for simply adding up the figures of the judges Othniel through Eli and coming to a total of "about 450 years" just because this method does not conform to modern practice. His note in Acts 13:20 may in fact provide one more argument for the need to understand the Bible most fundamentally on its own terms.

CHAPTER 13

"God Gave Them Up": A Study in Divine Retribution

S. Lewis Johnson, Jr.

P reaching to his Sunday congregation in Bern, Switzerland, at the Münster on Romans 1:18–32, Walter Lüthi said, "In the words that we have just read we are told the whole truth about our condition. There may well be people among us who cannot bear to hear the truth, and would like to creep quietly away out of this church. Let them do so if they wish."[1] There is much justification for Lüthi's words, for Paul's canvas on which he has pointed his picture—dark, foreboding, threatening, flashing with lightning, and crashing with thunder—is crammed with forms and figures, lights and shadows, of sin, wrath, and judgment. And the revelation of wrath is total and complete, encompassing all and rendering all without excuse and under condemnation, both individually and collectively.

Isaiah spoke of judgment as God's "strange work" and His "strange act"[2] (Isa. 28:21, KJV), and the idea that it is strange because contrary to His goodness and grace, while a popular contemporary misunderstanding of his words, it is not only out of harmony with the context of Isaiah 28:21, but it also does not agree with the total picture of the being and attributes of God in Scripture. His retributive justice is one of His essential properties, and in this passage in Romans it comes to the center of the stage. In the threefold παρέδωκεν (KJV, "gave up"; vv. 24, 26, 28) the problem is plainly before the reader. It is the purpose of this chapter to analyze and, if possible, clarify the meaning of the term, setting it within the context of the theology of the being and attributes of God. But first a word regarding the flow of the Pauline thought in this section of the letter.

After having introduced this message to the Romans (cf. 1:1–7) and stated his theme, namely, the gospel (1:16–17), the apostle skillfully and in detail developed the case history of human sin

134

and condemnation (1:18–3:20). The section moves from the declaration of Gentile sin[3] (1:18–32) through Jewish sin (2:1–3:8) to the climax of the apostolic diagnosis that "all the world" is guilty, with every mouth stopped, speechless in the terror of condemnation before a holy and righteous God (3:9–20).

In the immediate context Paul, in his endeavor to prove that the only righteousness available to man is that obtained by faith, declared that God's displeasure toward sin has been revealed from heaven (1:18). It follows, of course, that all who are charged with ungodliness or unrighteousness stand under His wrath and cannot obtain acceptance before God by their character or conduct. That the Gentiles are guilty and therefore inexcusable is evident, because they have rejected it (1:19–20).[4] And not only have they rejected the light of this truth; they have also given themselves up to idolatry (1:21–23). The Pauline picture of the religious history of mankind is one of retrogression, not progression; of devolution, not evolution; downward, not upward. In unbelief the human race has passed from light to futility to folly. Thus the divine wrath has found its justification in human rejection of "the truth of God" (1:18, 25).

There remains, therefore, only one alternative for God and mankind, divine retribution, and the apostle solemnly and yet vigorously[5] proclaimed this in the final section of chapter one (1:24–32). The διά ("wherefore") makes the connection. In the light of the rebellion just described the inference of vindicatory justice is drawn. Sin justly brings judgment,[6] a judgment expressed most clearly in 1:24, 26, 28.

"Therefore God gave them over [παρέδωκεν] in the lusts of their hearts to impurity, that their bodies might be dishonored among them."

"For this reason God gave them over [παρέδωκεν] to degrading passions; for their women exchanged the natural function for that which is unnatural."

"And just as they did not see fit to acknowledge God any longer, God gave them over [παρέδωκεν] to a depraved mind, to do those things which are not proper."

The Interpretation of the Revelation

The essence, the heart, the *Leit Motif* of the passage and the divine judgment is expressed in the threefold παρέδωκεν (KJV, "gave up," vv. 24, 26; "gave over," v. 28), repeated as a terrifying refrain.[7] Considerable debate has raged over this term, and it is to the elucidation of it that this chapter is addressed. Generally speaking, there are three contending viewpoints.

First, perhaps the favorite interpretation of the term is one that has prevailed since the time of Origen and Chrysostom, in which the παρέδωκεν is taken in the permissive sense. According to this view God passively permitted men to fall into the retributive consequences of their infidelity and apostasy. The active force of παρέδωκεν is surely contrary to this view. It is not that God permitted rebellious men to fall into uncleanness and bodily dishonor; He actively, though justly in view of their sin, consigned them to the consequences of their acts. It is His divine arrangement that the unregenerate by their apostasy should fall into moral impurity, sin being punished by further sin, and He maintains the moral connection between apostasy and impurity by carrying out the judgment Himself.[8]

Second, another popular view, which became current after the time of Augustine, takes παρέδωκεν in the privative sense. According to this interpretation God deprived mankind of an aspect of His work of common grace. He withdrew His hand that had restrained men from evil. Godet has expressed and illustrated this interpretation about as well as it can be set forth. Wherein did His action consist? he asks. And the answer follows:

> He positively withdrew His hand; He ceased to hold the boat as it was dragged by the current of the river. This is the meaning of the term used by the apostle, Acts 14:16: "He suffered the Gentiles to walk in their own ways," by not doing for them what He never ceased to do for His own people. It is not a case of simple abstention, it is the positive withdrawal of a force.[9]

At bottom this view is the practical equivalent of the permissive view. This is evident from the fact that Godet uses Acts 14:16 as illustrative of the sense. However, in that passage the verb used is εἴασεν ("suffered," KJV), which normally means simply to permit. As Meyer pointed out a long time ago,

> Therefore Chrysostom not only explains it by εἴασεν, but illustrates the matter by the instance of a general who leaves his soldiers in the battle, and thus deprives them of his aid, and abandons them to the enemy. Theodoret explains it: τῆς οἰκείας προμηθείας ἐγύμνωσε,[10] and employs the comparison of an abandoned vessel. Theophylact illustrates the παρέδωκεν by the example of a physician who gives up a refractory patient (παραδίδωσιν αὐτὸν τῷ ἐπὶ πλέον νοσεῖν[11]).[12]

These illustrations express quite well the privative view, but the Pauline language is stronger than this. The expression, "God gave them to . . . impurity," describes a judicial act,[13] a "judicial abandonment."[14] The active force of παρέδωκεν must not be glossed over.[15]

Therefore it becomes clear that the term must be given a judicial sense.[16] The meaning is not simply that God withdrew from the wicked the restraining force of His providence and common grace, though that privative sense is included in the judicial sense, but that He positively gave sinners over to the judgment of "more intensified and aggravated cultivation of the lusts of their own hearts with the results that they reap for themselves a correspondingly greater toll of retributive vengeance."[17] The usage of the word in both this epistle (4:25; 6:17; 8:32) and in the other Pauline epistles (cf. 1 Cor. 5:5; 1 Tim. 1:20) supports this force.[18] The interpretation is also in harmony with the occurrence of the precisely identical form in Acts 7:42, where, in speaking of Israel's apostasy in the days of Moses, Stephen said, "But God turned away and delivered them up [παρέδωκεν] to serve the host of heaven." Both the Romans and the Acts passages describe the act of God as a penal infliction of retribution, the expression of an essential attribute of God's nature and being, and it is thoroughly consistent with His holiness.

Another striking occurrence of the identical form of the verb is in Ephesians 4:19, and that verse serves to remind the interpreter that the infliction of punitive justice does not compromise the free agency and responsibility of man. Speaking of the sin of the Gentiles, Paul wrote that "they, having become callous, have given themselves over to sensuality, for the practice of every kind of impurity with greediness." In the midst of the retributive action of God there is no coercion. God does not entice or compel to evil.[19] Individuals remain responsible and can even be said to be giving themselves over to uncleanness while God gives them up to the judgment of their sin.

Concluding Questions

There are hardly any passages in the Bible that say more plainly than Romans 1:24, 26, 28 that moral depravity is the result of the judgment of God. And this raises an interesting question that concerns the present moral condition of the nations of the world, and particularly the United States. The question is, What is the real significance of the spread of immorality, crime, and violence in Western civilization? To compound the problem, the newspapers are filled with stories of clergymen encouraging sexual license. Many Christian ministers, contrary to the Apostle Paul's teaching, no longer regard homosexuality and other sexual aberrations as a sin. To them, it is a sickness or a weakness. In an article in one of the national news magazines homosexuality was referred to by the author as "an undesirable handicap."[20] To many today it is nothing more than a deviation from the customary sexual patterns. Occasionally, in what must seem to the Christian the ultimate evil, homosexuality is traced to God Himself, for, it is said, He made men and women what they are.[21]

Years ago the famous Harvard sociologist, Pitirim Sorokin, in his book *The Crisis of Our Age*, warned that increases in crime, suicides, mental breakdowns, revolutions, and war have been symptoms of civilizations in the midst of death pangs. In another article on homosexuals in *Time* magazine the author wrote, "At their fullest flowering, the Persian, Greek, Roman and Moslem civilizations permitted a measure of homosexuality; as they decayed, it became more prevalent."[22] Later Sorokin in *The American Sex Revolution* pointed out that sex anarchy leads to mental breakdowns, rather than the other way around, as the Freudian psychologists have taught.[23] Further, he pointed out that increasing sexual license leads to decreasing creativity and productivity in the intellectual, artistic, and economic spheres of life.

What, then, are the sources of the problems of the present age? As Howard indicates,

> Spengler had a biological answer: civilizations grow old and die like any other living thing. Toynbee has a religious answer: civilizations fail to respond to the higher challenges of the Spirit and therefore fossilize. In his *Civilization and Ethics*, Albert Schweitzer tried to find an ethical answer. St Paul had still a different answer.[24]

The Pauline answer is plain, and Romans 1:24 expresses it most impressively and succinctly. When people rebelled and sinned, God "gave them up" to uncleanness in the lusts of their hearts so that by their own activities their bodies might be dishonored. Sexual rebellion, license, anarchy are the retributive judgment of God. The civilization of the Western world, including the United States, is not a civilization in danger of contracting a fatal disease. That civilization has already contracted a malignant and fatal cancer through its unbelief of the message of God in

Christ. It is now hurrying on with increasing speed to final climactic destruction. Civilizations do not die because of violence, crime, immorality, and anarchy. These things are the evidences that death already is at work, a death brought on by disobedience to the revelation of God. Hodge was referring to these principles when he wrote, in reference to the Christian body of truth, "Religion is the only true foundation, and the only effectual safeguard for morality. Those who abandon God, He abandons. Irreligion and immorality, therefore, have ever been found inseparably connected."[25]

It should be carefully noted that the apostle was not speaking of eternal punishment in these three verses. What he specifically had in mind is a judgment that pertains to this life, not to the life to come. But on the other hand it is also plain that Paul's words lead on to the doctrine of everlasting torment (cf. v. 32).[26] The vindicatory judgment inflicted by God is continued in the life to come in a more terrible and permanent form if the escape through the gospel of the cross is neglected. The doctrine of eternal punishment has never been popular, and it is less so now. Even some evangelical seminaries seem embarrassed by it.[27] There is an old story about Boswell and Samuel Johnson that contains solemn truth. When the latter once appeared overfearful as to his future, Boswell said, "Think of the mercy of your Savior." "Sir," replied Johnson, "my Savior has said that He will place some on His right hand, and some on His left."

It is doubtful that there is a doctrine in the Bible easier to prove than that of eternal punishment (cf. Matt. 25:46[28]), a fact that reminds one of an incident involving Henry Ward Beecher and William G. T. Shedd, both eminent leaders of their day. *The North American Review* engaged the two men for articles on the subject of eternal punishment, knowing their differing views. Beecher had once commented, "I believe that punishment exists, both here and hereafter; but it will not continue after it ceases to do good. With a God who could give pain for pain's sake, this world would go out like a candle." Shedd was asked to write an article supporting the doctrine, and Beecher was asked to answer it. When the proof sheets of Shedd's article were sent to Beecher he telegraphed from Denver to the magazine's editors, "Cancel engagement. Shedd is too much for me. I half believe in eternal punishment now myself. Get somebody else." The reply was never written by anyone. Shedd remained unanswered.[29] There is no answer, biblically, logically, or philosophically to the doctrine of eternal punishment.

A final question one might ask regarding Romans 1:24 and its declaration of divine retribution is this: When did the retribution occur? That is, when did God "give up" the nations? Was the apostle referring to a specific event or time in the past, or was he simply interpreting human history broadly? In the collective sense the rebellion of men against God had its inception at Babylon, and it has been surmised that Paul may have had in mind the construction of the tower of Babylon and its destruction, with mankind's scattering by God (Gen. 11:1–9). It is doubtful that Paul had this in mind. On the other hand, two things point to the fall of man in the Garden of Eden as the event the apostle was thinking about. First, the fact that Paul traced the entrance of sin into the human race specifically to Eden in Romans 5:12 suggests that 1:24 is to be understood in the light of that important event. It was there that the human race, in Adam and Eve, rebelled against light, the light of both natural and special revelation, and turned to darkness. And it was there that judgment was inflicted on account of sin, a judgment that consisted of wrath and death, accompanied by consequent immorality and wickedness, as history indicates.

Second, the terminology of Romans 1:22–23 points fairly clearly to the Genesis account. For example the phrases to "birds and four-footed animals and crawling creatures" (v. 23) is surely reminiscent of "the birds of the sky and over the cattle and over all the earth, and over every creeping thing that creeps on the earth" (Gen. 1:26; cf. vv. 20–25). And, further, the words "the glory of the incorruptible God for an image [lit., the likeness of an image] in the form of corruptible man" seem to come from the Genesis account. "Let us make man in our image, according to our likeness" (1:26). It thus seems that Paul was thinking of the Genesis record in the Romans passage, and this would support the view that he regarded God's giving up of man to uncleanness as occurring at the time of the Fall, recorded in the early part of that same Genesis record.[30] There, then, humanity fell into sin, judgment, and condemnation, with their inevitable companion, the retributive justice of immorality, crime, and all manner of evil.

One must conclude from Romans 1:24, 26, and 28 that retributive justice is an attribute of the living God and a necessary feature of His actions toward unbelieving mankind. To the question, Can God really give man up to judgment? this passage provides a resounding yes answer. But in fact it is not the final and convincing answer to the question. That comes from the cross of Jesus Christ, which in the cry it elicited from Him, "My God, my God, why hast thou forsaken Me?" (Matt. 27:46), unmistakably affirms the fact that God can give man up to judgment. It was there that the sinless Man bore the judgment of God on sin, and it forever proclaims the true nature of sin—it is worthy of the penalty of spiritual and physical death—and God's hatred of it with His necessary condemnation of it.

One might wonder, Does God, then, really care? The answer to this question also is obvious, and it too comes from the Cross. God gave His Son as the vicarious Sacrifice; God initiated the work that produced the remedy for sin and condemnation. And the Son voluntarily bore in agony the depths of the vindicatory judgment for sinners. And if that is not sufficient evidence of God's love and concern, one can reflect further on the fact that He revealed to sinners their lost condition and the significance of the atoning death, inscribed its interpretation in the written Word of God, and preserved that Word for countless millions to read and ponder. Isaiah was right. Though righteous and necessary, judgment is His "strange work" and His "strange act."

CHAPTER 14

Romans 8:28–29 and the Assurance of the Believer

D. Edmond Hiebert

> And we know that God causes all things to work together for good to those who love God, to those who are called according to His purpose. For whom He foreknew, He also predestined to become conformed to the image of His Son, that He might be the first-born among many brethren.

Paul's words in Romans 8:28–29 express a ringing Christian assurance to the believing heart; they have brought comfort and encouragement to many troubled and afflicted believers down through the centuries. The opening words, "And we know," introduce a crucial assertion for victorious Christian living that is apprehended by faith. The verb "we know" (οἴδαμεν) denotes "the knowledge of faith and not mere intellectual investigation."[1] As Watson remarks, "As axioms and aphorisms are evident to reason, so the truths of religion are evident to faith."[2] The assurance expressed in Romans 8:28–29 is not a logical deduction of cold reason but rather an inner conviction of the believing heart wrought by the Holy Spirit on the basis of Scripture and verified in personal experience. In setting forth the great truths of the gospel in the first eight chapters of Romans, Paul used the verb οἴδαμεν six times (2:2; 3:19; 7:14; 8:22, 26, 28). Romans 8:28 states the crowning certainty of the Christian life.

Many indeed have found the sweeping assertion, "all things work together for good" (Rom. 8:28, KJV), difficult to believe. Faced with the sufferings and catastrophic experiences of life, many believers and even Christian leaders have found it difficult to accept this categorical assertion. During World War II a prominent preacher designated Romans 8:28 as "the hardest verse in the Bible to believe." While willing to admit that the countless ravages that have befallen the human race are the logical consequences of mankind's sin and rebellion against God, many a devout believer, when some shattering experience has befallen him, has cried out in bewilderment, "Why does God allow this to happen to me?" How can this kind of experience be reconciled with Romans 8:28? When Jacob's sons, who had gone to Egypt to buy needed food, came back without their brother Simeon, and reported to their father that the next time Benjamin must also go to Egypt, the patriarch cried out in despair, "All these things are against me" (Gen. 42:36).

And today Christ-rejecting, secular humanists in their spiritual blindness may reject the assertion that "all things work together for good." Such individuals, unconscious of any beneficent activity of God in their lives, while observing a tumultuous world with weary eyes, may readily conclude that human life has no higher meaning. They may be prone to agree with the cynical poet who wrote:

> The world rolls round forever like a mill,
> It grinds out life and death, and good and ill,
> It has no purpose, heart, or mind, or will.
>
> Man might know this thing, were his sight less dim,
> Life whirleth not to suit his petty whim,
> For it is quite indifferent to him.
>
> Nay, doth it use him harshly, as he saith?
> It grinds for him slow years of bitter breath,
> Then grinds him back into eternal death.[3]

How utterly contrary such a cynical evaluation of human life is to the declaration of Paul in Romans 8:28–29! No one can truly accept the gospel of Jesus Christ and accept such a cynical, godless interpretation of human existence. Instead the ringing assurance declared by Paul offers a message of inner certainty and reality that imparts meaning, power, and encouragement to the believing heart. The assurance that "God causes all things to work together for good to those who love God" is a message that the indwelling Holy Spirit vitalizes in the believing heart. It is a reality that "Christians know intuitively, though they may not always fully understand and sense it experientially."[4] The importance of the truth declared in Romans 8:28–29, as well as the questions, perplexities, and unwarranted assumptions that have been made, make clear the need for a careful study and interpretation of these verses in the light of the context.

The Contextual Setting

The particle δε in verse 28 clearly marks a close connection with the preceding verses. Verses 28–30 form a kind of climax to the teaching in verses 18–27, while verses 31–39 form a concluding paean of praise celebrating the redemption in Christ, delineated in the first eight chapters of Romans, as establishing a bond of love that can never be broken.

The force of the connecting δὲ has been understood in two ways. The rendering "but" in some English versions[5] indicates that its force is understood as adversative. Thus Godet suggests that δὲ marks the contrast between the present groaning of creation, the source of suffering in the present age, and "the full certainty already possessed by believers of the *glorious goal* marked out beforehand by the plan of God."[6] But Meyer feels that if such a contrast was intended "it must have been marked in some way or other (at least by the stronger adversative ἀλλά)."[7] Nor does the admission in verse 26 that "we do not know how to pray as we should" offer a basis for an assumed contrast. It is more natural to hold that δὲ here has the force of "and"[8] or "further,"[9] adding ground for encouragement amid the sufferings of this present life. This accords with the contents of verses 18–27.

In verse 18, Paul asserted his evaluation of the believers' present sufferings as "not worthy to be compared with the glory that is to be revealed to us." In verses 19–25 he supported his evaluation from creation's yearning for deliverance from corruption by pointing to the believers' present yearning for full redemption; in verses 26–27 he pointed to the present intercession of the Holy Spirit. Thus Lenski notes that to this intercession, "which aids us in our weakness in this distressing world, δὲ adds another mighty comfort."[10] That truth is "that God causes all things to work together for good to those who love God, to those who are called according to His purpose." "We know" indicates that this asserted knowledge is accepted by believers as a truth not to be gainsaid. It is an inner assurance vitalized and strengthened by the indwelling Holy Spirit. Hendriksen suggests that this knowledge is probably based on "two additional grounds: (a) *Experience;* that is, the effect on him of knowing how God had dealt with him and with others in the past. . . . And (b) Acquaintance with *specific biblical passages* which teach that in God's providence all things result in blessing for God's children, evil being overruled for good (Gen. 45:5, 7, 8; 50:20)."[11]

The Central Assertion

The central assertion of verse 28 (NIV) is the truth that "in all things God works for the good" (πάντα συνεργεῖ εἰς ἀγαθόν). Taken alone, these four words may equally well be rendered as in the King James Version, "all things work together for good." The neuter plural πάντα, "all things, everything," has no indicated restrictions. In itself the term naturally includes all the experiences, whether sad or glad, that come into the lives of God's people. Yet in the light of the context (vv. 18–27) the primary reference of πάντα is to "every kind of painful experience in Christian lives, all those that press groans from our lips and make us groan inwardly in unuttered and unutterable distress. Some of the things that Paul has in mind he states in vv. 38, 39."[12]

According to a peculiar law of Greek grammar a singular verb may have a neuter plural subject.[13] Therefore the neuter plural πάντα, standing before the singular verb συνεργεῖ, naturally may be accepted as its subject. The present tense verb, "work together," denotes a continuing or protracted activity of unspecified duration, with the result that all things work "unto good" (εἰς ἀγαθόν) in the experience of the recipients. Paul's terse assertion does not further define the nature or scope of this "good," except to declare a beneficial impact.

Dunn notes that "the pious hope that everything will work out for the best for the godly is 'a common axiom of antiquity' (Käsemann)."[14] Thus Paul's words would not strike his readers as a new and strange assertion. It is an assertion that believers in all walks of life have found an assuring and comforting truth. But the axiomatic nature of Paul's assertion makes it necessary to guard against unwarranted interpretations.

Paul's assertion must not be taken to mean that all things automatically work for the good of all people. That would be a fatalism for good, a view denied by Scripture and human experience. This statement does not sanction the view of enthusiasts, whether religious or secular, who blithely exult, "Hip, hip, hurray, let come what may, all things will be OK!"

Nor did Paul mean that all things that come into believers' lives are in themselves "good." Paul was not blurring moral distinctions between the various experiences of this life. The fiery persecutions, or the slanderous accusations to which Paul's readers were subjected by a Christ-rejecting world, were not in themselves good. Even the unjust assertions or unkind deeds of fellow believers, motivated by misunderstanding or ill will, cannot be declared to be good, or for one's good, in themselves. Even some of the things experienced as the result of one's own deeds or choices are not always in themselves good.

Nor did Paul mean that everything believers experience is God's will for them. Paul did not necessarily mean that those undesirable things that cannot be averted are God's will. Paul was not telling believers that when a thief stole a Christian's goods and escaped, the believers must piously say, "God willed it." God never condones sin in deed or attitude.

Paul's assertion that "all things work together for good" (KJV) must be understood in the light of the context. It is also desirable to look more closely at the original statement, πάντα συνεργεῖ" εἰ" ἀγαθόν. The common view is to take πάντα as the subject. However, the entire statement in verse 28, as well as a significant textual variant, indicate that πάντα may be taken as the emphatic object of the verb, with the singular subject of the verb ("He") being the true subject of the sentence. So understood, the sentence may be rendered, "And we know that to those loving God all things He works together unto good, to those according to purpose called ones being." That various early scribes and interpreters so read the verse is clear from the fact that the words ὅ θεὸς ("God") were added as the expressed subject of the verb in Papyrus 46 (dated about A.D. 200), uncials A (fifth century) and B (fourth century), cursive 81 (ca. 1044), and the Sahidic Coptic version, and used in two of five known quotations of Romans 8:28 in the writings of Origen.[15] Though this textual evidence is too weak to accept ὅ θεὸς as the original reading, its presence indicates that "God" rather than "all things" was understood as the subject of the sentence. Since in the original Paul had already used the noun "God" (τόν θεὸν), to have written ὅ θεὸς as the expressed subject of the verb συνεργεῖ would have resulted in making Paul "a rather clumsy stylist."[16] But the textual variant establishes that Paul, having just mentioned God, would expect the reader to understand that "God" (ὅ θεὸς) was the intended subject of the singular verb. This interpretation is expressly indicated in the NIV rendering and various other English versions.[17]

Another identification of the intended subject has been suggested. This view asserts that the true subject of the verb in verse 28 is "the Spirit," named in verse 26. That the Holy Spirit is accepted as the subject of the verb here is evident from the rendering of verses 26–28 in the New English Bible. In his interpretive rendering Barclay names the Holy Spirit as the subject: "We know that through the work of the Spirit all the different events of life are being made to work for good, for those who keep on loving God, those whom his purpose has called."[18] But the view that the Spirit is the intended subject of the verb "work together" runs into difficulty in verse 29, for that verse would then read, "For whom He [the Spirit] foreknew, He also predestined to become conformed to the image of His [the Spirit's] Son." "This," Hendriksen notes, "is impossible, for nowhere in Scripture is Jesus Christ called the Son of the Holy Spirit."[19]

Most probable is the view that God is the intended subject of the verb συνεργεῖς: "He works together with all things unto good." Clearly Paul's thought is not that "all things" as impersonal realities by themselves work together constructively; rather it is God's providential working in and through these various things that assures that all things work together for good. This is expressly asserted when ὁ θεός is placed into the text. "This certainty," Grundmann remarks, "which is proper to all Jewish piety and derives from its consciousness of God, acquires here its fullness from the action of God."[20] This reading of Romans 8:28 is strongly supported by Paul's assertion in Philippians 1:6.

The present tense verb συνεργεῖς declares God's continuing activity in working all things "unto good" in the lives of His people. "For good" (εἰς ἀγαθόν) denotes the goal of the divine working, but the verb does not indicate when or how soon that goal is attained. The verb may mean that God "cooperates with" all these things to attain His goal for His own, but the expression εἰς ἀγαθόν suggests that in the providence of God all things "work together with or cooperate in" the achievement of the intended "good." Watson suggested a medical analogy:

> Several poisonous ingredients put together, being tempered by the skill of the apothecary, make a sovereign medicine, and work together for the good of the patient. So all God's providences, being divinely tempered and sanctified, work together for the best to the saints.[21]

The "good" that God works to bring about in the lives of His people is not just a physical good, such as food, comfort, health, or pleasures of one kind or another experienced in this life. God works to fulfill His "purpose" for His own as outlined in verse 29. Thus Dunn remarks, "In the context here, where Paul has in view the eschatological climax which God has purposed for 'all things,' the ἀγαθόν will have an eschatological reference (cf. 14:16)."[22]

Yet Scripture and Christian experience confirm that even in this life God in His infinite way works "all things for good" for His own. Lenski refers to two biblical stories in support of this fact.

> The Old Testament story of Joseph is a striking example of the mysterious and the wonderful way in which God makes the evil done to us eventuate for our good. Another instance is the story of the persecution precipitated by Saul. It scattered the great congregation at Jerusalem to distant parts, it seemed to be a calamity but served only for the good of the church by planting it in a hundred new places to flourish more than ever.[23]

On a small scale Christians through the ages have testified to this reality in their own lives. After completing seminary training it was my joy to be invited to join the Christian training department in a midwestern Christian college. In the middle of the second year of a delightful ministry there a sudden and severe illness brought me to the brink of death; the hospital stay stretched into 110 days. Recovery was slow and often discouraging. Before long the threat of physical deafness was evident and two years later deafness became total. Before that time some calls to administrative service came for which I did not feel adequate. With total deafness such calls were effectively terminated, leaving me free for concentrated study of the Scriptures and their systematic exposition in the college and seminary classroom and in a written ministry. In looking back over the years I can gladly testify that I could not have chosen a more delightful ministry.

The Careful Limitation

Paul carefully limited his confident assertion that "God causes all things to work together for good" to a distinct class of people. Paul added two limiting clauses, one placed before and the other following his central assertion, as seen in the rendering of Rotherham: "We know further that unto them who love God, God causeth all things to work together for good—unto them who according to purpose are such as He hath called." The first marks a clear limitation from the human side, the second states a limitation from God's side.

THOSE WHO LOVE GOD

Those for whom God works all things for good are emphatically identified as "those who love Him" (τοῖς ἀγαπῶσιν τὸν θεὸν, "to those loving God"). The present tense articular participle characterizes these people by their abiding love for God, while the article with God ("the God") designates the true God whom Christians now love and serve. "Despisers and haters of God," Watson reminds, "have no lot or part in this privilege."[24] This abiding love for God is the difference between the regenerated individual and the unsaved.

This is the only place in Romans where Paul wrote of the believers' love for God; elsewhere the reference is to God's love for them. The verb for "love" (ἀγαπάω), here used to identify true believers, "is the word for the highest type of love, that of comprehension coupled with corresponding purpose."[25] Hogg and Vine call it "the characteristic word of Christianity."[26] It is not merely a love of emotion but a purposeful love that actively desires the welfare of others and sacrificially works toward that end. It reflects the love of God Himself toward needy sinners. Those who "love God" thus reveal an attitude and activity in accord with the very nature of God Himself. God is at the center of such a love-dominated life.

Such love in the hearts of believers is not meritorious; their love for Him does not prompt God to begin working all things for their good. Such a love is not native to the human heart; it can only be known as the result of God's love being poured out in the believers' hearts through the Holy Spirit (Rom. 5:5). As John wrote, "We love, because He first loved us" (1 John 4:19). It is this infusion of divine love that created the fundamental distinction between the saved and the unsaved. Thus Paul placed this factor forward. This criterion of "love to God is both the most elementary and the highest mark of being in the favor of God."[27] The believers' love "is nothing but the direct flowing back of the heavenly love which has been poured out upon" those whom God has called and saved.[28] Those who are lovers of God experience the reality that everything which may happen to them is being divinely used to further their highest good.

THOSE WHO ARE CALLED ACCORDING TO GOD'S PURPOSE

Paul's second limitation, placed after his basic assertion, passes from the human experience to the divine purpose and reaches into eternity past. Again the articular participle construction (τοῖς κατὰ πρόθεσιν κλητοῖς οὖσιν, literally, "to those according to purpose called ones being") again indicates the character of the distinct group in view. They are now defined exclusively in terms of God's purpose (κατὰ πρόθεσιν). The noun πρόθεσιν (literally, "an act of setting forth") here denotes God's pretemporal purpose, which is now working in and through history and moving toward the accomplishment of His intended goal. God, not men, determines the nature and progressive development of that purpose. He has taken the initiative in the lives of these individuals, not only inviting them but also effectively calling them in accord with His purpose for them. As a result they now are the subjects of the outworking of His purpose, and as such are the "called" (κλητοῖς). As Lenski notes, "The verbal is passive and involves God as the agent who called and the gospel as the divine means and the power by which he called."[29] Those in whose lives God is now working in accord with His redemptive purpose are assured that the outcome will be for their ultimate good, since His purpose is filled with His love.

A Christian's assurance concerning the beneficent result of the outworking of God's purpose is grounded not in fluctuating love for Him nor steadfast obedience to His call, but in His unchanging love for believers as His "called ones." This realization gives purpose and encouragement for daily life. But one must remember that what God is now doing is the outworking of His eternal purpose, not the believers' limited and fallible plans and aspirations. This brings present assurance and peace when believers cannot comprehend His dealings with them. At such times they can rest in the assurance Jesus expressed in John 13:7, "What I do you do not realize now, but you shall understand hereafter." Often God gives His own a clear or growing understanding of His purposes for them in this present life; but when they cannot understand His purposes in permitting frustrations, sufferings, and persecutions to assail them in this life, by faith they can accept that fact that He is working out His eternal purposes. But if one stops with verse 28, and fails to go on to verse 29, he generally fails to realize what God's ultimate purpose is.

The Clarifying Goal

In verse 29 Paul delineated God's comprehensive activities and ultimate purpose for those who are the subjects of His redemptive plan. The opening "for" (ὅτι) introduces the reason why all things work together for good to those who love God and have been called according to His purpose. The words "called according to His purpose" already contain the assured outcome, but Paul now "draws it out and details it in full because every part of it is so convincing and thus so comforting in the face of ills."[30]

THE COMPREHENSIVE ACTION

In verse 29 the purpose of God is unfolded in terms of His foreknowledge and foreordination of the redeemed. "For whom He foreknew, He also predestined to become conformed to the image of His Son." The use of the personal relative pronoun "whom" (οὕς), as well as the triple use of the demonstrative pronoun "these" (τούτους) in verse 30, underlines the truth that God's plan relates to individuals, not merely to the experiences they undergo. The two verbs rendered "foreknew" and "predestined" indicate that God's plan for the redeemed began in eternity past and reaches into eternity future.

"Whom He foreknew" (οὕς προέγνω) means more than that He knew about believers before they came into being. As Kelly remarks, "His foreknowledge is of persons, not of their state or conduct; it is not what, but whom He foreknew."[31] The Greek verb "foreknew" (προέγνω) means "to know in advance, to foreknow." The preposition προ does not change the meaning of the verb γινώσκω; it only dates the knowledge. God's knowledge of those He chose goes back to eternity past (1 Peter 1:2, 20). In His omniscience God knew, knows, and foreknew all men. But, unlike οἶδα, this verb does not imply mere intellectual apprehension; it also indicates an active and affectionate desire to bless. "That this character, in which they were foreknown to God, presupposes the subjection to faith (the ὑπακοὴ πίστεως, 1:5), was self-evident to the Christian reader."[32] Paul's focus in Romans 8:29 is on the terminus, not on the intermediate stages (cf. 5:30).

The second verb, "He also predestined" (καὶ προώρισεν), likewise records God's activity on behalf of Christians; the action also relates to the eternal past but looks forward to what He wanted to achieve with them. The simple verb ὁρίζω means "to mark out or determine the boundaries" (cf. the English "horizon"), hence "to determine or appoint." Used of persons it means to set out or determine the goal or destiny of those foreknown; the preposition προ again marks this divine action as taking place in eternity past. The indicated action cannot be restricted to one point but covers all that is involved until the consummation of the

goal. Again the indicated action relates to individual persons, not
necessarily what happens to them. This predetermined goal cannot
be separated from the fact of God's self-motivated love for them.
As Behm notes, this is "the New Testament faith in providence in
its most individual form."[33]

THE CHRIST-CENTERED GOAL

The indicated goal, "to become conformed to the image of His
Son" exhibits "not only the dignity of the ordination but also the
greatness of the love from which the appointment flows."[34] Dunn
declares, "It is the sureness of the end as determined from the
beginning which Paul wishes to emphasize."[35]

God's purpose for His children is their conformity "to the
image of His Son" (τῆς εἰκόνος τοῦ υἱοῦ αὐτοῦ). "His Son" (cf.
"His own Son," 8:3) denotes Christ's unique and eternal Sonship.
Motivated by His love for lost humanity, God sent forth His Son
"in the likeness of sinful flesh and as an offering for sin" (8:3). In
His sinless life, His vicarious atonement, and His triumphant
resurrection, the incarnate Son perfectly realized the divinely
intended destiny of the chosen sons of God. On the basis of
Christ's perfection as the incarnate Son it is now God's purpose to
form a great family of sons, all of them patterned after the "image"
of the incarnate Son of God. The word "image" (εἰκών) denotes a
derived likeness in believers. In the saints this image "is not
accidental but derived as the likeness of the child is derived from
its parents. Through the new birth we become children of Jesus
Christ (Heb. 2:13) and thus inherit His image."[36] Thus the goal of
God for His chosen sons is that they shall be conformed to and
manifest something not merely like Christ but "what He is in
Himself, both in His spiritual body and in His moral character."[37]

Interpreters differ on whether Paul had in mind "(a) *only* the
final conformation; that is, only that part of transformation into
Christ's image that will take place at his Return; or . . . to (b) the
entire process of transformation, beginning already when the
sinner is brought out of the darkness into the light."[38] If the
reference is merely to the great eschatological change that will
occur at the resurrection, then the first view is to be preferred.
Thus Lenski holds that "Paul is pointing his readers from their
sufferings to their comfort amid trials and to their assured hope,
and this means their coming glory."[39] But in view of Paul's
reference to Christ as "His Son" and His asserted uniqueness in

that day, the moral element in the conformity cannot be overlooked. More than bodily conformity to Christ's image is involved. Dunn holds that "the implication of Paul's language here and elsewhere is of an image to be formed in Christians by process of transformation."[40] Since their conformity "to the likeness of His Son" was the goal of their predestination from eternity past, it is logical that this conformity involves not only their bodily transformation but also the moral transformation during the period before His return.

Clearly the bodily transformation of believers into the image of the risen Christ will be the glorious climax of their being "conformed to the image of His Son," but if only this is in view here then Paul passed over a fundamental aspect of redemption in Christ. In 2 Corinthians 3:18 Paul spoke of a present spiritual transformation of believers into the image of Christ through the work of the Spirit. This present transformation into the image of Christ is based on having the mind of Christ (Phil. 2:5–8) and is experienced in sharing the suffering of Christ in this life (3:10). Clearly both aspects of the believer's transformation into the image of Christ are included in the eschatological likeness to Christ portrayed in 1 John 3:2–3.

This blessed hope—that believers will be conformed to the image of His own Son—explains God's dealings with them as His chosen sons in this present age. He is ever at work to reproduce the moral image of Christ in them. All that now comes into their lives He uses for their good to further that glorious goal. His aim for them now is not to make them happy, materially prosperous, or famous, but to make them Christlike. He now uses "all things," the sad as well as the glad, the painful as well as the pleasant, the things that perplex and disappoint as well as the things they eagerly strive and pray for, to further His eternal purpose for them. In His infinite wisdom He knows what is needed to bring about that transformation. For some of His own He may need to use hotter fire and strike with harder blows than in His dealings with others to effect the formation of Christ's image in them. This may be because some believers may be more resistant to His molding activities or are more prone to insist on their own efforts.

When believers understand and accept the Father's loving purpose of developing Christlikeness in them as His beloved children, thus preparing them for that future day when the blessed Savior will come again to take them home, then they can rejoice and thank Him for all He is doing in them. Christians may not now understand how all that comes into their lives works together for their good. Yet they can trust God's love and unreservedly entrust themselves to Him. As they increasingly experience the reality of this profound Christian assertion from the pen of Paul, they can gladly join in proclaiming its reality to others.

The closing statement in verse 29 adds the glorious truth that the ultimate aim in God's redemptive program is the preeminence of Jesus Christ as "the first-born among many brethren." The expression involves both His distinctiveness from and identity with the vast redeemed family of God.

In that coming day the presence of God's Son surrounded by "many brethren" conformed to His likeness declares their union with Him. He is the pattern for the entire family of sons, each conformed to His nature. The bodies of their humiliation will have been conformed to the body of His glory; all will manifestly be sons of the resurrection, either raised from the dead or instantly transformed into His likeness at His coming (1 Cor. 15:42–55). Spiritually made like Him, these "many brethren" will demonstrate God's redemptive purpose "to have a family of sons, beloved even as Christ is; and like Him in body, in spirit, in glory, in inheritance; dwelling as the Royal Family in the mansions Christ has gone before to prepare."[41]

But the reference to Christ as "the first-born" declares His abiding distinctness from all the other sons. They are conformed to His image; He is and remains distinct and unique as the Father's "first-born" (πρωτότοκον). This distinctive designation of Jesus Christ expresses His position of priority to and preeminence over all the other members of the family. In the Old Testament the term was used of the oldest son of his father; he was the object of special parental affection and inherited special rights; he was expected to further the welfare and concerns of the entire family. In the New Testament the term is five times applied to Christ in a spiritual sense to set forth His uniqueness as the eternal Son of God. Vine points out the chronological sequence of these references as follows:

> (a) Col. 1:15, where His eternal relationship with the Father is in view, and the clause means both that He was the Firstborn before all creation, and that He Himself produced creation . . . ; (b) Col. 1:18 and Rev. 1:5, in reference to His resurrection; (c) Rom. 8:29, His position in relationship to the Church; (d) Heb. 1:6, R.V., His Second Advent (the R.V. "when He

again bringeth in," puts "again" in the right place, the contrast to His First Advent, at His birth, being implied); cp. Ps. 89:27.[42]

In light of the marvelous statement of assurance in Romans 8:28–29, believers rejoice in knowing that all that God is now doing and will yet do in bringing many sons to glory will ever redound to the praise and honor of the blessed Lord and Savior Jesus Christ as the Firstborn of the Father. May this ringing message grip each believer's heart and mind, stimulate his devotion and service, and bring unceasing glory and honor to the matchless Savior and Lord!

CHAPTER 15

Should Women Wear Headcoverings?

Kenneth T. Wilson

F irst Corinthians 11:2–16 is among the most challenging passages in the Bible. Key words and the thrust of the passage lend themselves to numerous, often conflicting opinions. Because of the controversial and difficult nature of this section, any interpretation must be held with a certain degree of caution.

The Structure of 1 Corinthians 11:2–16

This passage is composed of three major units. In the first (11:2–6) and third (11:13–15) units Paul presented reasons for proper decorum in public worship. In the second unit (11:7–12) he discussed male-female functional distinctives within the framework of essential equality as a part of God's created order. An opening statement (v. 2) and concluding exhortation (v. 16) round out the passage.

Paul clearly appealed to cultural issues in the first and third units, where the explicit statement is made that women should cover their heads. The issues are the shame associated with an uncovered head (vv. 4–6) and the teaching of "nature" (vv. 13–16). Yet in the middle section, where he appealed to noncultural issues (vv. 7–12), he avoided calling for women to cover their heads. Instead he asked that they have "authority" on their heads, though this breaks the parallel structure maintained in the other sections.

Comments on 1 Corinthians 11:2–16

In 7:1–11:1 Paul answered questions concerning the church's moral life, and then in 11:2–34 he addressed problems pertaining to the worship of the church. He then discussed spiritual gifts (chaps. 12–14) and the resurrection (chap. 15).

AN EXPRESSION OF GOODWILL (11:2)

Paul introduced a new section in verse 2 with the use of δὲ ("now").[1] Does this section continue Paul's replies to the Corinthians' questions, which began in 7:1, or was Paul now dealing with things that had either been reported to him or that he felt were important?[2] Perhaps he was referring to their letter by means of a quotation in this section,[3] and then he moved on to clarify their concern as he had done in 8:1. In any case, the discussion of worship and the Lord's Supper in chapter 10 would certainly have brought further issues of public worship to mind, and the discussion of practices at the Lord's Supper fits well in the flow of the argument at this point, providing a smooth transition to the use of spiritual gifts in the worship service in chapters 12–14.

After Paul encouraged the Corinthians to be imitators of him (11:1), he praised their conduct because they remembered him (v. 2). This unexpected commendation of the Corinthians has raised questions about Paul's purpose here. This could be the typical Pauline pattern of beginning a difficult section with encouragement (cf. 1:1–9). Some have supposed that Paul was being sarcastic, as he was earlier in 4:8.[4] Others feel that Paul may be quoting something the Corinthians wrote in their letter. It seems best to take this as a true commendation, in view of the literary device whereby Paul introduced a section with praise when possible and then gave a needed rebuke and correction.[5]

The nature of this commendation is twofold. First, the Corinthians' remembrance of Paul is commended (v. 2a). Second, their remembrance was evident in that they held "firmly to the traditions" (τὰς παραδόσεις κατέχετε). To "hold firmly" is to observe something faithfully.[6] Παραδόσεις probably does not refer to mere "traditions" that have no authority in the church, since Paul mentioned them as ones he had conveyed. Some writers feel that the traditions were all the teachings Paul had given the Corinthians, either while he was at Corinth (Acts 18:1–17) or in the letter referred to in 1 Corinthians 5:9 that has not survived.[7] Godet feels these traditions are only the ecclesiastical traditions of the church without reference to doctrine.[8] Yet Paul used this word (παράδοσις) with reference to his oral teachings as well as his letters, which contained both practice and doctrine (cf. 2 Thess. 2:15). Παράδοσις is literally "a handing down"[9] and this can mean either teachings handed down from an apostle or from

Christ. Whatever the case, these are authoritative teachings and Paul commended the Corinthians for obeying them. With the positive foundation set by this commendation, Paul then rebuked the Corinthians for violations in their worship (11:2–14:40).

A REFLECTION OF GOD'S CREATIVE DESIGN MANDATED (11:3–16)

Some have suggested that the question of headcoverings in the church was not an important issue with Paul.[10] Yet his tone reveals otherwise. That the Corinthians needed strong exhortation in this area is seen in the asyndeton (lack of connectives) in verses 13–15. By the use of asyndeton "the point of the sentence . . . is heightened by the brevity of the components."[11] The importance of the issue is also shown by Paul's extended discussion and numerous reasons for maintaining proper practice in the use of headcoverings.

An argument from design and disgrace (11:3–6). This section begins with a contrastive δέ ("but" or "now"), which shows that this was something about which the apostle could not praise the Corinthians.[12] Paul wanted them to know the principle of headship. A hierarchical structure exists in the universe.[13] This structure begins with God and moves downward to Christ who is over man, who in turn is over woman (v. 3). This doctrine of headship is foundational to the entire passage. This is in keeping with Paul's practice of affirming a theological principle as the basis for Christian behavior. The rejection of this doctrine is what led the Corinthian women to throw off the customary symbol of this order.

The order in which the examples of hierarchical relationship appear—Christ-man; man-woman; God-Christ—places the relationship under discussion in the middle for emphasis. This may also have been an intentional ordering to avoid placing woman at the bottom of the list (as also in vv. 12–13).

The word "head" (κεφαλή), used to describe the relationship between the members of the structure, has posed numerous problems. The term can refer to the source of something, similar to the "headwaters" of a river. It may also refer to the authority of one person over another. Some see in the term a reference to both source and subordination to authority.[14]

Those who understand headship in this passage as a reference to source alone appeal to the discussion of man being the source of woman in creation (v. 8). This is a strong argument.[15] The grounds for taking it instead as a reference to subordination to authority with no reference to origination or source center on the fact that God is said to be the "head" (κεφαλὴ) of Christ (v. 3). A case is then made for God being the authoritative Head of Christ and not His Source. It is also pointed out that to say that Christ originated in God is to be guilty of the heresy of Arianism.[16]

Two points should be made in defense of the view that κεφαλὴ refers to source as well as authority. First, Paul seemingly picked up both meanings of κεφαλὴ in the following verses. Verses 3–6 deal with subordination to authority and verses 7–12 deal with source. Second, Paul used the term elsewhere to refer to both subordination (Col. 2:10) and origin (2:19). In response to the Arian charge, one should note that though Paul taught that Christ is subordinate to the Father in His Sonship (1 Cor. 3:23; 15:28), Paul was not teaching that Christ originated from God. Nor did John teach this when he affirmed that Christ was "the only begotten from the Father" (John 1:14).[17] Here Paul was showing the order of God in relation to both origin and subordination.[18]

Paul then made two claims that relate to the covering of men and women. His first assertion deals with the men of the church. Paul asserted that "every man who has something on his head while praying or prophesying disgraces his head" (1 Cor. 11:4). There is some ambiguity regarding what was on their heads. A literal translation reads, "having down from the head" (κατὰ κεφαλῆς ἔχων). What is down the head? This may be the man's hair, which would mean that the man should not have long hair. But this does not make sense in the context, which demands that what is down the head is a covering. This meaning can be seen in the context, for clearly this is parallel to the headcovering of the woman (v. 5). Therefore this verse is claiming that a man is not to have his head covered when he prays and prophecies.

The reason men were not to wear a headcovering is related to the principle of headship Paul had just established—a man would thereby disgrace his head (v. 4). The question is whether this is a disgrace of the literal head or of the One who is head over the man (i.e., Christ). Those who think this is a reference to a man's head see the connection between "head" (κεφαλὴ) in the first part of this verse and its use here.[19] Those who say this is a reference to the hierarchical head, Christ, appeal to the use of κεφαλὴ in verse 3.[20] It seems preferable to see here a reference to both the hierarchical and the literal head. "Head" is a key word in this passage and the difficulty in determining the meaning seems to be that Paul had both in mind. Therefore the man who prays with his head covered dishonors Christ and himself. The reference to the literal head names the part for the whole. If the head is dishonored, so is the entire person.

The custom for women in New Testament times was to cover their heads. Not to do so was to ignore the distinction between male and female. It would also seem that headcoverings (perhaps something like a modern-day shawl) showed submission to a visible authority.[21]

Paul next described what the women's practice of headcoverings ought to be in light of the principle of headship (vv. 5–6). The extent to which Paul emphasized women in this passage seems to indicate that his reference to men was simply to point out the contrast and that the women were in violation of his instruction.[22]

Though there is much dispute about the practice of headcoverings in Corinthians, two things are clear: (a) men did not wear them and women did, and (b) the headcovering was a sign of distinction between men and women.[23] Talbert concludes that "where the covering was worn, it appears to have been a social symbol attesting one's femaleness."[24] Lowery summarizes the issue well: "It cannot be unequivocally asserted, but the preponderance of evidence points toward the public covering of women as a universal custom in the first century in both Jewish culture and Greco-Roman."[25] This is also supported by Paul's appeal to nature.

These headcoverings were in the form of hoods pulled up from a shawl, rather than full facial coverings.[26] It seems that the Corinthian women had abandoned headcoverings in worship because of misunderstanding the equality of all who are "in Christ."[27] Paul had taught elsewhere, and likely also at Corinth, that in Christ "there is neither male nor female" (Gal. 3:28). This may have caused the Corinthian women to conclude that, like the angels, they need not concern themselves with male-female distinctions. Paul countered this by showing women their need to wear headcoverings, thereby maintaining the sign of distinction between men and women. Their redemption did not override the creative order.[28]

Paul wrote that "every woman who has her head uncovered . . . disgraces her head" (v. 5). If the woman does not have a headcovering,[29] she dishonors her "head" (κεφαλὴ). As in the case of the men (v. 4), the word "head" refers to both the literal and the hierarchical head. She dishonors her hierarchical head, for she is claiming to be equal to him rather than distinct from him.[30] "Head" (κεφαλὴ) is again being used as a part for the whole. Hence the woman was bringing dishonor to herself.

Verse 6 contains the first class condition of εἰ followed by the indicative mood (εἰ . . . αἰσκρὸν),[31] translated literally, "If it is a disgrace for a woman . . . and it is, then. . . ." The point is that it was indeed a disgrace for the woman to have her head uncovered. Examples of this disgrace ranged from temple prostitutes whose heads were uncovered to women who were found to be adulteresses.[32] In that culture not wearing a headcovering was an act of shame.

Paul then argued that if a woman abandoned her headcovering, she might as well "have her hair cut off" (καὶ κειράσθω, v. 6). Wallace identifies "cut off" as a permissive middle, which would mean if a woman willfully refused to wear a headcovering, then she should willingly submit to having her hair cut.[33] For her to do this, however, would be to place herself among the dishonored. Therefore since she would not be willing to be dishonored in that way, she should wear the headcovering and not act as if she were dishonored.

Who is the "woman" (γυνή) in verses 5–6? Some say she is a woman who is married to the man referred to in verse 4. Others see this as a reference to all women in their relationship to men in the meetings of the church.[34] The best alternative seems to be that this is a reference to all women because (a) marriage is not mentioned in this passage, (b) the principles seem to illustrate the fact that men in general are the head of women in general, and (c) the issue involves male-female distinctiveness.

Paul next dealt with the question of when this headcovering of women was to be done. The problem is in the use of the words "while praying or prophesying" (v. 5). If these words were applied only to the men mentioned in verse 4, then the occasion would be the meetings of the church. But Paul used the words in reference to women. If this was a reference to church meetings, Paul seems to have contradicted himself when he wrote in 14:34–35 that women should be silent in the church. This problem has been solved in a number of ways. (1) Some believe the meeting in 11:5 is not a meeting of the congregation. This is supported by the fact that the phrase "because you come together" does not appear until verse 17. (2) Another view is that 14:34–35 refers to "speaking in ecstatic language."[35] These writers refer to Paul's usage of the words in chapter 14. (3) Others think Paul was restricting actions that he would later forbid.[36] (4) Another solution is that Paul forbade women to teach men, as stated in 1 Timothy 2:11–15. (5) Many believe that Paul was here giving a true exception to the general rule that was set forth later. That is to say, women are allowed to speak only (a) when their heads are covered and (b) when they are prompted by the Holy Spirit to speak.

Most likely Paul had in mind the meeting of the gathered church in light of the broader context in which worship and the Lord's Supper were discussed in chapter 10. The mention of the practices of the church in 11:16 is further support that this is the gathered church. How then can this be harmonized with Paul's call in 14:34–35 for the women to be silent? The solution seems to be that in 14:34–35 Paul was regulating the participation of the women in church in evaluating the prophets.[37] Women were not to participate in this evaluation as the men did, but were to ask questions of their husbands at home. Support for this is in the structure of 1 Corinthians 14:26–35. The context deals with the regulations surrounding the exercise of the two spiritual gifts being addressed in that passage, including tongues-speaking in verses 27–28 and prophecy in verses 29–35.[38]

According to this view, women could pray and prophesy in the church meetings so long as they were wearing their headcoverings. They were not to participate in any evaluation of other prophets. This view seems to fit perfectly with Paul's other instruction that women are not to exercise authority over men, because evaluation of their prophesying would certainly be an exercise of authority.

Christian women in Corinth were allowed to pray, but they were not allowed to teach or exercise authority over men (1 Tim. 2:12).[39] They could also prophesy (1 Cor. 11:5), but the meaning of this is debated. It may mean the delivering of revelation from God, which today would limit them to the public reading of Scripture. It may also refer to delivering a message given spontaneously in response to God's leading.[40] Whatever the meaning, they were permitted to do so, so long as it was not teaching or exercising authority over men and so long as their heads were covered.

An argument from creation (11:7–12). Paul began this section by stating, "For a man ought not to have his head covered" (v. 7a). The word "ought" (ὀφείλει) is used in the sense of an obligation. Some controversy surrounds the exact translation of οὐκ ὀφείλει. Did Paul mean a man "is not obligated,"[41] or was he saying the man "ought not."[42] It is better to view this as a command, because as Paul did not leave women a choice, so it is not likely that he was giving men liberty to do as they pleased.

Why was the man obligated not to cover his head? The answer, as Paul said, is that man "is the image and glory of God" (v. 7b). What did Paul mean by these words? Genesis 1:26 states that man was created in the "image" and "likeness" of God. It should be noted that the Old Testament applies these terms to the woman as well as the man (Gen. 1:27), which means that the woman is also made in God's image. But Paul's point is found in the use of "glory" (δόξα), also used to describe the woman's relationship to man. "Image" in 1 Corinthians 11:7 indicates a reflection.[43] So for a man to veil the reflection of God in a service in which he is praying to Him or delivering a prophetic word from Him would be inconsistent. To cover the reflection of what one is worshiping is counterproductive.

When Paul used the word "glory," he was not alluding to a specific Old Testament verse as he had done in the case of "image." Rather he was summarizing what the Old Testament teaches. Paul used the participle "being" (ὑπάρχων) with reference to the man, rather than the verb "is" (ἔστιν) which he used to describe the relationship of the woman to the man. Though the reflections are similar, they are not identical. Some conclude that the terms "image" and "glory" are practically synonymous.[44] Since Paul used the term "glory" and not the synonym "likeness," he may be suggesting some other meaning for "glory." Hurley points to Paul's use of "glory" in 15:40–41 in which he refers to the honor of the celestial bodies.[45]

"In Greek thought an 'image' gives tangible, perceptive expression and substance to that which is invisible."[46] Thus man gives or reflects the glory of God.[47] In some manner this glory is resident or reflected from the head of the man and should not be covered.

Paul next said women must wear headcoverings because of the order of God's creation: "but the woman is the glory of man" (11:7c). What does this mean? The thought may be as Findlay notes, "But the woman (ought to have her head veiled, for she) is the glory of man."[48] Another option, presented by Fee, argues that the other side of the formula is intentionally left until verse 10, where Paul used the term "ought" in reference to women.[49] This latter understanding fits well and is displayed in the following layout by Fee.

A   Man ought not to have his head covered,
  B   since he is the image and glory of God;
      on the other hand
  B' Woman is man's glory
      for this reason
A'   She ought to have authority on her head because of the
      angels.[50]

In parallel thought to verse 7b, Paul claimed that in some way "the woman is the glory of man" (v. 7c). The reason for this is given in verses 8–9.[51] These verses show that the sequence of creation demonstrates how woman brings glory to man—she comes from him and completes him. Paul's use of prepositions in verses 8–9 is crucial. He claimed that the woman is "out of" ($\dot{\epsilon}\xi$ NASB, "from") man and not vice versa. This is an obvious reference to the original creation of the first woman, in which she was formed from the rib of the man (Gen. 2:22–23). Therefore, as Paul wrote, woman brings man glory, for she was actually created "out of" his body.

A second reason the woman is the glory of the man is that she was created "for the man's sake" ($\delta\iota\grave{\alpha}$ $\tau\grave{o}\nu$ $\check{\alpha}\nu\delta\rho\alpha$, v. 9). The translation of $\delta\iota\grave{\alpha}$ varies. Ellicott has "because of the man."[52] Others translate, "on account of the man."[53] Grosheide calls this the purpose for which Eve was created.[54] The reference is to Genesis 2:18, where God recognized that the man needed a companion who would complete him,[55] and so He created Eve. Thus since woman was created because of man's need for a companion, she brings him glory.

In 1 Corinthians 11:10 Paul gave an imperative for the woman. As the man was to have his head uncovered, "therefore the woman ought to have . . . authority on her head, because of the angels." This statement has two closely related problems: (1) What is the meaning of "authority" ($\dot{\epsilon}\xi o\upsilon\sigma\acute{\iota}\alpha$)? (2) What is the meaning of "because of the angels" ($\delta\iota\grave{\alpha}$ $\tau o\grave{\upsilon}\varsigma$ $\dot{\alpha}\gamma\gamma\acute{\epsilon}\lambda o\upsilon\varsigma$)?

Does "therefore" ($\delta\iota\grave{\alpha}$ $\tau o\hat{\upsilon}\tau o$) point backward toward the discussion of the order of creation,[56] or does it point forward, simply giving another reason for the woman's headcovering?[57] The fact that Paul in the following verse clarified the order of creation and its significance suggests that he did not break his thought and then return to it. Instead, since the reference to the angels is closely related to the discussion of the order of creation, the word "therefore" points backward to the reason Paul expressed in the preceding verses and also forward[58] to the reason presented in the following verses.

"Authority" (ἐξουσία) was a key word for the Corinthians (8:9; cf. 9:4–6, 12, 18). There are several possible meanings for it: (a) freedom of choice, right to do as one wishes, (b) ability to do something, (c) authority to do something, or (d) power exercised by rulers. The question here is whether the "authority" is the woman's or the man's. Those who feel that ἐξουσία is a metonymy for the headcovering, or that this is a "sign of the authority" of the man over the woman, point to the meaning of the headcovering in the culture of that day.[59] Yet that does not explain why Paul used "authority" instead of "headcovering" or "sign of subjection." The fact that Paul did not refer specifically to the headcovering here indicates that the issue is not the exact use of the headcovering but the larger issue of the disregard of distinctions. This clearly shows that cultural conditioning is present in the passage.

Thus it seems appropriate to understand "authority" here to refer to the woman's freedom or authority and not the man's. Specifically it is her authority to participate in the worship of the church. In the synagogue women were not allowed to speak, but now in Christ they have freedom or authority[60] to speak in worship.[61] Thus the woman should wear a sign of her authority in order to allow her to have the freedom and authority to pray and prophesy in the presence of the man who is "head" over her. "The sign of authority refers to the head covering which serves as a social symbol of the woman's femaleness. . . . Paul's point is that wearing the veil means acceptance of one's created sexuality."[62]

Placing the symbol of authority on the head was a cultural practice. The fact that the symbol was worn on the head also allowed Paul to pursue a wordplay on the word "head," as noted earlier. The use of "on the head" therefore does not demand that a symbol on the head be retained today, but only that the symbol in that day was to be on the head.

At least five options have been suggested for the meaning of "because of the angels" (διὰ τοὺς ἀγγέλους). (a) Because the ministers of the church may be tempted by the beauty of the women to lust, women should cover their heads.[63] (b) Because evil angels may lust after women, their heads should be covered.[64] (c) Good angels may be tempted to lust.[65] (d) Since angels are guardians of the created order, to violate that order explained in the preceding verse would offend the angels.[66] (e) Since the angels are present in worship, women should conduct themselves properly so as not to offend them.[67]

The first option (the temptation of ministers) should be rejected in light of the findings of Hurley concerning the type of headcoverings as well as the consistent use of ἀγγέλους in Corinthians to describe angelic beings, not earthly messengers. Hurley concludes that because a full facial veiling was not in practice, the headcovering would not prevent the ministers from lust.[68] The second and third options are also to be ruled out because evil angels would not be the normal meaning of ἀγγέλους with the article.[69] It is also unlikely that elect angels would lust after women, for nowhere else in Scripture are they pictured as doing this.

The last two explanations are the only likely options. Of these the first has a few problems. Waltke cites Moffatt as basing this interpretation on the midrash of Genesis 1:26–27.[70] However, Genesis 1:26–27 does not refer to the presence of angels in creation at all. Rather the midrash was a Jewish misunderstanding of the plural form used for God in the beginning chapters of Genesis. If this view is accepted on the basis of Paul's understanding of the midrash, then he was basing his argument on something that was not true. This is incompatible with a high view of Scripture. This leads to the conclusion that the last view best accords with the evidence. Angels are presented elsewhere as spectators of the affairs of humans (1 Cor. 4:9; Eph. 3:10; 1 Tim. 3:16). Thus the meaning is, "If a woman thinks lightly of shocking men, she must remember that she is also shocking the angels, who of course are present at public worship."[71] The angels would be shocked not because they are the guardians of creation, but simply because they have knowledge of the order of creation and what it involves (Job 38:7).

The reference to angels takes on new meaning in light of the Corinthians' apparent feeling that they had arrived at an angelic status.[72] Paul mentioned angels a number of times in 1 Corinthians (4:9; 6:3; 11:10; 13:1).

In 11:11–12 Paul paused to clarify the statement he had just made about the order of creation and its significance.[73] The idea of clarification is introduced in verse 11 by the adversative "However" (πλὴν). He had used the prepositions ἐκ and διὰ in dealing with the source of the woman in reference to original creation (vv. 8–9). In verses 11–12 he again used important prepositions in underscoring the equality of men and women in Christianity. In verse 11 Paul stated that men and women are not "independent" (χωρις) of each other, and in verse 12 he affirmed that man and woman each depend on the other. Woman "originates from [ἐκ] the man," a clear reference to verse 8 and to Genesis 2:21. Also the man is said to be "through [διὰ] the woman," a reference to his birth through her. As in Genesis 2, man and woman complete and need each other. They are equal in light of the fact that both depend on God, for they "originate from God" (v. 12b). The equality of believing men and women "in the Lord" (v. 11) is illustrated in the birth of the man through the woman and the creation of the woman out of the man.[74]

The dependence of both sexes on each other and their common dependence on God shows in the natural world what is true in the spiritual world—men and women are equal. This does not in any way discard the command for them to recognize male headship. Headship deals with *functional subordination*, not with equality. This is clear in light of the headship ascribed to the Father in relation to the Son in verse 3. Paul's instruction, then, was to maintain the practice that recognizes that though male and female are dependent on each other, in God's plan they are distinct.

Paul supported his instruction by two lines of reasoning—the principle of headship and the order of creation. Both principles show that women should wear their headcoverings in public worship and that men should not have their heads covered. Returning in verses 13–15 to his main point, Paul discussed another reason why headcoverings should be worn by the women.

An argument from nature (11:13–15). In these verses Paul reached the climax of his argument. Grammatically it is noteworthy that the apostle here used a figure of speech called asyndeton. Bullinger describes asyndeton as "without any conjunctions."[75] This figure has an emphatic use. "The resolution of a sentence into unconnected components produces a more powerful effect than would a more periodic form proper. The point of the sentence moreover is heightened by the brevity of the components."[76] In verses 7–12 Paul used the "periodic form" by using numerous coordinating conjunctions (γάρ, δέ, πλήν, διά τοῦτο, and ὥσπερ). The shift in verses 13–15 is evident because connectives are few, and generally the ones used connect parts within the sentence rather than the sentences themselves.

Paul called on the Corinthians to "judge for yourselves" (v. 13), that is, to take note of what he was about to say. "For yourselves" (ἐν ὑμῖν) can mean either a decision reached by the church, without reference to outsiders, or it may refer to a decision reached within oneself.[77] Since Paul appealed to the teaching of "nature" (v. 14), it would seem that the appeal here is to individuals.

Paul raised questions the Corinthians should be able to answer without any help from him. The first deals with the matter at hand, that is, headcoverings. In light of the reason he put forth at this point the Corinthians should decide that it was not proper for a woman to pray with her head uncovered (v. 13). The meaning of "proper" (πρέπον) is general, what is known to be right and appropriate.[78] From what they now knew, they should see that women worshiping without a headcovering was not appropriate. This appeal to a sense of propriety is another indication that at least some cultural conditioning is present in the passage.

As added support Paul wrote of the teaching of "nature" (v. 14), which would serve as a final catalyst in the Corinthian believers' decision. Two related questions—one pertaining to the length of men's hair, and the other to women's hair—call for a positive answer.[79] Findlay calls "nature" (φύσις) "a constitutional feeling,"[80] while Grosheide calls it "the general notion which all people have by virtue of their being human beings."[81] Godet on the other hand feels that "nature" refers to the physical organization of women,[82] a view that lacks evidence. The claim that men's hair does not grow as long as women's hair, even if true (and it is not), would not have been known by the Corinthians in the first century.

Grosheide's view of "nature" as that which all have as human beings is inadequate, since not all felt that long hair was a shame, even in the ancient world.[83] So it is preferable to take the meaning of Bauer's first reading, that which is "inherited from one's ancestors."[84] Fee gives this sense when he writes, "By 'nature' Paul meant the natural feelings of their contemporary culture."[85] Their culture taught that as a general rule, men have short hair and women have long hair. This is seen in Paul's vow, which indicates that it was unusual for men to have long hair (Acts 18:18). Thus people at that time understood that "if a man has long hair, it is a dishonor to him" (v. 14). Robertson and Plummer attest that "at this period, civilized men, whether Jews, Greek, or Romans wore their hair short."[86] This again points to Paul's grounding in the culture of his day in making this special appeal about covering or not covering one's head. The second question pertained to the length of women's hair (v. 15). The question here is how the hair of the woman is "glory" (δόξα) for her. Some interpret glory as meaning "pride."[87] This seems to be the sense of the passage so long as one does not suggest any negative connotations. Why is a woman's hair her glory? It has been given to her "for a covering" (ἀντὶ περιβολαίου) and thus distinguishes her from man, allowing her to function properly in her created role. The word "covering" (περιβολαίου) differs from the word for headcovering in the earlier verses. Some have missed this point altogether.[88] To suggest that the hair replaces the headcovering is to ignore the message Paul was communicating, namely, that women needed to wear headcoverings in congregational worship.[89] The argument that ἀντὶ should be translated "in place of" loses force when this fact is realized. Society informed women that their hair had been given as a covering and was thus their "glory." To apply this directly to the issue of headcoverings is to miss Paul's point. Long hair is the proper woman's covering in the *natural* realm.

The apostle's point is this: Since a woman has a covering in the physical realm, which is taught by nature, she should also have a covering in the spiritual realm, which is the headcovering.

The difference in words for the coverings raises the question of what kind of headcovering Paul was speaking about in this passage. Hurley is helpful here, even though he takes the position that the hair replaces the covering. He shows from many extrabiblical sources that the coverings used in Paul's day covered the head. As stated earlier, they were not full facial veils; they were often attached as hoods to the women's garments.[90]

A final word (11:16). Alford says that this verse "cuts off the subject already decided abundantly, with a settlement of any possible indifference by appeal to universal apostolic and ecclesiastical custom."[91] As indicated by the first class condition, Paul addressed a reality,[92] not a mere possible situation. "Contentious" (φιλόνεικος) describes the manner in which the man "thinks" (δοκεῖ). The word φιλόνεικος, used only here in the New Testament, means quarrelsome, or one who disputes.[93] The point is that if anyone, whether one in the church or one who comes and introduces himself as a teacher, is thinking in a contentious manner, he is here put down by the authority of the apostolic company.[94]

Such a person should succumb to Paul's instruction because "we have no other practice, nor have the churches of God" (v. 16b). This statement can mean either that there was no custom of being quarrelsome, or that there was no custom of women praying with their heads uncovered. The first option is that of early expositors cited by Ellicott.[95] It seems better, in light of the forcefulness with which Paul concluded, to say, as do the majority of the interpreters,[96] that the second view is preferable.

When Paul wrote "we" (ἡμεῖς), he meant either himself and the apostolic circle, or himself alone in an editorial sense. In light of the emphasis in the following phrase, it seems better to understand this as an editorial "we." He then moved on to enlarge the circle of support by mentioning the "churches of God," thus showing that he was not asking anything special of the Corinthians, for this was how all God's people conducted themselves.

Was Paul basing his "practice" (συνήθειαν) on a mere custom of the church, being disturbed because the Corinthians were violating an optional custom? This seems unlikely. Rather, Paul was dealing with practices important in the church.

Contemporary Applications

If this passage is perceived as addressing the question of what headcoverings women are to wear in church worship settings, then the conclusion is likely to be that headcoverings must be worn by women today. If the issue of the passage is the problem of throwing off the accepted symbol of male-female role distinctions, then the cultural factor becomes more significant and other appropriate symbols are more likely to be accepted. To state this differently, Paul was either telling the Corinthians to wear headcoverings as a sign of God-ordained male-female role distinctives or he was telling them to wear the proper cultural symbol of God-ordained male-female role distinctives. In this second option Paul was telling the Corinthians not to abandon the culturally accepted symbol of male-female role distinctives.

While these two possibilities may have led to the same application for the Corinthians, their application today will vary. The first option demands that women today wear coverings in recognition of God's creative order. The second option demands that women not wear an expression of a false theology and thus signify a rejection of God's creative order.

The question before the interpreter is not whether this passage should be applied today. It should. The question is *what* should be applied. Should women wear headcoverings, or should they dress in such a way that they do not obliterate the God-ordained distinction between men and women? The common appeal that this is simply a symbol and that the attitude is what really counts is clearly to be rejected. Symbols have always been significant for God's people. The entire sacrificial system of the Old Testament was symbolic as well as the two ordinances observed by the church today, baptism and the Lord's Supper. The symbolic nature of headcoverings is no basis for rejection of the practice.

This article has concluded that Paul did indeed require women believers in the Corinthian church to wear headcoverings when they attended worship services, and he required the men not to have their heads covered. Man's head is not to be covered, because he reflects God's glory, but the woman's head was to be covered as an indication of her role as a woman. Otherwise she would detract from her glorious role of completing the man.

In a broader sense Paul can be understood as asking for appropriate dress in the church—dress that reflects God's intent in the headship of Christ over man and the headship of men over women.

The headship established by God should not be disregarded. To overlook God's distinctive function for men and women is disgraceful. That is true in any culture. The expression of disregard in the Corinthian culture was the removal of women's headcoverings. Paul's response was to tell them to wear what was the normal cultural expression of male-female distinction. In the Greco-Roman culture that distinction revealed by women wearing headcoverings.

However, to require women today to wear headcoverings in church is to ask them to do something abnormal rather than normal. This is exactly what Paul wanted to avoid. He wanted women to do what was normal in their culture in reflecting their womanhood and the creative order and distinction set forth in verse 3. To be obedient to this passage Christian women should not dress in a way that blurs the distinction between male and female. Fee's comments on this section support this understanding.

Although various Christian groups have fostered the practice of some sort of headcovering for women in the assembled church, the difficulties with the practice are obvious. For Paul the issue was directly tied to a cultural shame that scarcely prevails in most cultures today. Furthermore, we simply do not know what the practices were which they were abusing. Thus, literal "obedience" to the text is often merely symbolic. Unfortunately, the symbol that tends to be reinforced is the subordination of women, which is hardly Paul's point. Furthermore, it would seem in cultures where women's heads are seldom covered, the enforcement of such in the church turns Paul's point on its head.[97]

If women are asked to wear headcoverings in church *today*, they are asked to do what is abnormal, though Paul was asking them to do what was normal.

In light of the fact that Paul based his instruction on the universal concepts of headship, the order of creation, and what the Corinthians knew to be true about proper headcoverings in the physical realm, as well as a universal practice, this writer concludes that the principles of this passage are indeed valid for today. It seems that Paul was asking the Corinthians to follow a normal cultural practice that in that day reflected an understanding that God has created men and women to function in different roles. As long as men and women today are not communicating by their dress that the creative order and distinctions are done away, they are being obedient to this passage. Whereas this passage does not require women to wear headcoverings today,[98] the application of the principle of the passage is still called for.

In addition to the exegetical considerations presented above, the following practical points should be observed. It is apparent that the present-day practice of women wearing headcoverings in church does not immediately communicate Paul's thought. Yet one must determine whether this is sufficient grounds for rejecting the practice as a whole. Almost all symbols require education for their meaning to become clear. This is true in the symbolic practices of baptism and the Lord's Supper, which do not immediately communicate the ideas of initiation and fellowship.

"In the culture of the early church, while headcoverings may not necessarily have been universally worn by women in public settings, their meaning was nonetheless clear."[99] Today, however, pastoral experience has revealed that the presence of headcoverings results in confusion for visitors and those unfamiliar with the meaning of the symbol. This violates the principle that the church should not do things seemingly strange to "some who do not understand or some unbelievers [who] come in" (14:23, NIV).

If the practice of women wearing headcoverings is maintained, the church must wrestle with the difficulties this presents in reaching and retaining newcomers. The strong communication of the principle of headship that Paul was addressing remains, but confusion cannot be avoided when headcoverings are worn.

If a symbol is to be maintained, a suitable alternative to the wearing of headcoverings could be the presence of a male leader in the services in which women participate.[100] Other alternatives include the wearing of a wedding ring or hair pins; yet consideration must be given to whether these communicate the intended meaning any more clearly than a headcovering without further teaching.

The present writer has concluded that faithfulness to the teaching of this passage can be maintained so long as the participants in worship services do not follow a practice that denies God's creative order reflected in male-female distinctions. This results in the conclusion that no symbol is actually called for in the passage. Instead, the passage is forbidding the presence of a symbol or practice that denies male-female distinctions and roles.

CHAPTER 16

The Chronological Problem of Galatians 2:1–10

Stanley D. Toussaint

Without a doubt, the outstanding problem in reconciling Paul's Epistle to the Galatians with the Book of Acts is relating Galatians 2:1–10 with Luke's record. Knox calls this "the central problem of Acts."[1] Simply stated, the problem is this: Which of Paul's visits to Jerusalem recorded in Acts is discussed in Galatians 2? Can the Acts account be squared with Paul's autobiography in Galatians without facing hopeless discrepancies?

According to Luke's record Paul was in Jerusalem five times following his conversion. First was the visit to Jerusalem after Paul left Damascus (Acts 9:26–30). It is clear this corresponds with Galatians 1:18–20. Second, there was the famine visit recorded in Acts 11:27–30 and 12:25. Third, Paul visited Jerusalem at the time of the Jerusalem Council (15:1–30). The fourth brief visit to Jerusalem following Paul's second missionary journey is recorded in Acts 18:22. The fifth visit occasioned Paul's Cesarean imprisonment (Acts 21:15–23:35).

It is almost certain Galatians 2:1–10 is not viewing Paul's fourth visit of Acts 18:22 and it cannot be describing the fifth.[2] Unless Luke omitted one of Paul's visits to Jerusalem,[3] a rather unlikely alternative, the reconciliation of Galatians 2:1–10 with the Acts record is limited to two possibilities: in Galatians Paul was referring either to his second or to his third visit to Jerusalem.[4]

In either case Luke's reliability has been called into question because of the difficulties involved in reconciling Galatians with Acts. Bruce states concerning Luke's record of the Jerusalem Council: "His account of this occasion has been impugned by a number of scholars as tendentious and largely unhistorical, mainly because of the difficulty that has been felt by more conservative scholars as well."[5] Burton is a case in point. In his outstanding

174

commentary on Galatians, he takes Galatians 2:1–10 as a description of Acts 15 but says Luke was inaccurate in his record of both the second and third visits.[6] Undoubtedly there are problems, but they are by no means insurmountable and certainly no solution needs to accuse either Luke or Paul of errors or inaccuracies.

Galatians 2 and the Jerusalem Council

It is possible that Paul was describing the Jerusalem Council in Galatians 2. A considerable amount of evidence is amassed in favor of this position.[7] First, the issues discussed are the same in both passages. The question revolves around the necessity of circumcision and the keeping of the Mosaic Law.

Second, the same people are involved in both. James, Peter, Paul, and Barnabas are all mentioned in both Acts and Galatians 2. While Titus is referred to in Galatians 2:3 and is not named in Acts 15, he would be included in the "certain others" of Acts 15:2. The "false brethren" of Galatians 2:4 correspond with the "certain ones from Judea" in Acts 15:1.

Third, the same geography is considered in both accounts. Antioch and Jerusalem both figure prominently in Acts 15 and Galatians 2.

Fourth, Galatians is similar to Romans and 1 and 2 Corinthians and therefore must have been written about the same time. Romans and the Corinthian epistles were certainly written after the Jerusalem Council. Galatians 2 therefore looks back to this important milestone in the early church.

Fifth, the aorist tense of ἐσπούδασα ("were eager") implies the famine visit had taken place a considerable time before the agreement described in Galatians was reached.[8] It is assumed the aorist tense refers back to the famine visit and the accord that was reached at the Jerusalem Council. This however is an unwarranted assumption. The present tense of μνημονεύωμεν ("remember") with the aorist ἐσπούδασα gives the impression that Paul should *continue* to remember the poor just as he had endeavored to do. It actually makes better sense to refer the entire verse to the famine visit since charity was the business at hand at the time.

This view faces a number of objections. One difficulty is this: If Galatians 2 refers to the Jerusalem Council, why did Paul not refer to its official pronouncement? There is no reference in the entire epistle to the decree of the Jerusalem Council. This objection is answered by saying Paul was attempting to prove his independence of the church at Jerusalem and the apostles. For Paul to acknowledge the power of the decision of the Council would be to subject himself to human authority. However, Acts 15:3–16:5 indicates Paul did use the decrees of the Council when his position had to be vindicated in the face of opposition from Judaizers.

Another formidable difficulty is found in the omission in Galatians of any reference to the famine visit to Jerusalem if Galatians 2:10 is made to correspond with the Jerusalem Council. This is very important. In this section of Galatians, Paul was carefully showing his independence of human authority in his reception and proclamation of the gospel. One by one he discussed his contacts with Jerusalem. If Galatians 2:1–10 refers to the Jerusalem Council and Galatians 1:18–20 corresponds with Acts 9:26–30 (a fact no one disputes), then Paul purposely omitted reference to his second visit to Jerusalem. He leaped from the first to the third contact with the church at Jerusalem. This objection is answered by asserting Paul did not see any apostles in the famine visit; he saw only elders (Acts 11:30). Paul, it is stated, was concerned in Galatians with mentioning only his contacts with the apostles, none of whom he saw in the famine visit. Because of the severe persecutions in Jerusalem at that time, it is assumed the apostles were driven out of the city. However, this is an assumption that is difficult to prove. In Acts 8:1 during a time of persecution, all were scattered except the apostles. In fact Acts 12:17 strongly implies "James and the brethren" were in Jerusalem at the time of the persecution and Peter certainly was.

How then can the lack of mention of apostles in Acts 11:30 be accounted for? It was simply a matter of responsibility.[9] The church at Antioch sent relief to the elders at Jerusalem so that the elders could direct the distribution. This is not the work of the apostles (6:2–4). Moreover, Acts 11:30 does not say Paul saw no apostles. It simply states the relief was turned over to the elders in Judea just as the church at Antioch had directed Paul and Barnabas to do. To say therefore that Paul omitted any reference to the famine visit in Galatians tends to make his defense in Galatians 1:17–2:10 rather inaccurate.

The third objection relates to the kind of conferences described in Galatians 2 and Acts 15. The Acts account describes a public conference whereas Galatians 2 looks at a private meeting. The two therefore must be different. Those who feel Galatians 2 and Acts 15 are to be reconciled account for this difficulty by saying the private conference preceded the public one. Paul, it is argued, would not endanger his whole position in a public council without having first discussed it in private with the apostles. This is possible but it tends to give the impression the Jerusalem Council, which Luke so strongly emphasized, was little more than a rubber stamp.

Galatians 2 and the Famine Visit

The proponents of the view which equates the visit of Galatians 2:1–10 with Paul's second or famine visit also claim weighty support for their position.[10] First, one gains the distinct impression as he reads Galatians 1:17–2:10 that Paul was carefully listing in order his contacts with Jerusalem. The famine visit would correspond then with his second contact described in Galatians 2:1–10.

Second, Galatians 2:2 asserts Paul went up to Jerusalem by revelation and this fits with the circumstances of Acts 11:27–28. It must be acknowledged, however, that Paul also could have gone to the Jerusalem Council by revelation, though no such fact is mentioned by Luke. In Acts 9:29–30, Luke wrote that Paul fled from Jerusalem because his opponents were seeking his life. Nothing is said of a revelation. However, Paul in Acts 22:17–21 testified he left Jerusalem because of a vision. It is possible therefore for Luke to have omitted any reference to a special revelation in Acts 15. Nevertheless the prominence given to revelation in both Acts 11:27–28 and Galatians 2:2 argues for their identification.

Third, Peter's vacillation as described in Galatians 2:11–14 is easier to explain if it occurred before the Jerusalem Council than after it. To this it is replied that the response of Peter in Galatians 2:11–14 is completely in character with his vacillating personality. But the fact remains, it is easier to explain Peter's actions if they transpired before the Jerusalem Council than after it.

Fourth, it is easier to explain Luke's omission of a private conference in Acts 11 than it is to account for Paul's omission of a visit to Jerusalem in Galatians.

Fifth, Paul's use of πάλιν in connection with Jerusalem in Galatians 2:1 indicates he was marking out his contacts with Jerusalem, not merely his conferences with the apostles.

This view also has some problems. The first and primary difficulty involves chronology. It is known the famine occurred between A.D. 44 and 48 because Josephus said the famine occurred in the procuratorships of C. Cuspius Fadus (44–46) and Tiberius Alexander (46–48). It is probable then that the famine visit took place about A.D. 46. If the three years mentioned in Galatians 1:18 are added to the 14 years of Galatians 2:1, the famine visit may have taken place about 15 years after Paul's conversion.[11] Paul's conversion would have occurred then in A.D. 31. This would hardly leave sufficient time for the growth of the church described in Acts 1–7 to take place. It is very possible, however, to say the 14 years of Galatians 2:1 are to be reckoned from Paul's conversion. From this great turning point in his life Paul would have measured everything. If this method of measuring is followed, then the chronology is no real problem.

A second objection to this view is the reference to the former visit in Galatians 4:13. It implies Paul made two trips to Galatia before he wrote this epistle; therefore the Jerusalem Council preceded the writing of Galatians. This objection can be met by noting the itinerary of Paul's first journey. The apostle retraced his steps through the cities of Galatia on his first journey so he in effect visited them twice. Needless to say, this view assumes the South Galatian theory.

To this writer it seems best to say Galatians 2:1–10 refers to the famine visit. The problems are not insuperable and the evidence in its favor is strong.

A Sequence of Events

If the conclusion of the preceding discussion is accepted, then the following represents the probable succession of events. (1) Paul and Barnabas returned to Antioch of Syria from the famine visit to Jerusalem described in Acts 11. (2) They embarked on their first missionary journey and returned to Antioch. (3) Reports of Judaizers working in the Galatian churches founded by them came to the missionaries. (4) Paul wrote Galatians from Antioch of Syria. (5) The Jerusalem Council was held shortly after the writing of Galatians.

This sequence of events would date the epistle about A.D. 48 and would make it Paul's earliest extant epistle. This series of events also helps explain why Paul could not deal with the heresy in the Galatian churches personally. The press and importance of the Jerusalem Council would necessitate his presence in Jerusalem and a trip to Galatia would have been impossible at that time.

If ease of explanation and logical order is to be considered in Galatians, it seems best to equate the visit of Paul to Jerusalem described in Galatians 2:1–10 with the famine visits of Acts 11.

CHAPTER 17

The Mystery in Ephesians 3

Charles C. Ryrie

The mystery of Ephesians 3:1–12 is a touchstone of interpretations. Amillennial eschatology is quite certain that in this passage Paul was not saying that the mystery is something that was not revealed until New Testament times but is a further revelation of the covenant promises made with Abraham. Allis, for instance, says, "It was new and unknown in a relative sense only, being in its essentials an important theme of prophecy from the time of Abraham. . . ."[1] A more recent writer speaks in the same vein. "What he [Paul] does mean is that this mystery truth, although known and written in kernel form in the text of the Old Testament, was not fully comprehended nor understood until the times of the New Testament, and so can be spoken of, relatively speaking, as being hidden."[2]

Covenant premillennialists hold essentially the same interpretation. Payne, for instance, writes, "Second, the Greek *musterion*, 'mystery,' does not necessarily imply discontinuity. . . . A 'mystery' need not even have been unknown or unappreciated previously, except perhaps relatively so. . . ."[3]

The purpose of this sort of interpretation is to obviate the necessity of recognizing the distinctiveness of the church, the body of Christ, by attempting to show that the church was revealed, at least partially, in the Old Testament. This idea also implies, of course, that the church as spiritual Israel is the continuation of God's redemptive program through Old Testament Israel.

On the other hand dispensational premillennialism has insisted that the mystery is something unrevealed in the Old Testament (though now revealed) in order to demonstrate the distinctiveness of the church from Israel and to emphasize its unique place in God's program for this age. Pentecost, for instance, writes as follows: "Paul then, is explaining, not limiting the mystery there set forth. The concept must stand that this whole age with its program was not revealed in the Old Testament, but constitutes a new program and a new line of revelation in this present age."[4]

Ultradispensationalists complicate the interpretive picture by insisting not only on the distinctiveness of the church but also on the fact that this was not revealed until sometime in the ministry of the Apostle Paul. Extreme ultradispensationalists believe that the mystery was made known by Paul during his first Roman imprisonment, while moderate ultradispensationalists hold that it was revealed earlier in his ministry—either at the time of his conversion or during his first missionary journey. Ultradispensationalists are agreed on the fact that Paul was the initial revelator of the mystery, but they do not agree among themselves as to when he first revealed it.

What is a mystery? What is this mystery in Ephesians 3? Is the church distinct to this age or were Old Testament saints in the body too? Did the Old Testament reveal this mystery? What was Paul's relationship to its revelation? These are some of the questions germane to an understanding of the mystery in Ephesians 3.

The Concept of a Mystery

In classical Greek, μυστήριον means something hidden or secret. In the plural the word was used to designate the sacred rites of the Greek mystery religions—secrets that only the initiated shared. In the Old Testament the Aramaic equivalent appears only in Daniel 2:18–19, 27–30, 47; 4:9. In the second chapter of Daniel the mystery was the dream and its interpretation; in the fourth chapter the mystery was apparently only the interpretation, for the king remembered the dream. The secret (mystery) that the king wanted revealed was the interpretation; thus this was the content of the mystery. It seems unwarranted to include that in 4:9 "the *musterion* is not something unknown (Nebuchadnezzar knows the facts of the dream) but is only something which the king does not understand."[5] Just because the mystery in Daniel 2 was the dream *and* the interpretation does not require that this be the case in chapter 4. After all, the content of the various mysteries in the New Testament must be determined from the passages in which the word is used, and the content is not the same in each occurrence. Thus we may assume in the Old Testament a mystery was something unknown until revealed.

In the Dead Sea Scrolls the same Old Testament word, רז, plus a synonym, פלא, are used in a number of references to indicate not so much something unknown but wisdom that is far above finite understanding.

The word "mystery" therefore means a secret containing high or deep truth. In the New Testament the word μυστήριον occurs 27 times with both ideas of something secret and something deep. The idea of supernatural wisdom in a mystery is found in the only uses of the word in the Gospels in relation to the mysteries of the kingdom (Matt. 13:11; Mark 4:11; Luke 8:10). The idea of a mystery being something secret in Old Testament times but revealed in the New Testament is clearly seen in a passage like Colossians 1:26. Four occurrences are found in Revelation (1:20; 10:7; 17:5, 7) and the other 20 are in the writings of Paul.[6] All seem to involve some higher wisdom which God reveals.

Thus the concept of a mystery is basically a secret which only the initiated share. This includes two ideas: a time when the secret was not known followed by a time when it became known; and deeper or higher wisdom which is revealed to the one initiated into an understanding of the mystery.

The Content of the Mystery

The content of the mystery is expressly stated in Ephesians 3:6: "That the Gentiles are fellow-heirs, and fellow-members of the body, and fellow-partakers of the promise in Christ Jesus through the gospel." In other words, the mystery concerns Jews and Gentiles as joint-heirs, in a joint-body, and joint-sharers of the promise in Christ. That the mystery contains the fact that Gentiles are included in God's plan of redemption is clear, and most nondispensational writers stop at this point. But is this all there is to the mystery? If so, there is little mystery in that, for the Old Testament made this clear (Gen. 12:3; Isa. 42:6–7). If this is the mystery, then Paul was wrong to label it a mystery, for it is neither something new nor some higher truth. The heart of the mystery is that there would be a "joint-body" for Jews and Gentiles. Thus the crux of the interpretation of the mystery in this passage is whether the one body for Jews and Gentiles is an Old Testament revelation.

A concordance examination of the use of the word "body" reveals conclusively that the idea of the body of Christ or of any body into which the redeemed were placed is nowhere found in the Old Testament. Indeed, almost all the uses of the word "body" are of the physical body. The first occurrence of the word "body" in connection with the body of Christ is in the extended discussion of that concept in 1 Corinthians 12:12–25. The next occurrence is in Romans 12:5, and the remainder occur in Ephesians and Colossians. The concept of one body or of any body was unknown in the Old Testament.

Ephesians 3 cannot be dealt with accurately without considering some features in the extended discussion of the body in 1 Corinthians 12. Two important features of the body of Christ are detailed in 12:13. First, Jews and Gentiles are not distinguished in the body of Christ. This is the emphasis of the mystery of Ephesians 3. Second, entrance into that body is effected by the baptism of the Spirit. That baptizing work did not occur in the Old Testament nor during the earthly ministry of Christ. Even after the resurrection the Lord said that it was still future (Acts 1:5). It did take place for the first time in the history of the world on the day of Pentecost (Acts 11:15–16). Therefore the inescapable conclusion is that the body of Christ did not come into existence until the day of Pentecost when the first members of that body were joined to the risen Head.

If by stretch of the interpretive imagination the body could be said to have existed before Pentecost, then it was without a head, for it was not until after the resurrection and ascension of Christ that He was made head of the body which is the church (Eph. 1:22). In His capacity as risen Head, He gives gifts (Eph. 4:9–11) which further underscores the distinctiveness of the body to this age. That body-church is called a "new man" (Eph. 2:15), not a continuation or remaking of Israel, but something new and distinct from the Israel of the Old Testament.

There is certainly continuity of the body of Christ with the redeemed of all ages simply because those in the body are redeemed people. But there is also discontinuity in that the redeemed today are in the body of Christ and not some sort of Israel. Just as the redeemed before Abraham's day (like Enoch and Noah) were not a part of Israel, so the redeemed of this age are not either. Enoch and Noah and other pre-Abrahamic saints belong to the family of God's redeemed, but they never belonged to the commonwealth of Israel. So today redeemed Jew and Gentile belong to God's family of saints without being members of any kind of Israel. They are members of the body of Christ, a new man, entered by the baptizing work of the Spirit, and all believers in this age, whether Jew or Gentile, have equal standing. This is the content of the mystery of Ephesians 3:6.

The Relationship of the Mystery to Old Testament Revelation

Was this mystery revealed in the Old Testament? Covenant theologians respond in the affirmative, and the dispensationalists in the negative. What did Paul say? In this passage he declared that the mystery "in other generations was not made known to the sons of men, as it has now been revealed to His holy apostles and prophets in the Spirit" (Eph. 3:5). Covenant theologians have seized on the word "as" as proving the validity of their contention that the church was in the Old Testament, while dispensationalists have sought to explain the verse otherwise.

Before investigating the possible meaning of the "as" phrase, it is important to notice that in the parallel passage in Colossians 1:26 there is no "as." The statement there is unequivocal—the mystery was not known at all in Old Testament times. It is also rather significant that nondispensational writers on this subject never mention the Colossians passage in connection with their discussions of Ephesians 3, for it would obviously damage their position.[7]

But exactly what was Paul saying in Ephesians 3:5? First, let it be said that even if the clause means that there was some revelation of the church in the Old Testament, it does not necessarily follow that the church was in existence in those days. The second coming of Christ is revealed in a number of Old Testament passages but it has not come to pass yet. In fact, the considerations given above concerning the body of Christ prove that the church was not operative in Old Testament times.

Second, it should be noted that the Greek word for "as" has several meanings. Undoubtedly the most frequently used sense is a comparative one. If this is the use in Ephesians 3:5, then Paul was saying that the mystery was not revealed in the Old Testament to the extent that it is in the New, but it was revealed in the Old. Such an interpretation would stand in contradiction to Colossians 1:25 and the use of the word "body" (meaning the church) in the Scriptures.

But "as" has another meaning which would not impose a contradiction. It may express an adjectival or declarative force which simply means that the "as" clause merely adds additional information. For instance, "as you suppose" in Acts 2:15 adds additional information to the sentence and can in no way be understood as a comparative. Furthermore with a negative in the preceding clause (as in Eph. 3:5) "as" may have the meaning of "but." A clear example of this is found in 1 Corinthians 7:31. Thus Paul may very well have been saying in Ephesians 3:5 that the mystery was not made known to the sons of men in other ages, but it is now revealed. Of course this would be in harmony with the clear passage, Colossians 1:25.

It is true that the Old Testament testifies to the coming of Christ which is involved in the mystery since the church is His body. That the Old Testament witnesses to Him is what is meant in a passage like Romans 16:24–25, but this witness was not comprehended until the mystery had been revealed in the New Testament (1 Peter 1:11–12). Dispensationalists do not deny that the Old Testament predicted the coming of Messiah and blessing on Gentiles, but one looks in vain to find a revelation in the Old Testament of the body of Christ, the church, and of equality of Jews and Gentiles. Even in the millennial kingdom there will not be equality.[8] Covenant theologians seem to imply that since the Old Testament foretold the coming of Christ it also revealed these other truths. The mystery in Ephesians 3 is not that Messiah would come nor that Gentiles would be blessed, but it is that Jews and Gentiles would find an equal position in the new and unique body of Christ.

The Relationship of the Mystery to the Apostle Paul

Ephesians 3:5 is a favorite passage of ultradispensationalists (followers of the teachings of Bullinger, O'Hair, Stam), for in it they believe they have proof that Paul was the first to reveal the mystery of the body church to the world. Three considerations in this passage alone disallow such a conclusion.

First, Paul explicitly stated that the mystery was revealed to "His holy apostles and prophets by the Spirit." In other words, others (plural) understood the mystery and not through the agency of Paul but through the ministry of the Spirit. Paul did not receive it first and then reveal it to the others. They received it, as he did, from the Spirit. The ultradispensationalists' point would be proved if the verse said that the mystery was revealed to his holy apostles and prophets "by me." But it does not say that.

Second, the verb "revealed" in verse 5 is in the aorist tense. In conjunction with the word "now," this indicates that the revelation of the mystery was "made definitely at a former period in these [New Testament] times."[9] This definitely contradicts the extreme type of ultradispensationalism which teaches that the mystery was not revealed to Paul until the time of the imprisonment during which Ephesians was written.

Third, in declaring that he had received this revelation, Paul gave himself no priority (v. 3). "To me" is an unemphatic form (μοι) and it does not stand in a place of emphasis in the sentence. In verse 8 when he wrote of his proclaiming the mystery he did use the emphatic form and placed it in the emphatic position at the beginning of the sentence. Thus when speaking of receiving the mystery he gave himself no priority, while in the matter of preaching it he emphasized the prominent part he played. The constructions ought to be reversed if the claims of the ultradispensationalists are correct.

The mystery of Ephesians 3 is the equality of Jews and Gentiles in the body of Christ. This equality and this body were not revealed in the Old Testament. They were made known only after the coming of Christ by the Spirit to the apostles and prophets including Paul but not excluding others.

CHAPTER 18

"The Husband of One Wife" Requirement in 1 Timothy 3:2

Ed Glasscock

With the divorce rate in America approaching nearly 50 percent of all marriages, the church is being forced to deal more frequently with converts who have divorced and remarried. Can these Christians serve in the body of Christ? To what degree does their divorce and remarriage affect their spiritual activity? The issue of this study questions whether the phrase "the husband of one wife" (1 Tim. 3:2; cf. v. 12) eliminates from Christian service a man who has been divorced and remarried, or a man who has married a woman who was divorced.

Since 1 Timothy 3 provides a list of requirements for those who desire to serve in the offices of elder (vv. 1–7) or deacon (vv. 8–10), it should be noted that whatever one concludes about the meaning of the phrase under discussion, it does not follow that these restrictions automatically apply to all areas of Christian service but only to these two high offices which Paul named specifically.

Four Common Interpretations of 1 Timothy 3:2

Among the variety of explanations of Paul's phrase γυναικὸς ἄνδρα (1 Tim. 3:2, 12; Titus 1:6) four common views will be discussed.

MARRIAGE AS A REQUISITE

Some commentators hold that the phrase "husband of one wife" implies that a man who wishes to serve as an elder or deacon must be married. If one accepts the translation "husband of one wife" then this could possibly be a legitimate view. One who desires the office of elder "must be . . . the husband of one wife," δεῖ . . . εἶναι μιας γυναικὸς ἄνδρα. Δεῖ is an impersonal verb meaning "it is necessary, one must, or has to."[1] According to

187

this view only married men are eligible to serve as elders. Some would also insist that elders also must have children (1 Tim. 3:4). The reasoning is simple: a man cannot manage God's household if he cannot manage his own. By observing the way a man manages his own family, one can determine whether he is capable of helping to manage the local church. Thus, it is argued, a man must be married and have children in order to be an elder or deacon.

Though this seems to be a logical as well as literal application of the requirement "husband of one wife," it seems to contradict 1 Corinthians 7:8, 25–33. Paul apparently encouraged celibacy to avoid "the present distress" (v. 26) and other concerns that distract one from the Lord's service (v. 32). But he also acknowledged the need for marriage and urged that a person not gifted with celibacy should have his own wife (vv. 2, 7, 9, 17). Some would argue that Paul's comments were intended only for the church at Corinth at that particular time. Luck states, "This phrase directly refers to local conditions. The Corinthian Christians were facing difficult times of oppression and persecution."[2] This, however, may not be the case since the Lord had already told His followers they would always suffer persecution (John 15:20), and Paul acknowledged that all godly saints would be persecuted (2 Tim. 3:12). History also clearly shows that the church in all ages has lived in danger and hard times. This writer feels that Calvin expressed the proper view.

> There are some, however, that view the term *necessity* as referring to the age of the Apostle, which was, undoubtedly, full of trouble to the pious: but he appears to me to have had it rather in view to express the disquietude with which the saints are incessantly harassed in the present life. I view it, therefore, as extending to all ages, and I understand it in this way, that the saints are often, in the world, driven hither and thither, and are exposed to many and various tempests, so that their condition appears to be unsuitable for marriage.[3]

Furthermore, though Paul did refer to the "present distress" (τὴν ἐνεστῶσαν ἀνάγκην, 1 Cor. 7:26), there is no reason to assume that he was referring to "the great distress" (ἀνάγκη μεγάλη, Luke 21:23) preceding the Lord's second coming. Paul used the same term elsewhere in reference to his distresses (2 Cor. 6:4; 12:10; 1 Thess. 3:7). Paul's advice is as appropriate today for many Christians who live in hostile environments as it was in his own day. Also it seems that 1 Corinthians 7:32 states Paul's general view that single men have an advantage in serving the Lord. Paul did not require marriage as essential for Christian service; on the contrary, he saw advantages in the Lord's servants remaining single. Therefore if one accepts the translation "husband of one wife," he must face an inconsistency in Paul's view, for it surely would not be consistent to *require marriage* to serve the Lord as an elder or deacon (1 Tim. 3:2, 12), *yet encourage one to stay single* so as not to be distracted from serving the Lord (1 Cor. 7:32).

Another reason this first view could be rejected is that it is more probable that Paul was concerned not so much with a man's marital status as he was with his character. Also it will be shown later that the words "husband" and "wife" may not be the best translations for ἄνδρα and γυναικός.

ONE WIFE IN A LIFETIME

Other scholars point to the numerical requirement of *"one* wife." This too may be a legitimate understanding of the phrase. However, this view goes further by teaching that the restriction eliminates any man who has married a second wife for any reason, including the death of his wife.[4] Besides restricting a divorced man who has remarried from holding these high offices, those defending this view add that even widowers who marry a second wife cannot be elders or deacons.

> A second marriage, although perfectly lawful and in some cases advisable, was so far a sign of weakness: a double family would in many cases be a serious hindrance to work. The Church could not afford to enlist any but its strongest men among its officers; and its officers must not be hampered more than other men with domestic cares.[5]

Several questions challenge this interpretation. If one assumes that a widower cannot remarry because of the burden of a double family, what is to be said concerning the burden a widower has in caring for children without a mother? Is the widowed elder who cares for his work, his church, and his children at home not facing a greater burden if he is not married? If it is considered a weakness to marry a second wife, is it not also out of weakness that one married his first wife? If God chooses to take a man's wife from him through death, where does Scripture teach that God cannot provide a new helpmate for him?

Another consideration is Paul's example of a woman's freedom to remarry after her husband's death to illustrate believers' freedom from the Law so that they may be bound to Christ (Rom. 7:1–6). Thus if one is set free from the previous marriage bond by death (v. 2) and is free to remarry without guilt or offense (v. 3), it hardly seems fitting to imply that remarriage after the death of one's wife would make a man unfit to serve as an elder or deacon. Certainly a godly widower who marries a godly woman is not committing a sin nor is he guilty of impropriety.

First Timothy 3:2 does not say "an elder must be married only once" nor does it say "an elder cannot remarry." Since the phrase is admittedly somewhat ambiguous, to place this type of stern restriction on a godly man because of such an unclear phrase seems quite unjust. One should avoid the Pharisaical error of binding men with unnecessary and oppressive burdens (Matt. 23:1–4; Acts 15:10) and should seek to be gracious at every opportunity. Surely no one seriously believes that if a man's wife dies he is still bound to her in marriage; thus if he marries a second time, he still has only one wife, that is, he is truly still "the husband of one wife." If Paul had stated ἔσχώ μιᾶς γυναικὸς μονῆς ("having had only one wife"), it would be easier to argue that Paul meant possessing only one wife in one's lifetime up to the point of his being examined. However, Paul did not make such a statement. Plummer wrongly felt that Paul was expressing concern about the elder being hampered with "domestic cares." Certainly Paul acknowledged that these elders would have family responsibilities (1 Tim. 3:4), but he was not expressing concern for their involvement with these household duties. An elder with one wife may have had, say, eight children, which would mean an extra burden in domestic cares compared to an elder who was married and had two children. But Paul was not limiting the number of dependents an elder can support: rather, his concern was only that he manage his domestic affairs well.

NO DIVORCE

The third and perhaps most common view is that Paul was prohibiting divorced men from being elders or deacons. Those holding this view also say that remarriage after a divorce makes one ineligible to serve in either of these capacities. The restriction is usually extended to prohibit a man who, though he has never been previously married, is married to a woman who is divorced from a previous husband. It is also common to see men in these situations forbidden to teach Sunday school classes or serve in other areas as well.

One can sympathize with a concern for maintaining a pure testimony in church ministries, but to expand this phrase to exclude those in other areas of ministry in the church is adding to God's Word. Some would treat divorce and remarriage as the unpardonable sin and practically force some genuine, godly Christians to a life of spiritual exile, treating these forgiven children of God as though the blood of Christ could not thoroughly cleanse them. How sad it is that even some good scholars refer to these believers as being "a part of the garden of God—in shadow,"[6] as though they are not quite as pure as other Christians. This writer is unaware of any scriptural reference to some Christians whose former sins keep them "in shadow." Rather, Scripture includes all believers as "sons of light" (Eph. 5:8). Scripture does not justify excluding any born-again member of Christ's body from active service in His work so long as that member has been forgiven and cleansed from his sin. On the contrary, Ephesians 4:16 states that "every joint" is to be contributing to the body of Christ. Regardless of one's view of the phrase being discussed, the qualifications cited in 1 Timothy are not for Sunday school teachers, committed chairmen, or other church workers. Every member of the body of Christ has been given "the manifestation of the Spirit for the common good" (1 Cor. 12:7). Paul did not exclude those who have divorced and remarried. Even if μιας γυναικὸς ἄνδρα were a prohibition against divorce and remarriage, the phrase applies only to these two offices and not to other outlets of service in the church. If the divorce and remarriage view is assumed here, then the prohibition is not against one who is divorced, but only against one who has remarried. Along this same line, there is no problem against an elder's wife having been previously married.

Paul only said that an elder must be a husband of one wife (or, literally, a one-woman man) and yet expansions of the requirement have been expounded to cover a large variety of areas and conditions. Since the issue of divorce and remarriage has become such a critical problem, churches should reevaluate their positions and seek to avoid exaggerations of biblical qualifications. As to whether this phrase is actually concerned with a divorced man remarrying is still highly questionable and dogmatic assumptions should be guarded. Though it may possibly be a prohibition against a man marrying a second wife and holding the office of either elder or deacon, there remains another alternative which seems better grammatically, biblically, and logically.

FAITHFUL TO ONE'S WIFE

This view holds that the translation "husband of one wife" is not the best understanding of the Greek phrase μιᾶς γυναικὸς ἄνδρα, but that it should be translated "a man of one woman" or "a one-woman man." This understanding emphasizes the character of the man rather than his marital status. Thus even a single man or a man who has been married only once must demonstrate that he is not a "playboy" or flirtatious, but that he is stable and mature in character toward his wife or other women. A man who demonstrates a character of loyalty and trustworthiness in such personal relationships is qualified in this area. He, being a one-woman type of man, can be placed in this position and trusted to deal in maturity and with discretion in a situation involving female members. This view shifts the emphasis away from an event that took place in a man's life before his conversion and properly concentrates on the character and quality of his life at the time of his consideration for this high office.

Paul's Emphasis on Character

The importance of understanding what Paul meant by a "one-woman man" is critical. The lives and Christian service of hundreds of Christian men are affected by one's view. Some say it is safer simply to have a standard that forbids anyone who is divorced (or married to someone who has been divorced) to enter Bible colleges, seminaries, or Christian organizations, or to hold church offices. But this approach is impersonal and possibly unjust and comes close to being apathetic toward God's standards. In an age when almost half of American marriages end in divorce, each church, school, and other Christian organization should offer consistent and honest instruction concerning the role and position of these divorced men who are brought to new birth by God's saving mercy, who are cleansed and made new by Christ's blood, and who are instructed to serve their Lord. These instructions must not be based on emotional overreaction to the world's immorality, but rather on true grammatical, contextual, historical, and theological grounds.

A ONE-WOMAN KIND OF MAN

Paul's instruction includes only three words, μιᾶς γυναικὸς ἄνδρα, as one of several requirements for being an elder (1 Tim. 3:2; Titus 1:6) or a deacon (1 Tim. 3:12, where the plural ἄνδρες is used). Γυνή refers to any adult female, including wives and widows.[7] The King James Version translates it "woman" 129 times and "wife" 92 times.[8] The noun γυναικὸς is in the genitive and therefore deals with attribution. It may refer to relationship or quality, for "the genitive defines by attributing a quality or relationship to the noun which it modifies."[9] Dana and Mantey define the genitive as "the case which specifies with reference to class or kind."[10] The genitive here is used to define or describe the noun ἀνήρ.

This should not be considered a possessive genitive, for that would mean that the word in the genitive indicates one who owns or possesses the noun it modifies.[11] In that case the translation should be "a man owned by one woman." Nor can this be considered as a genitive of relationship ("a man who has [possesses] one wife") for there is not indication within the phrase or context that that relationship is implied.

It is best to understand this γυναικὸς as being a genitive of quality,[12] that is, giving a characteristic to the noun it modifies. The noun being modified is ἄνδρα, accusative singular of ἀνήρ. Ἀνήρ is translated "man" 156 times in the King James Version and "husband" only 50 times[13] (including the passage under discussion). This accusative functions here as an object of the main verb "be" along with a long list of other accusative nouns and participles. Stated simply, the clause is "Therefore . . . an elder must be . . . a man. . . ." The words "one woman" modify "man" to explain what kind, or to qualify the noun by attributing to him this character. Robertson adds that the genitive of quality (also called attributing genitive) "expresses quality like an adjective indeed, but with more sharpness and distinctness."[14] He also points out that usually the genitive follows the limiting substantive, "but the genitive comes first if it is emphatic,"[15] as is the case here. Since the other qualifications in 1 Timothy 3 deal with man's character and since the grammatical structure is more naturally consistent with this emphasis, it seems best to understand the phrase as meaning that he is a one-woman type of man.

If, on the other hand, one understands the phrase to mean that he possesses only one wife (though this does not seem best grammatically), then other qualifications must be made. First, it must be decided if this means only one wife in a lifetime or one wife at a time. Since neither the grammar of the phrase nor any reference in the context implies that Paul was discussing a once-in-a-lifetime situation, then that idea must not be forced into the text. As suggested earlier, if Paul had said something like ἔσχων μιᾶς γυναικὸς μονῆς, then one could speak more assuredly that Paul meant having had only one wife ever. Paul, however, simply said he must "be" (εἶναι, present tense) a man of one woman. If, indeed, Paul was reacting to the problem of divorce and remarriage, as White suggests,[16] it would have been more easily and clearly said by μὴ ἀπολελύμενον, even as he did write μὴ πάροινον, prohibiting the abuse of wine, and μὴ πλήκτην, prohibiting physically violent men. In prohibiting these men, the negative μὴ is used with the phrase under consideration; however, here Paul was concerned with a positive character, not with a prohibition. Though this argument does not prove that Paul was not referring to divorce and remarriage, hopefully it shows that there is no room for dogmatic limitations based on this verse. One should guard against enforcing authoritative assumptions.

Another consideration that leads to this view is that the nouns being used are without the definite article. Some translators feel this anarthrous construction is important. Wuest explains, "The two nouns [for 'woman' and 'man'] are without the definite article, which construction emphasizes character or nature."[17] He concludes, "Thus one can translate, 'a one-wife sort of a husband,' or 'a one-woman sort of man.'"[18] Though the absence of the article does not "prove" the translation, it certainly supports it. Robertson explains that the qualitative force of a noun is "best brought out in anarthrous nouns."[19] Dana and Mantey offer this explanation:

> Sometimes with a noun which the context proves to be definite the article is not used. This places stress upon the qualitative aspect of the noun rather than its mere identity. An object of thought may be conceived of from two points of view: as to identity or quality. To convey the first point of view the Greek uses the article; for the second the anarthrous construction is used.[20]

The context is discussing "the overseer" (τὸν ἐπίσκοπον) and therefore is definite; so then the absence of the article with the word ἄνδρα can rightly emphasize the idea of character. In other words what Paul was emphasizing is the man's character, not his marital status. In the excessive moral laxity of the Greek culture Paul was planting young, fragile churches; and during that period of church development issues which today may be taken for granted had to be clarified. Getz follows this thought as he offers his understanding of Paul's qualification. "In a culture where men frequently cohabited with more than one woman, Paul needed it very clear that an elder in the church was to be a 'one-woman man'—loyal to his wife and her alone."[21] Earle is another commentator who sees the point of Paul's phrase as meaning that "the overseer must be completely faithful to his wife."[22]

FORGIVENESS OF THE PAST

Divorce and remarriage, when committed outside the provisions for them in the Bible, are sins; but like any other sins, they can be forgiven and the believer cleansed. Once a person has come to Christ, all sins are forgiven and to claim that so long as a man stays married to his second wife, he is still living in sin is to ignore God's provision of mercy, to degrade the power of Christ's work, and to overlook God's forgiveness. Chafer explains the extent and power of God's forgiveness.

> It is the taking away of sin and its condemnation from the offender or offenders, by imputing the sin to, and imposing its righteous judgments upon Another. . . . divine forgiveness is never extended to the offender as an act of leniency, nor is the penalty waived, since God, being infinitely holy and upholding His government which is founded on undeviating righteousness, cannot make light of sin. Divine forgiveness is therefore extended only when the last demand or penalty against the offender has been satisfied.[23]

Everyone who has been born into God's family has experienced this forgiveness which is based on God's satisfaction that Christ's sacrifice was adequate compensation for the violation of God's holiness. A person's second marriage may have indeed been sin, but after conversion one cannot divorce his second wife in hope of returning to his first wife, for that would involve a new sin in itself. Further, it is inconsistent to allow a divorced and remarried man to become a member of a church on the grounds that his previous sins have been adequately paid for through Christ and yet forbid him a leadership role because of his *previous* sins (which Christ removed by His death). If a church is bound to judge its members on the consequences of their lives before conversion, who then could meet the majority of the qualifications in 1 Timothy 3? Are churches as quick to forbid a man the office of elder or deacon because before his conversion he was not "above reproach" or because he was "pugnacious"?

Certainly one cannot attempt to make the qualifications of

1 Timothy 3 apply to a man's life before he is saved. If God has forgiven him and made him a part of His church, why do Christians hold his past against him? When one is saved, *all* his sins are forgiven (Col. 2:13); he becomes a member of the body of Christ (1 Cor. 12:13); his body becomes a temple of the Holy Spirit (1 Cor. 6:19); he receives a new nature created after God's own holiness (Eph. 4:24); he becomes a new creature (2 Cor. 5:17); and he becomes a part of God's "spiritual house" (1 Peter 2:5) and "royal priesthood" (1 Peter 2:9). Before a man is saved, he is dead toward God and His holy standards. He has no power over sin, no knowledge of God's Word or will; thus to judge one's life before his new birth is totally unjust. Paul wrote that even adulterers (as in divorce and remarriage) were "washed . . . sanctified . . . justified" (1 Cor. 6:9–11).

Paul's concern in 1 Timothy 3:1–10 is that if a man desires the office of elder he must be qualified *at that time*, not before his conversion. For those concerned with the testimony of the church, let them consider which glorified God more—that He takes an unworthy, defiled human and makes him pure enough to become His own servant (cf. 1 Tim. 1:12–16) or that though God forgives, He does not let a man's past sins be forgotten? Even divorced and remarried Christians can trust the great promises of Psalm 103:12–13 and Isaiah 38:17. If God has made a man clean, how can the church consider him unworthy to serve God even on the highest levels? Is the church guilty of Peter's prejudice (Acts 10:9–16) so that God must also rebuke believers and say as He did to Peter, "What God has cleansed, no *longer* consider unholy"? It does not seem possible that by Paul's phrase in 1 Timothy 3:2 he intended to hold a man's preconversion sins against him.

WAS POLYGAMY BEING OPPOSED?

Some commentators hold that Paul was referring to a man having only one wife at a time. Though some rigorously deny that polygamy was a threat to the church in Paul's day, at least among the Greeks or Romans, yet there is evidence that it existed in the culture from which the saints were being saved. Though Plummer rejects the view that Paul was thinking of polygamy, yet he says, "It is quite true that polygamy in St. Paul's day still existed among the Jews."[24] To substantiate his claim he quotes Justin Martyr in his *Dialogue with Trypho*: "It is better for you to follow God than your senseless and blind teachers, who even to this day allow you each to have four or five wives."[25] Gentile believers could have easily been misled by Jewish teaching since both groups studied the same Old Testament Scriptures, which the Jews used to show the polygamous habits of David, Solomon, and other Old Testament heroes.

Another support for defending the polygamy view is that it was the common interpretation of early church writers. White sums up this argument: "on the other hand, it must be conceded that the Patristic commentators on the passage . . . suppose that it is bigamy or polygamy that is here forbidden."[26] Calvin refers to Chrysostom's view as "the only true exposition" on the issue.

> The only true exposition, therefore, is that of Chrysostom, that in a bishop he expressly condemns polygamy, which at that time the Jews almost reckoned to be lawful. This corruption was borrowed by them partly from a sinful imitation of the Fathers, (For they who read that Abraham, Jacob, David and others of the same class were married to more wives than one at the same time, thought that it was lawful for them also to do the same). . . . polygamy was exceedingly prevalent among them; and therefore with great propriety does Paul enjoin that a bishop should be free from this stain."[27]

Again Calvin stated in his summary, "Paul forbids polygamy in all who hold the office of a bishop, because it is a mark of an unchaste man, and of one who does not observe conjugal fidelity."[28]

Even though there is obviously some support for this view and though it would surely correspond to the idea of a one-woman requirement, this writer does not believe that polygamy was Paul's major concern.

Apparently those who prohibit a remarried man from serving as an elder or deacon overlook the obvious point of the list in 1 Timothy 3. Paul's list deals primarily with the *character* or *attitudes* of men seeking these high services in the church. The requirements are based on what the man *is*, not what may have transpired in his past. Thus Paul wrote, "an overseer, then, must be" (δεῖ οὖν . . . εἶναι). He expressed the same idea in Titus 1:6 (εἴ τίς ἐστιν). Even as "temperate," "prudent," "respectable," and other qualifications deal with his character, so also a "one-woman (kind of) man" is a character trait demonstrated by a chaste and mature attitude toward his wife and other females. Lenski offers a similar explanation: "The emphasis is on *one* wife's husband, and the sense is that he have nothing to do with any other woman. He must be a man who cannot be taken hold of on the score of sexual promiscuity or laxity."[29] Lenski points out that converts did not always immediately withdraw from their pagan customs and become instantly perfect in sexual purity;[30] thus Paul set up this standard of moral character.

Indeed, to say that a man's character means that he is content with his one wife is not lowering God's standard; it is putting the emphasis where it belongs—on the quality of a man's moral attitudes after his conversion. To judge a man's spiritual qualities on the basis of a sin committed before he was saved, before he was capable of understanding God's will or Word, and before he had the power of Christ's life within him is to create a false standard that detracts from God's wonderful grace and that also fails to deal with the real issue of 1 Timothy 3.

In 1 Timothy 5:9, Paul wrote that before a widow can be added to the official widow's list of the church, she must meet certain qualifications, including "*having been* the wife of one man" (ἑνὸς ἀνδρὸς γυνή), the converse of "a man of one woman." Plummer insists that this means "a woman who after the death of her husband has not married again."[31] Though Plummer may have a legitimate argument against the polygamy view, this verse does not prove that a widow could not have remarried for the phrase may be translated as "a one-man type of woman." In other words this phrase is just as ambiguous as the one in 1 Timothy 3:2. Calvin makes a fair point in contrasting the two phrases by pointing out "in this very Epistle, where he treats of widows . . . he expressly makes use of the participle of the past tense."[32] The participle to which Calvin refers is γεγονυῖα (a perfect participle from γίνομαι). If it does govern the phrase ἑνὸς ἀνδπὸς γυνή, it would mean "having become one man's wife" or "having been a one-man type of woman." Obviously this still does not prove that Paul was saying that she must have been married *only once* in her life. Even if one insists that it must be translated "having been married to only one man," Calvin's point remains valid. In this verse, the issue is governed by a perfect participle which implies a state that was initiated before her consideration for the role of a genuine church widow, but in 1 Timothy 3:2 the only verb for consideration is a present tense infinitive (εἶναι, "be"). Thus the condition in 1 Timothy 5:9 is the widow's condition *before* her present consideration, and the condition in 1 Timothy 3:2 is the man's condition *at the time of* his consideration. When a man is being considered for the position of elder, he must be a one-woman man.

However, is γεγονυῖα to be taken with ἑνὸς ἀνδρὸς γυνή or with the first phrase μὴ ἔλαττον ἐτῶν ἑξήκοντα? If it does belong to the first phrase, then the requirement is that she, "having become not less than 60 years of age," is now to be a one-man woman, having a reputation for good works, and so forth. So 1 Timothy 5:9 does not offer firm proof for the meaning of 1 Timothy 3:2. Any conclusion thus derived is based mostly on assumptions arising from predetermined ideas. This writer sees no conclusive reason for excluding a widow who over her many years may have had a second husband after her first husband died. In fact Paul's advice to a young woman whose husband died was that she remarry (1 Tim. 5:14). After a healthy and joyful marriage of many years, if her second husband died and she was left alone, is she no longer eligible for the widow's list because she followed the apostle's advice? Nothing in Paul's statement would eliminate her, for she may still have proven herself to be a "one-man type of woman" (ἑνος ἀνδρὸς γυνή).

Conclusion

As one considers the many facets of the arguments related to the phrase "one-woman man," it must be admitted that there is no simple absolute answer. One may *assume* Paul meant to prohibit divorced and remarried men from serving as elders, but one should honestly admit that Paul did not *say* "he cannot have been previously married" or "he cannot have been divorced." What he did say is that he *must be* a one-wife husband or a one-woman type of man. Paul was clearly concerned with one's character when a man is being considered for this high office; Paul was not calling into review such a person's preconversion life.

If God forgives sin and cleanses and restores lost sinners, if a believer is made new in Christ, then is this not what the church should stand for? This writer knows that emotions run high on this issue and there is no desire to stir up hard feelings with those who may differ with the views presented here. It is only hoped that each reader will be challenged to consider prayerfully the facts of this phrase, μιᾶς γυναικὸς ἄδρα.

CHAPTER 19

The Thorn-Infested Ground in Hebrews 6:4–12

Thomas Kem Oberholtzer

T he third warning in the Book of Hebrews is in 5:11–6:12—a passage infamous for its interpretive problems. The various theological perspectives on this portion of God's Word are as numerous as any in the New Testament.

The eschatological section of the passage is found in 6:7–8 in the illustration of the soil, rain, fruit, and thorns. Even a casual reading of the passage reveals that a judgment is in view. It is the thesis of this chapter that the judgment is of true believers, in which disobedience may result in divine discipline in this life and in loss of future rewards in the millennium. The passage motivates Christians to live according to Scripture and to experience life to the fullest in the present and in the coming kingdom.

The Relationship of Hebrews 5:11–6:3 to 6:4–12

Hebrews 5:1–10 discusses Christ's qualifications to be a high priest, since His priesthood comes not from the Aaronic line but from the order of Melchizedek. Following a brief introduction concerning Melchizedek, the author shifted his discussion to the warning of 5:11–6:12.[1] The readers' spiritual dullness and immaturity might cause them to misapprehend the truth about Melchizedek.[2]

Hebrews 5:11–14 rebukes the spiritual immaturity of the readers and their failure to apply the principles of the Word of God to discern good and evil. The readers obviously had been exposed to the teaching of doctrine for an extended period of time (διὰ τὸν χρόνον, "because of the time," v. 12), yet they had failed to mature in their faith.[3] They should have matured to the point of being teachers but instead needed τὰ στοιχεῖα τῆς ἀρχῆς ("the elementary principles"). These principles were the ABCs of the revelation that had come through Christ (1:1),[4] which would include His teachings on the coming kingdom (2:3).

200

Hebrews 6:1–3 exhorts the readers to move from spiritual basics to maturity. The author did not review the basics, but he encouraged his readers to "press on" to τελειότῆ ("maturity," v. 1). The readers are admonished not to "lay again a foundation" or basis for their faith. The writer listed six objective genitives grouped in three pairs:[5] repentance from dead works and faith toward God (6:1), instruction about washings and laying on of hands (6:2a), and resurrection of the dead and eternal judgment (6:2b). Maturity and growth in faith involves human responsibility and God's sovereignty. "This we shall do, if God permits" (6:3). In other words spiritual maturity depends on the believers' obedience and God's working in their lives. Pressing forward is a present possibility if God permits. However, if the readers "fall away," renewal to repentance is not possible (6:6).

The Warning of Hebrews 6:4–12: The Thorn-Infested Ground

HEBREWS 6:4–6

The causal conjunction γὰρ ("for") in 6:4 connects the previous section on moving toward maturity with the following warning about the alternative to progress.[6] Those who had "fallen away" are described by five participles in 6:4–6a. Each of these five participles is governed by the article τούς ("those who"). The use of the single article indicates that only one group of individuals is in view.[7] The individuals are described as follows:

1. ἅπαξ φωτισθέντας ("once been enlightened," 6:4a)
2. γευσαμένους τε τῆς δωρεᾶς τῆς ἐπουρανίου ("have tasted of the heavenly gift," 6:4b)
3. μετόχους γενηθέντας πνεύματος ἁγίου ("have been made partakers of the Holy Spirit," 6:4c)
4. καλὸν γευσαμένοῦ θεοῦ ῥῆμα δυνάμεις τε μέλλον- τος αἰῶνος ("have tasted the good word of God and the power of the age to come," 6:5)
5. καὶ παραπεσόντας ("and have fallen away," 6:6a)

These readers had "once been enlightened." The term φωτισθέντα" ("being enlightened") is also used in 10:32, where regeneration of the readers is clearly stipulated. The author was equating enlightenment with the reception of the full knowledge of the truth.[8] This argues strongly for the view that the enlightenment refers to regeneration.[9] "This is a natural way to refer to the conversion experience (cf. 2 Cor. 4:3–6). The writer's only other use of the verb 'enlightened' (10:32) is used where the reference to true Christian experience can hardly be doubted."[10]

The second fact about these readers is that they had "tasted the heavenly gift." The verb γεύομαι ("to taste") is to be understood in verse 4 in the sense of "to come to know something."[11] The same word is used in 2:9 of Christ, who "tasted" death for everyone. It is inconsistent to have 2:9 mean "drink it all" and 6:4 mean "sampled," as some suggest.[12] The term δωρεᾶς ("gift") may be understood in a technical sense as equal to grace.[13]

These individuals are also referred to as "partakers of the Holy Spirit." The concept of being a μέτοχος ("companion") resurfaces.[14] Μέτοχος is used in 3:1 of a "partaker" of the heavenly calling. Here in 6:4 the individuals are seen as "partners" in the Spirit's activities.

Hebrews 6:5 says these individuals had "tasted the good word of God and the powers of the age to come." The term "good word of God" deals with the present age and "powers of the coming age" directs the audience to the future. The "good word of God" may refer to Jesus' teachings about the kingdom (Heb. 2:3).[15] The signs, wonders, and miracles of 2:4 were a foreshadowing of the δυνάμεις τε μέλλοντος αἰῶνος ("powers of the coming age," i.e., the millennial kingdom). The readers had "tasted" (γευσαμένους) or "experienced" this power in their assembly.

The ominous expression καὶ παραπεσόντας ("and have fallen away") now appears. The participle παραπεσόντας is governed grammatically by the single article τούς ("those"), which also governs the previous four participles. Apparently certain individuals had actually fallen away (cf. 10:25); the warning is not "hypothetical."[16]

The word παραπίπτω ("fall away") occurs only here in the New Testament. This verb is formed from παρά ("beside") and πίπτω ("to fall"). What certain readers had fallen aside from is not specified. Therefore the context becomes the determinative factor as to the meaning of the participle. From Hebrews 3:6, 14; 10:23–25, 35–39, the "falling away" relates to the readers' withdrawal from their Christian confidence and worshiping function in God's house.[17]

The internal dullness and immaturity of the readers may have as its outward manifestation the "falling away." A volitional choice to abandon their Christian confidence and worship function may place them in the position of judgment described in 6:7–8. The Apostle Paul knew of believers who had abandoned their confession of faith and had become subjects of discipline (1 Tim. 1:20; 5:15; 2 Tim. 2:17–18).

For those who "fall away" it is πάλιν ἀνακαινίζειν εἰς μετάνοιαν ("impossible to renew them again to repentance," Heb. 6:6). The subject of the infinitive ἀνακαινίζειν ("to renew") is not stated. Since God is sovereign and is able to do as He pleases in human affairs, it is incorrect to assume that God is the subject of the infinitive. It seems best to supply ἥμας ("us") or τίνα ("anyone") as the intended subject. The verse would then read, "It is impossible for *us*, or *anyone*, to renew them again to repentance." This translation parallels the writer's admonition in 3:13 in which the readers are urged to encourage each other daily to avoid a hardened heart. The warning in chapter 6 concerns the danger of spiritual dullness and immaturity. This immaturity may result in falling away from their confidence and worship participation in God's house detailed in 3:1–4:13. If this were to occur, those individuals would be beyond encouragement by others in the community to repent and press on to Christian maturity. They would be "hard of hearing" and beyond human persuasion.

The following participles—ἀνασταυροῦντα" ("crucifying") and παραδειγματίζοντας ("openly disgracing")—are the reasons repentance is impossible.[18] The term ἀνασταυροῦντας is best understood as "recrucifying."[19] Morris notes, "The author is saying that those who deny Christ in this way are really taking their stand among those who crucified Jesus. In heart and mind they make themselves one with those who put him to death on the cross at Calvary."[20]

They subject the Son of God to "open disgrace." Realigning themselves with those who hated the Messiah would result in a public disgrace of the name of Christ. These actions are the result of a spiritually dull heart. These individuals become impervious to all efforts by others in calling them to repentance.

This alignment seems to have been with a sectarian form of Judaism similar to that of Qumran.[21] This action is so heinous that a reversal appears impossible from the human perspective. The only option facing those who "fall away" is judgment. An analogy with nature describes the inevitable judgment.

HEBREWS 6:7–8

The illustration from nature forms the only prophetic or eschatological statement in the warning.[22] The illustration clearly shows that a judgment is in view. Is this judgment temporal discipline of believers[23] or a final judgment resulting in eternal damnation?[24]

The conjunction γάρ ("for") links the illustration of 6:7–8 with the previous section, showing that the readers of 5:11–6:6 are still in view.

The clause, "For ground that drinks the rain which often falls upon it," is understood as the subject of verses 7–8.[25] The same "ground" (γῆ) is in view in both verses. The difference is found in the produce that results from the rain. The ground in verse 7 produces vegetation, green plants, and herbs. This produce is useful and receives "a blessing from God." The rain-soaked ground fulfills its God-designed function by providing produce for the farmer, which results in a blessing being received from God. This illustrates the individual believer who obediently chooses to press on to spiritual maturity. The concept of usefulness is seen in natural produce. This produce is described in verse 10 as the ministries of work and love among the readers. These activities, like proper produce, result in a believer receiving God's blessing.

Hebrews 6:8 shows the negative side of the illustration. The γῆ ("ground") of verse 7 is the antecedent of the participle ἐκφέρουσα ("yields") in verse 8. Thus the same land is in view but this time the rain yields "thorns and thistles," not useful produce. This condition is analogous to the readers' dullness and immaturity described in 5:11–14. Spiritually immature and dull believers will produce thorns and thistles.

Three phrases describe the uselessness of the land that grows thorns and thistles: ἀδόκιμος ("worthless"), κατάρας ἐγγύς ("near to being cursed"), and ἧς τὸ τέλος εἰς καῦσιν ("its end is for burning").

Ἀδόκιμος occurs in classical Greek, the Septuagint, and eight times in the New Testament. It generally refers to being disqualified or unapproved. In 1 Corinthians 9:27 Paul referred to his efforts to be faithful in the Christian life. He used the metaphor of competing in games for which he disciplined himself so as not to be ἀδόκιμος ("disqualified").

Some scholars understand the "curse" of Hebrews 6:8 to recall the incident of man's fall (Gen. 3). However, the curse in Genesis 3 resulted in thorns and thistles, whereas in Hebrews 6:8 thorns and thistles resulted in the curse. There is a cause-and-effect inversion between the curse in Genesis and Hebrews.[26] The curse in Hebrews is the consequence of the rain-soaked earth failing to fulfill its natural function, the production of useful vegetation.

Moses taught Israel the principle that obedience results in blessing, and disobedience results in cursing (Deut. 28–30). The Old Testament cursings were temporal, not soteriological in nature and did not result in eternal damnation. The teaching of blessing for obedience and cursing for disobedience was an integral part of Jewish law and thought. It is reasonable to understand that the Jewish readers of Hebrews, after becoming Christians would view this principle in an individual sense instead of in a national sense.

This principle parallels the teaching concerning the produce of the soil. If the soil yields useful produce, it receives God's blessing (Heb. 6:7). If the soil produces thorns and thistles, it becomes disqualified, worthless, and is near to being cursed. The analogy is lucid—obedience in the life of a believer results in blessing; disobedience in the life of a believer results in a useless life for God and the possibility of receiving temporal discipline from the Lord (12:5–11).

The agricultural imagery continues: "it ends up being burned" (6:8). The metaphor of burning has caused many to think this verse refers to hell.[27] To insist that burning denotes "the future of the damned" is to ignore the immediate context and to press the agricultural illustration beyond its intent. Soteriology is not being discussed in this passage. The context is a call for believers to press on to maturity. The danger is a dullness of hearing which may result in a disqualification and temporal discipline. Further, the analogy of burning relates only to the worthless thorns and thistles, not to the land itself. The fire would destroy only the worthless fruit, not the soil. The Elder Pliny (ca. A.D. 112) attested to the fact that land was burned to remove weeds and stubble.[28] The purpose of the burning in Hebrews 6 is to remove the thorns and thistles (i.e., the results of disobedience) by means of temporal judgment (cf. 12:5–11).

The specifics of this temporal discipline are not stipulated. Biblically God's discipline of His children is for the purpose of bringing them back to usefulness and productivity (1 Cor. 5:5; 1

Tim. 1:20; Heb. 12:5–11).

An eschatological perspective is implicit within the burning imagery. For believers in Christ there will be a "burning" of all their useless motives, thoughts, and actions at the judgment seat of Christ (Rom. 14:10–12; 1 Cor. 3:10-15; 2 Cor. 5:10). Paul used identical imagery in 1 Corinthians 3:9–15: "you are God's field . . . each man's work will become evident; for the day will show it, because it is to be revealed with fire; and the fire itself will test the quality of each man's work. . . . If any man's work is burned up, he shall suffer loss; but he himself shall be saved, yet so as through fire."

Although temporal judgment for disobedience is in view in Hebrews 6:5–8, an eschatological perspective appears implicit also. Terms such as ἀδόκιμος ("worthless") and καῦσιν ("burning") imply eschatological loss.

Salvation is settled on the basis of grace through faith alone (Eph. 2:8–10; Titus 3:3–7). Believers will never be judged to determine their eternal destiny (John 5:19–29; Rom. 3:21–30; 8:1; 2 Cor. 5:17; 1 John 5:13). However, the Scriptures teach that believers will be evaluated for reward or loss of reward for their motives, thoughts, and actions as disciples of Christ.

For the readers of Hebrews, failure to press on to maturity might result in temporal discipline. It seems reasonable from Hebrews 3:1–4:13 that this might sometimes include the loss of physical life (cf. 1 Cor. 11:30; 1 John 5:16–17). Theologically it is clear that present unfaithfulness will result in loss of reward at the judgment seat of Christ. The result for the believer is not loss of eternal salvation but a forfeiting of inheritance-rest, reward, and position in the coming millennial kingdom.

HEBREWS 6:9–12

Following the ominous words of warning are words of comfort and encouragement. Hebrews 6:9 refers to the readers as ἀγαπητοί ("beloved"), a term used in Scripture only of believers. The author wrote with tender pastoral encouragement when he said, "We are convinced of better things concerning you." Hodges writes:

> The author did not want his readers to believe that he had despaired of them. Instead, he was convinced of *better things in your case*. The words are like those of a pastor who, after warning his congregation of a dangerous course of action might say: "But I am sure you people would never do that!" The words are not a theological proposition, as they are sometimes wrongly taken, but an expression of hope.[29]

The writer was confident of "better things that accompany salvation." The σωτηρία ("salvation") is to be understood in the same way as in 1:14; 2:3, 10; 5:9; 9:28—as referring to eschatological victory, glory, and ruling with the Messiah. The author was confident that his readers would press on to maturity and receive these blessings.

The writer's confidence was founded on God's faithfulness and the readers' work and love toward other believers (6:10). This work and love parallel the earlier exhortation in 3:13 to encourage one another daily. The readers were not beyond renewal.

Hebrews 6:11 encourages the readers to "demonstrate" or "show" (ἐνδείκνυσθαι) diligence. The purpose of this demonstration is the full and final realization of hope. Michel explains that the readers may not realize the "full hope," "conviction," or "certainty" if they failed to be diligent. The possibility of loss is real,[30] but perseverance would result in eschatological blessing (6:9).

In 6:12 the purpose of the exhortation is that the readers not be νωθροὶ ("sluggish"). The same term is used in 5:11. Their "sluggishness" or "dullness" as a manifestation of their immaturity was to be replaced by diligence. In contrast they are to be imitators of those who through faith and patience inherit the promises. Hebrews 6:13–20 describes Abraham as one whose faith is to be imitated: "Having patiently waited, he obtained the promise" (v. 15).

The concept of "promise" occurs throughout the epistle (4:1; 6:12–13, 15, 17; 7:6; 8:6; 9:15; 10:23, 36; 11:9 [twice], 11, 13, 17, 33, 39; 12:26). Sixteen of the 18 references refer to the millennium.

The author of Hebrews clearly states that perseverance is essential for inheriting the promises. This inheritance of the promises should not be equated with eternal salvation. The inheritance cannot be soteriological, for eternal salvation is by grace through faith. Throughout Hebrews perseverance is said to be essential for enjoyment of the eschatological promises (3:6, 14; 4:1; 5:9; 6:11–12; 10:23, 36).

Since the readers had not yet entered into a permanent state of dullness, it was possible through God's working in them and their perseverance for them to inherit the promises related to the coming age (i.e., rewards and positions in the kingdom).

Conclusion

The warning of Hebrews 5:11–6:12 is addressed to regenerated individuals and is given to motivate them to spiritual maturity. They were in danger of falling away from their Christian confidence and worship function in the house of God. If they were to "fall away," it would be impossible for their community to call them to repentance because of their spiritual dullness. The analogy of rain-soaked ground and its produce suggested both temporal and eschatological judgment.

With a pastor's heart the writer encouraged his readers to move toward maturity through their ministry of love and good works. Through present diligence they would realize their full eschatological hope as those who would inherit the promises of rewards and position in the millennial kingdom.

CHAPTER 20

An Exegetical Study of 2 Peter 2:18–22

Duane A. Dunham

P eter's second epistle has not been a well-mined field of study in recent investigations. The number of commentaries is not large, even when included with 1 Peter and Jude. This second chapter of the epistle is no exception to the general neglect as Cavallin has observed: "For the last 20 years I have found only two papers . . . on problems in 2 Peter 2. . . ."[1]

This neglect is not due to a lack of interesting problems. This second chapter discloses several difficulties of both exegetical and theological import. Perhaps the most complex is raised by the words of verses 18–22:

> For they by uttering pompous words of vanity, in lusts of flesh by excesses, entice those recently escaping those living in error (and) while promising liberty to them, they themselves are slaves of corruption. For by what anyone is overcome, he is enslaved to this. So then, if after escaping the stains of the world by the knowledge of our Lord and Savior, Jesus Christ, they are again entangled and overcome, the latter things have become worse for them than the former. For it would be almost better for them not to have come to know the way of righteousness, than after knowing to turn from the holy commandment delivered to them. The true proverb has happened to them: a dog (is) returned to his own vomit, and a washed sow (returns) to the mud wallow (author's translation).[2]

Two major questions are often asked about this passage: What is the spiritual condition and effect of the failure indicated for the people involved? Can a true Christian lose his salvation? Barnes addresses these issues.

> This passage is often quoted to prove the "possibility of falling from grace, and from a very high degree of it too." But it is one of the last passages in the Bible that should be adduced to prove that doctrine. The true point of this passage is to show that the persons referred to never were changed; that whatever external reformation might have occurred, their nature remained the same; and that when they apostatized from

209

their outward profession, they merely acted out their nature, and showed in fact there had been no real change.[3]

He then concludes, "This passage . . . can never be made to prove that one true Christian will fall away and perish."[4] Most commentators build their views on one of two premises: These are true believers who are in danger of losing their salvation, or these are merely professors of faith, not truly saved, who are in danger of falling into deeper sin. Of course this raises the theological problem of perseverance. Can true believers lose their salvation? Calvinists say no, while Arminians disagree. However, this is not directly the question to be addressed here. The first problem is to determine what this passage teaches.

Tracing the Persons Involved

Any successful assault on the problem must begin by finding who is being addressed. All would admit that the opening of this chapter deals with two groups: (1) the addressees (church members and professing Christians; "you," 2:1, 3; cf. 1:1) and (2) false teachers who will enter their assemblies (ἐν ὑμῖν . . . ψευδοδιδάσκαλοι, 2:1). There is no reason why the same groups are not still in view in verses 18–22; yet most commentaries ignore any but the false teachers in this passage. The connection with the preceding sentences by the conjunction γὰρ in verse 18 and the αὐτοί of verse 19 makes it clear that the false teachers are still in view. However, the words "those scarcely/recently escaping" (τούς ὀλίγως ἀποφεύγοντας) indicate that another group must be involved. These, Peter wrote, are enticed by others (δελεάζουσιν, "they are enticing"). Those in this enticed group must be either the readers at large or a specific group of readers, that is, new converts in the assembly. If all the readers are involved, then, the ὀλίγω" would likely mean "scarcely" of degree, not of time. But against this is the fact that they were "confirmed in the present truth" (1:12) and were characterized by "steadfastness" (3:17). The general tone of the letter and the obvious threat of the false teachers might be argued against the new converts reference, but that would require straining the meaning of 1:12; 3:17; and other references. Furthermore, the ones most likely to be affected by the blandishments of the false teachers would be the newest members of the assembly. Lenski calls this group "the special victims of these vicious deceivers . . . the newly converted. . . ."[5] Moffatt undoubtedly agrees, but does not precisely say so. He asks, "What chance have recent converts from paganism against the specious argument of these religionists?"[6] Of course older carnal Christians may be fully as vulnerable as recent ones.

The identity of those whom these newly converted ones escape are not the false teachers, for that would make the grammar ponderous with the same persons being both the subject of the leading verb and the object of the direct object! This difficulty is avoided easily by taking them to refer to the heathen at large.

With these two important groups in view in verse 18, most commentators assume that in the following verses only the false teachers are in view. But in the next verse αὐτοῖς ("them") and αὐτοὶ ("they") refer to two different groups: "While promising liberty to them (αὐτοῖς, the new converts), they themselves (αὐτοὶ, the false teachers) are slaves of corruption." This is then buttressed by the general aphorism, "For by what anyone is overcome, he is enslaved to this."

The real difficulty arises with verse 20. Up to this point the subject has been the false teachers (v. 18, "they entice") and this followed through verse 19. To whom does the phrase ἀποφύγοντες τὰ μιάσματα τοῦ κόσμου ("escaping the stains of the world") refer? Many commentators identify these as the false teachers.[8] However, three clues in the passage point to these as new converts: (1) the use of a form of the verb of ἀποφεύγω ("escape") in both verses 18 and 20 of the noun ἐπίγνωσις ("full knowledge," v. 20); and (2) the verb ἐπιγινώσκω ("know fully," v. 21); and (3) the use of the descriptive term σωτήρ ("Savior") in verse 21.

The first clue indicates that the people referred to in verse 20 who have in some sense escaped the corruptions of the world are also the new converts spoken of in verse 18. Only one other time does this verb appear in the New Testament, and that is in 2 Peter 1:4, where the apostle expressed his desire that the readers escape the corruptions in the world. In classical Greek it meant "to escape," or in the forensic sense, "to be acquitted." In modern Greek it has the idea of "keeping clear of something." Huther admits that the use of this term in verse 20 "seems to refer back to . . . verse 18."[9] But then he objects to this by arguing:

> It would be more than surprising if the apostle did not, from here onward, continue the description of those of whom the whole chapter speaks, but should, all of sudden, treat of entirely different persons—and this without in any way hinting at the transition from the one to the other; in addition to this, there is the . . . ἥττηται ["is overcome," v. 19].[10]

Surely Huther overstates the case, for the entire chapter is written to warn the readers, not simply to describe a group of false teachers. Furthermore, there is more than a hint of transition in the preceding verses as Peter introduced the prospective victims of this false doctrine. Mayor suggests that the terms ἐπιγνώσει τοῦ κυρίου ("knowledge of the Lord") and ἐπεγνωκέναι τὴν ὁδὸν τῆς δικαιοσύνης ("to know the way of righteousness," v. 21) imply they have gone further in the Lord than those "scarcely escaping" (v. 18).[11] But this begs the very question at issue. To know the Lord and the way of righteousness does not require any extensive growth in the faith. Surely new converts know the Lord and the way of righteousness. The terms used in these constructions will be discussed later. But here it is concluded that the verb ἀποφεύγω in verse 20 is a strong clue to identify them with those in verse 18.

The second clue focuses on the noun ἐπίγνωσις in verse 20 and the verb ἐπιγινώσκω in verse 21. The noun occurs 20 times in the New Testament, four of which are in 2 Peter. In every use it indicates a careful and thorough knowledge, not a partial or incorrect one. Lenski argues:

> This is the same word that was used in 1:2–3, 8, the key word of this epistle; add *gnosis* used in 1:5–6. In those other passages we had the genitive of source: knowledge "from" our Lord; this genitive of source is also proper here: by the great gift of true knowledge that our Lord and Savior gives us we escaped.[12]

While this term is occasionally used in Scripture without an object, it is not so here. The object is "the Lord and Savior." It is not merely an abstract concept the people know; the Lord Himself is the object of their knowledge! The verb is used twice in verse 21, the only occurrences of the term in Peter's epistles.

While it is beyond the limits of this article to discuss at any length the differences, if any, between the simple terms γνῶσις and ἐπίγωσις and between γινώσκω and ἐπιγινώσκω in 2 Peter, both Liddell and Scott and Bauer, Arndt, and Gingrich indicate that there is a difference.[13] Even if one agrees with Bultmann, who argues persuasively against any discernible difference in meaning, the Old Testament usage certainly supports the meaning of "true" or "accurate" knowledge. Therefore to suggest that 2 Peter 2:20–21 refers to superficial or inaccurate knowledge would necessitate much more evidence from both Old Testament usage and Hellenistic literature than is forthcoming. In fact, it is difficult, if not impossible, to find one good, clear example of either γνῶσις or ἐπίγνωσις referring to superficial knowledge which later turns out to be false. This strengthens the view that the persons in view in 2 Peter 2:18–22 are new believers, not false teachers.

The third clue is the use of the term σωτήρ modifying Ἰησοῦ Χριστοῦ. Peter's reference to the Lord Jesus Christ as Savior is significant. He used this term four other times in this epistle (1:1, 11; 3:2, 18). Only Paul in Titus used it more (six times) in such a short book. Does not this term point to the validity of their salvation experience? It does in all four of the other usages in 2 Peter. If it refers in 2:20–21 to false teachers, this would seem to be a purely descriptive title with no personal effect (the view of some Calvinists) or to a personal effect that had gone awry (Arminians). Neither implication seems adequate. One would be hard pressed to find another New Testament occurrence of the words "the knowledge of the . . . Savior Jesus Christ" which does not imply a valid regenerating experience.

In summary, then, Peter opened this chapter with a warning to the entire church of difficulties to be faced when false teachers enter their assembly (2:1–3); then he vividly described the false teachers' character and activities (2:4–17); and then he applied the warning to those most likely to fall to the tactics of these pernicious heretics (2:18–22).

Handling the Difficulties

This writer takes the view that the following statements also refer to true Christians, the new believers referred to in verse 18: "the last things have become worse for them than the first" (v. 20), "it is almost better for them not to have come to know the way of righteousness" (v. 21), and "the true proverb" (v. 22). However, not all hold this view. For example Barnes says apostates are discussed by Peter. "Apostates become worse than they were before their professed conversion. Reformed drunkards, if they go back to their cups again, become more abandoned than ever. Thus it is with those who profess to become religious, and then fall away."[14] He then gives his rationale for this view:

> It would have been better for them, for (1) then they would not have dishonored the cause of religion as they have now done; (2) they would not have sunk so deep in profligacy as they now have; and (3) they would not have incurred as aggravated a condemnation in the world of woe.[15]

Thomas observes, "If the allusions in vv. 20–22 are to recent converts whom they lead astray, the description of hopelessness and ruin seems almost incredible. In the case of the teachers . . . such a description of utter ruin is entirely appropriate."[16] Lenski agrees with these ideas: "It is better to be a pagan, never to get out of pagan ignorance, than to become an apostate by sinking back into paganism."[17] One could ask of Thomas, "Does Peter really give a picture of hopelessness and ruin?" And Lenski merely assumes that apostasy is referred to here without defending his position.

If it were possible to prove a position by taking a vote, this writer's view would immediately be defeated. Since it is seemingly a minority view, a measure of caution and humility are necessary. The Scriptures rather than the commentaries must be one's primary consideration. Four questions need to be considered: (1) What is the nature of the sin of the new converts? (2) What is the meaning of the statement, "The latter things have become worse for them than the former"? (3) What is the intent of the statement, "It is almost better for them not to have come to know the way of righteousness"? (4) Why did Peter refer to the actions of a dog and a sow?

First, what is the nature of the sin of the new converts? If the nature of the sin of the new converts is total apostasy, that is, a complete rejection of the work of Christ, of faith in the Godhead, then one conclusion will be called for. If the sin is something else, then perhaps another conclusion will be more in line with the evidence of the text. Granted, if the persons involved in verses 18–22 are false teachers, adding up all the details of their character and activities of the chapter with the remarks in this portion would cause one to side with the majority of commentators. However, if one accepts the view espoused here that new Christians are addressed, then only the sins cited in these particular verses are appropriate in determining the nature of their sin. They are deceived (v. 18), they are entangled and overcome (v. 20), and they turn from the holy commandment (v. 21). Are these sins the equivalent of apostasy? Many assume so, probably because they view the passage as still dealing primarily with false teachers. What was the extent of their being deceived (v. 18)? Δελεάζω ("entice"), the term in question, is not used at all in the Septuagint, and it is used only three times in the New Testament. In its other two uses (James 1:14 and 2 Peter 2:14) it has no heavy theological overtones to imply apostasy.

The two terms ἐμπλακέντες ("entangled") and ἡττῶνται ("overcome") are in verse 20. The first is used only once in the Septuagint (Prov. 28:18) and only once in the New Testament outside 2 Peter 2:20, namely, in 2 Timothy 2:4. If anything supporting the apostasy view is to come from this text it would seem to be from ἡττάω. Huther refers to the term, but does not define it precisely; he assumes it means total slavery to corruption from which there is no escape.[18] It is difficult to argue from the usage of the verb in biblical Greek for it is rather rare, but the noun ἥττημας, while not more plentiful, is used in Romans 11:12. But the fall or loss there cannot be final, for that seems precisely opposite to Paul's argument.[19] There is good reason to interpret the term to mean "defeat," but to say that this is a final defeat is unsupported by either its usage or the context of 2 Peter 2.

Do the words ὑποστρέψαι ἐκ τῆς . . . ἁγίας ἐντολῆς ("to turn from the holy commandment") refer to apostasy? The aorist tense of the infinitive "to turn from" might be argued in favor of a final turning. But if that were so, then why are not the other aorists in the passage treated in the same way? The answer is that this would present some contradictions. The verb "they escaped" (v. 20) is aorist, yet they were in danger of turning back. So that aorist could not be final. The verb "knew" (v. 21) is aorist, but they can turn back from it. So that aorist cannot be final either. Further, this part of the sentence in verse 21 about turning from the holy commandment parallels precisely the grammatical construction that has the perfect infinitive ἐπεγνώκεναι. Both cannot be final, but preference would be given to the perfect tense, not the aorist.

What the new converts are said to know and leave is not the Savior. It is "the way of righteousness." It is a lifestyle that is in view, not a personal relationship. Of course the relationship is assumed, and it is expected that the believers will live like newborn creations, but here the question is one of action. If Peter intended to teach that their failure was apostasy, a final turning from God to Satan or a life of sin and rejection of their former faith, he has chosen some rather pallid terms with which to do it.

Second, what is the meaning of the clause, "The latter things have become worse for them than the former"? The crux of this problem is in determining what the terms "last things" and "the first" mean. Many assume these refer either to the final destiny of the apostate or to a more wicked condition than before they were saved. An example is Leaney: "It is striking that the apostate (the

Christian who has fallen away) is not back where he started but worse than before; it is a greater sin to reject the good when you have known it than to live in wickedness when you did not know the power of good available from God."[20]

This common view is unacceptable, not because the view of punishment is unscriptural, but because of the nature of the failure indicated in the passage. Peter was not writing about their returning to paganism or Judaism, nor about their utterly repudiating their faith in Christ. True, their temptation was heavy; their danger, acute. However, their danger was in falling into carnality, not into apostasy. While true faith results in proper living, it is possible (though obviously not desirable!) for a believer to live for a while like a sinner, failing to live up to his position in Christ.

Alford indicates that their turn from the "holy commandment" is a turn from the moral law.[21] Huther calls it "the law of the Christian life."[22] Lenski is not clear, for he first speaks of apostasy, indicating that it is worse than the original paganism, but later he says it is "moral filth."[23] Does a person's involvement in moral filth, however, necessarily indicate an unregenerate nature? Paul attacked the terrible sin of incest (1 Cor. 5) but he made no appeal for regeneration, nor did he imply that the lack of salvation might be the problem. On the other hand as he concluded a list of "the works of the flesh" he warned, "those who practice such things shall not inherit the kingdom of God" (Gal. 5:21). The Apostle John declared, "The one who keeps sinning is from the devil, for the devil keeps sinning from the beginning" (1 John 3:8). At times moral corruption practiced as a lifestyle may indicate an unregenerate nature, but other times it may not. More than a sinful life is necessary in a person if he is to be declared unregenerate.[24] Some Christians occasionally fall into sin. When Paul exhorted the Corinthian believers, not noted for their innocent lives, to examine themselves before participating in the Lord's Supper, he gave no hint of an unregenerate state as a cause for their misconduct (1 Cor. 11:27–32).

As to the use of the two superlative terms ἔσχατα ("last") and πρώτων ("first"), it is not required or even preferred to take them in an absolute sense in all the passages where they appear in Scripture. Deuteronomy 24:5–6 and Matthew 27:64 illustrate that these two terms can be used in a relative sense, that is, superlatives are used for comparatives. They mean "latter" and "former" in these cases.[25] Several points favor taking these meanings in 2

Peter 2:20. First, if "last things" is taken as ultimate and final, then grammar and logic would require that πρώτων means some ultimate "first." Taking them as comparatives, however, would resolve this problem. Second, the meaning of "former" and "latter" would follow the principle that the more general meaning ought to be examined first, before the more specific is considered. If context does not require the more technical meaning, then one ought to stick with the general meaning. Third, these meanings tie in better with the descriptions of the persons addressed and the temptations they faced.

If "former" and "latter" are the meanings here, what do they refer to? "Former" things undoubtedly refers to the time before the new converts were saved, that is, the action that characterized their unregenerate condition. "Former" things could not refer to their lives as Christians before they fell into "the sins of the flesh" (v. 18), for that would be so obvious as to need no statement.

The "latter" would refer to their current condition, which is said to be worse than before they were saved. Bigg cites a parallel in Matthew 12:43–45, which records the story of the man who, after being cleansed from the presence of one demon, was then filled with seven of them. Jesus concluded, "The last (latter) state of that man is become worse than the first (former)." Bigg's view is questionable, since the illustration in Matthew is not to show the danger of an ungodly lifestyle, but of the danger of caring only for the cleansing and not pursuing one's positive relationship with Christ.[26] But the passage does support the view that ἔσχατα and πρώτων can be comparatives, as in 2 Peter 2:20. Peter was saying that their current condition as Christians was in some way worse than their former one as unbelievers. Being a Christian and ensnared by sin is worse, *in some respects*, than being a non-Christian ensnared by sin.

Peter began verse 21 with the conjunction γὰρ ("for") to provide an explanation for the statement in verse 20. But the statement in verse 21 is even more remarkable than the one in verse 20. "For it would almost be better for them not to have come to know the way of righteousness, than after knowing to turn from the holy commandment delivered to them." This is the most difficult part of the passage, and it is especially important to the position advanced in this study. The key is found in the use of the verb in the imperfect tense, ἦν, which (with the word "better") may be rendered, "It would be almost better." The imperfect Greek tense usually indicates action occurring continuously in past time. If that were the case here, the clause would be rendered, "Not to have known the way of righteousness was better." The obvious question then would be, But what about now? Obviously the temporal emphasis is remote here and some other aspect is being emphasized.[27] There is little debate that the imperfect tense can be used in several other ways, including a nuance that would require the subjunctive mode in other tenses, but the imperfect is deficient here. It occurs only in the indicative. Robertson discusses the "potential" use of the tense and illustrates it this way: "An example is found in Romans 9:3, ηὐχόμην, where Paul almost expresses a moral wrong. He holds himself back from the abyss by the tense."[28] Moule uses a different designation, but has the same concept.

> Desiderative Imperfect . . . is chiefly used in expressing a wish. It seems to soften a remark, and make it more vague or more diffident or polite; as we might say "I could almost do so-and-so." Cf. ηυχομην Romans 9:3, I could almost pray to be accursed—the Imperfect softening the shock of the daring statement or expressing awe at the terrible thought.[29]

This should not be thought of as characteristic only of koine Greek, for Smyth indicates similar uses in classical Greek.[30] If this imperfect verb is understood as "potential" or "desiderative," then the idea would be (as it is translated above), "It would be almost better for them. . . ." Peter refused to make this statement bluntly, because it could be misunderstood by his readers.

Third, what is the intent of the statement, "It is almost better for them not to have come to know the way of righteousness"? People sin presumably because of the thrills and satisfaction it allegedly promises. A believer, having come to know God's way of truth and virtue and having found joy in holy living, by returning to a life of carnality would be even less likely to find satisfaction in sin than before he was saved. Now he has the indwelling Holy Spirit to convict him of the error of his ways. He is more tender to God's promptings than before; hence he is worse off in sin than the unsaved. Brooks asked, "What is a fine suit of clothes with the plague in it? And what is a golden cup when there is poison at the bottom?"[31] His fellow Puritan, Venning, wrote, "The pleasures of sin are grievous, and its honors are disgraces and shame. . . . The precious substance promised by sin ends in a pernicious shadow, and the spoils we get by sin only spoil us. Sin promises like a God, but pays like a Devil."[32]

Peter's point it that if one is looking for satisfaction in sin, it would be better not to come to Christ. But this thought is so awesome to contemplate that he softens the blunt statement by the use of the imperfect tense, and by mentioning the way of righteousness, not the person of Christ. Their real danger here is not in rejecting Christ, but in leaving the new way of holiness for the former path of carnality.

Fourth, why did Peter refer to the proverbs of the dog and the sow? Citing these two proverbs, the first probably from Scripture (Prov. 26:11) and the second from secular literature, is usually seen as a way of graphically describing the true character of these who have repudiated their faith in Christ. Seeing a dog eat its own vomit is not an unusual sight for those who have spent some time with dogs. Nor is it really unlikely that a sow would wallow in mud. However, these actions are *not characteristic* of these animals. Some dogs are very fastidious eaters, refusing certain fresh foods, to say nothing of vomit. It is a fact that hogs prefer to be clean, but on hot days there is usually no place for them to keep cool other than in some kind of mud wallow.

The question of the dietary habits of dogs and the bathing activities of hogs are not foremost here. Instead, Peter was illustrating before and after conditions. "After escaping the stains . . . they are again entangled," and "the latter things have become worse for them than the former" (v. 20). What satisfaction can a dog find in vomit if before that he could not even digest that food when it was fresh? The very thought is disgusting and is a picture of an irrational reflex action. If a sow washed herself and then returned to the mud, would not the mud not be even more odious than before? How can a mud wallow be expected to please and satisfy her after her bath? In each case there is the "before" condition: the dog had eaten undigestible food; the sow had been dirty. In each case a return is mentioned: eating vomit by the dog, and wallowing by the sow. They are similar to a Christian who has received Christ, repenting of his life of sin, but is then won back into his former habits by temptations from the false teachers. This illustrates going back to something with which one was dissatisfied previously. When such a great change has taken place in a believer's soul, how can he rationally expect to find satisfaction now, never having it even before? When a Christian turns back to sinful habits, he is acting like a dog returning to its vomit or a bathed sow to her mud wallow.

Conclusion

Peter was warning those most susceptible to the bait being offered by false teachers. He was not attempting to depict the awful consequences of apostasy. Nor was he dealing with the problem of whether one can lose his salvation in Christ. Instead he was warning those recently saved that the subtle enticements of false teachers and the wooings of their old natures not lead them into the snare of sin. In that sin they would find no peace and satisfaction. In fact, they would experience less peace than at any time before their commitment to Christ. "The latter things have become worse for them than the former." In fact, if they again are caught up into a life of carnality, "it could almost be better for them not to have come to know the way of righteousness," if it is fulfillment and thrills they seek. If they would turn back into the old life, it reminds one of the old proverbs: "A dog returns to its own vomit, and a washed sow returns to the mud wallow."

Every believer, then, should be wary of a too casual, cheap-grace view of sin. Believers have escaped its clutches by the enormously costly sacrifice of God's Son. Yet they may slip back into its seductive coils only to find that there is even less pleasure, less satisfaction, less fulfillment than before they were saved. It disgusts the Father to see His children foolishly seeking to return to a condition and activities which they once renounced for His kingdom. This is as disgusting as the thought of a dog eating its vomit or a clean sow hurrying back to her familiar mud wallow.

"Therefore, because of having such promises as these, beloved, let us cleanse ourselves from every kind of pollution of flesh and spirit, and perfect holiness in the fear of God" (2 Cor. 7:1).

Chapter Notes

Chapter 1

1. John Peter Lange, *A Commentary on the Holy Scriptures*, 25 vols., vol. 1: *Genesis* (reprint, Grand Rapids: Zondervan, 1960), p. 336.
2. Arthur C. Custance attempts to classify the characteristics of the major races in connection with this oracle (*Noah's Three Sons* [Grand Rapids: Zondervan, 1975], p. 43). It seems to this writer that much of the discussion goes beyond the evidence.
3. The second oracle in Genesis based on the character traits of sons comes at the end of the patriarchal material (Gen. 49).
4. David Neiman, "The Date and Circumstances of the Cursing of Canaan," in *Biblical Motifs*, ed. Alexander Altmann (Cambridge: Harvard University Press, 1966), p. 125.
5. Umberio Cassuto, *From Noah to Abraham* (Jerusalem: Magnes, 1964), p. 149.
6. Robert Brow, "The Curse of Ham—Capsule of Ancient History," *Christianity Today*, October 26, 1973, p. 10.
7. Gerhardus Vos, *Old and New Testament Biblical Theology* (Grand Rapids: Eerdmans, 1954), p. 35.
8. August Dillmann, *Genesis*, 2 vols. (Edinburgh: Clark, 1897), 1:302; John Skinner, *Genesis*, International Critical Commentary (Edinburgh: Clark, 1930), p. 182.
9. B. Jacob, *The First Book of the Bible*, *Genesis* (New York: KTAV, 1974), p. 68.
10. Skinner, *Genesis*, p. 181.
11. Clyde T. Francisco, "The Curse on Canaan," *Christianity Today*, April 24, 1964, p. 8.
12. Rabbi Abraham Ben Isaiah and Rabbi Benjamin Sharfmen, *The Pentateuch and Rashi's Commentary: Genesis* (New York: S. S. and R., 1949), p. 84.
13. The terms used in the passage reflect the description in Genesis 3.
14. Christ's first sign (John 2), changing water to wine, announces the age to come.
15. Sanhedrin 108a, 70a and b.
16. Isaiah and Sharfmen, *Genesis*, p. 85.
17. Leupold presents Noah as the seasoned man of God brought down

by a simple temptation (H. C. Leupold, *Exposition of Genesis*, 2 vols. [Grand Rapids: Baker, 1942], 1:345).

18. Gerhard von Rad, *Genesis* (Philadelphia: Westminster, 1972), p. 133. See also Skinner, *Genesis*, p. 183.
19. *Zohar*, 1:240.
20. D. C. Allen, *The Legend of Noah* (Urbana, IL: Illini, 1963), p. 73.
21. This view was proposed by Origen and Chrysostom earlier.
22. H. H. Cohen, *The Drunkenness of Noah* (Alabama: University of Alabama Press, 1974), pp. 3–8.
23. Cassuto, *From Noah to Abraham*, p. 160.
24. Gene Rice, "The Curse That Never Was (Genesis 9:18–27)," *Journal of Religious Thought* 29 (1972): 5–6.
25. Thomas O. Figart, *A Biblical Perspective on the Race Problem* (Grand Rapids: Baker, 1973), pp. 55–58.
26. J. Ernest Shufelt, "Noah's Curse and Blessing, Gen. 9:18–27," *Concordia Theological Journal* 17 (1946): 739.
27. The Torah found the account repulsive, Israelite conscience found it shocking, and it was not right to attribute such an act to Noah (Cassuto, *From Noah to Abraham*, pp. 150–52).
28. According to Philo Byblius, a legend among the Canaanites said El Kronos used a knife to prevent his father from begetting children.
29. Sanhedrin 70a. The Midrash here also tries to explain the problem by saying that a lion took a swipe at Noah on leaving the ark and destroyed him sexually, and that Ham discovered it.
30. F. W. Bassett, "Noah's Nakedness and the Curse on Canaan: A Case of Incest?" *Vetus Testamentum* 21 (1971): 232.
31. Rice, "The Curse That Never Was," p. 12.
32. Francisco, "The Curse on Canaan," p. 9.
33. John A. Bailey, "Initiation and the Primal Woman in Gilgamesh and Genesis 2–3," *Journal of Biblical Literature* 89 (1970): 149.
34. Cassuto, *From Noah to Abraham*, p. 151.
35. Calvin wrote, "Ham alone eagerly seizes the occasion of ridiculing and inveighing against his father; just as perverse men are wont to catch at occasions of offense in others, which may serve as a pretext for indulgence in sin" (*Commentaries on the First Book of Moses Called Genesis*, 2 vols. [Grand Rapids: Eerdmans, 1948], 1:302).
36. Kidner sees this as the reverse of the fifth commandment, which makes the national destiny pivot on the same point—a call to uphold God's delegated authority (Derek Kidner, *Genesis* [Chicago: InterVarsity, 1967], p. 103).
37. This idea of "seeing the nakedness" as a gross violation of honor is also related by Herodotus in the story of Gyges, who when

seeing the nakedness of Candaules' wife—which Herodotus said was a shame among the Lydians—either had to kill Candaules or be killed himself (Herodotus 1:8).

38. It seems to this writer that the listing of "Shem, Ham and Japheth" is not chronological. According to Genesis 9:24 Ham is the youngest of the three, and according to 10:21 Shem is the older brother of Japheth. So the proper order would be Shem, Japheth, and Ham. (However, the New International Version's translation of 10:21 suggests that Japheth was the older brother of Shem, in which case the order would be Japheth, Shem, and Ham. But either way Ham is still the youngest.)

39. Jacob, *Genesis*, p. 68.

40. *Theological Dictionary of the Old Testament*, s.v. "אָרַר," by Josef Scharbert, 1:408–12.

41. Herbert Chanan Brichto, *The Problem of "Curse" in the Hebrew Bible* (Philadelphia: Society of Biblical Literature and Exegesis, 1963), p. 217.

42. In Scripture the "word" is seen as the cosmic power of the Creator God (Walter Eichrodt, *Theology of the Old Testament* [Philadelphia: Westminster, 1967], 1:173; 2:69).

43. Brichto, *The Problem of "Curse*," p. 217.

44. Edwin M. Yamauchi, "Slaves of God," *Bulletin of the Evangelical Theological Society* 9 (1966): 36–39.

45. Jacob, *Genesis*, p. 68. In Genesis 27 the patriarch Jacob could not change the blessing he had given.

46. Kidner, *Genesis*, p. 104.

47. Dillmann, *Genesis*, p. 305.

48. John Bright, *A History of Israel* (Philadelphia: Westminster, 1959), p. 108.

49. George E. Wright and Floyd V. Filson, *The Westminster Historical Atlas to the Bible* (Philadelphia: Westminster, 1945), p. 36.

50. William F. Albright, *From the Stone Age to Christianity* (Garden City, NY: Doubleday, 1964). p. 214.

51. Cassuto, *From Noah to Abraham*, p. 154.

52. Skinner, *Genesis*, p. 105.

53. F. Delitzsch, *A New Commentary on Genesis* (Edinburgh: Clark, 1888), p. 296.

54. Von Rad, *Genesis*, p. 133.

55. For a brief discussion of the use of tents, see John P. Brown, "Peace Symbolism in Ancient Military Vocabulary," *Vetus Testamentum* 21 (1971): 20–23. J. Huftijzer presents the view that it represents forcible dispossession of someone as, for example, in 1 Chronicles 5:10; Job 11:14; 18:15; and Psalm 78:55 ("Some

Remarks to the Table of Noah's Drunkenness," *Old Testament Studies* 12 [1958]: 22–27).

56. Figart correctly affirms that "there is not one archaeologist, anthropologist, or Biblical scholar who has ever associated the Canaanites with Negroid stock. Canaan is listed in Genesis 10:15–19 as the father of eleven tribes, all Caucasoid with no Negro characteristics" (*A Biblical Perspective on the Race Problem*, p. 55).

57. Neiman, "The Date and Circumstances of the Cursing of Canaan," p. 126.

58. Speiser, *Genesis*, p. 63.

59. Herman Gunkel, *Genesis* (Göttingen: Vandenhoeck & Ruprecht, 1902), p. 70.

60. Neiman, "The Date and Circumstances of the Cursing of Canaan," p. 131.

Chapter 2

1. As in the Westminster Shorter Catechism, question 4.

2. Lewis Sperry Chafer, *Systematic Theology*, 8 vols. (Dallas, TX: Dallas Seminary Press, 1948; reprint [8 vols. in 4], Grand Rapids: Kregel, 1992), 1:191, 208.

3. Robert H. Pfeiffer, *Introduction to the Old Testament* (New York: Harper, 1948), p. 341.

4. Louis Berkhof, *Systematic Theology* (Grand Rapids: Eerdmans, 1941), p. 77.

5. On 1 Samuel 15:11, "I regret"; cf. Genesis 6:6, where God's repenting parallels His being "grieved in His heart." This might even be styled an "anthropomorphic" usage of the will of God, representing Him as a man, who changes his will, when the actual, overall, sovereign plan of Deity has not really altered.

Chapter 3

1. Albert Barnes, *Notes, Critical, Explanatory, and Practical on the Book of Psalms*, 3 vols. (London: Blackie & Son. 1868), 1:xxv–xxvi.

2. The cry of the martyred tribulation saints in Revelation 6:10 for God's vengeance, while similar to the psalmist imprecations, is not applicable to the Church Age.

3. Psalms 5:10; 6:10; 9:19; 10:2, 15; 17:13a; 28:4; 31:17b–18; 40:14–15; 55:9, 15; 68:1–2; 70:2–3; 71:13; 79:6, 10, 12; 94:1; 97:7; 104:35; 129:5–6; 140:9–11; 141:10; 143:12.

4. J. W. Beardslee, "The Imprecatory Element in the Psalms," *Presbyterian and Reformed Review* 8 (1897): 491.

5. H. C. Leupold, *The Psalms* (Grand Rapids: Baker, 1969), p. 18.
6. Roland K. Harrison, *Introduction to the Old Testament* (Grand Rapids: Eerdmans, 1969), p. 997.
7. Johannes G. Vos, "The Ethical Problem of the Imprecatory Psalms," *Westminster Theological Journal* 4 (May 1942):123.
8. Beardslee, "The Imprecatory Element in the Psalms," p. 491.
9. For an overview of other solutions that have been proposed see Roy B. Zuck, "The Problem of the Imprecatory Psalms" (Th.M. thesis, Dallas Theological Seminary, 1957), pp. 45–58.
10. Beardslee, "The Imprecatory Element in the Psalms," pp. 491–92.
11. G. Kittel, *The Scientific Study of the Old Testament*, p. 143, quoted in G. S. Gunn, *God in the Psalms* (Edinburgh: Saint Andrew, 1965), p. 102.
12. Beardslee, "The Imprecatory Element in the Psalms," p. 496.
13. Sigmund Mowinckel, *The Psalms in Israel's Worship*, trans. D. R. Ap-Thomas, 2 vols. (New York: Abingdon, 1962), 1:44–52.
14. Barnes, *The Book of Psalms*, 1:xxx.
15. E. Kautzsch, ed., *Gesenius' Hebrew Grammar*, trans. A. E. Cowley, 2d English ed. (Oxford: Clarendon, 1910), p. 322.
16. John Bright, *The Authority of the Old Testament* (Nashville: Abingdon, 1967), p. 238.

Chapter 4

1. See Leland Ryken, *How to Read the Bible as Literature* (Grand Rapids: Zondervan, 1984), esp. pp. 11–32.
2. Studies dealing with the definition and method of biblical rhetorical criticism include among others the following: James Muilenburg, "Form Criticism and Beyond," *Journal of Biblical Literature* 88 (1969):1–18; David Greenwood, "Rhetorical Criticism and Formgeschichte: Some Methodological Considerations," *Journal of Biblical Literature* 89 (1970): 418–26; Martin Kessler, "A Methodological Setting for Rhetorical Criticism," *Semitics* 4 (1974):22–36; and his "An Introduction to Rhetorical Criticism of the Bible: Prolegomena," *Semitics* 7 (1980): 1–27; Isaac M. Kikawada, "Some Proposals for the Definition of Rhetorical Criticism," *Semitics* 5 (1977): 67–91; Yehoshua Gitay, *Prophecy and Persuasion* (Bonn: Linguistica Biblica, 1981), esp. pp. 34–49; George A. Kennedy, *New Testament Interpretation through Rhetorical Criticism* (Chapel Hill, NC: University of North Carolina Press, 1984), esp. pp. 3–38; and N. J. Tromp, "Amos 5:1–17: Towards a Stylistic and Rhetorical Analysis," *Oudtestamentische Studiën* 23 (1984): 56–84.
3. Such an approach is illustrated by the work of Muilenburg and his

followers. Muilenburg in describing rhetorical criticism stated, "What I am interested in, above all, is in understanding the nature of Hebrew literary composition, in exhibiting the structural patterns that are employed for the fashioning of a literary unit . . . and in discerning the many and varied devices by which the predications are formulated and ordered into a unified whole" ("Form Criticism and Beyond," p. 8). Several studies by his followers are collected in Jared J. Jackson and Martin Kessler, eds., *Rhetorical Criticism: Essays in Honor of James Muilenburg* (Pittsburgh: Pickwick, 1974).

4. For examples of such studies see the works of Gitay, Kennedy, and Tromp mentioned in note 2. For a brief comparison of the two basic approaches mentioned here, see Gitay, *Prophecy and Persuasion*, p. 27.

5. Gitay, *Prophecy and Persuasion*, p. 45.

6. On the subject of the oral character of ancient texts, see Yehoshua Gitay, "Deutero-Isaiah: Oral or Written?" *Journal of Biblical Literature* 99 (1980): 190–97; H. van Dyke Parunak, "Some Axioms for Literary Architecture," *Semitics* 8 (1982):2–4; and Kennedy, *New Testament Interpretations through Rhetorical Criticism*, pp. 5–6.

7. See Herbert M. Wolf, "Implications of Form Criticism for Old Testament Studies," *Bibliotheca Sacra* 127 (1970):299–307.

8. See the critiques offered by Muilenburg, "Form Criticism and Beyond," pp. 1–7; Greenwood, "Rhetorical Criticism and Formgeschichte: Some Methodological Considerations," pp. 418–26; and Rolf Knierim, "Old Testament Form Criticism Reconsidered," *Interpretation* 27 (1973):435–68.

9. The limits proposed are well defined. Verses 8–30 are clearly structurally distinct from the preceding "song of the vineyard" (5:1–7) and the following call narrative (chap. 6).

10. On this positive, persuasive goal of chapters 1–12 as a whole, see Yehoshua Gitay, "Isaiah and His Audience," *Prooftexts* 3 (1983): 223–30.

11. For example, see Edward J. Young, *The Book of Isaiah*, 3 vols. (Grand Rapids: Eerdmans, 1965, 1969, 1972), 1:205–6; Hans Wildberger, *Jesaja 1–12*, Biblischer Kommentar, Altes Testament, 2d ed. (Neukirchen-Vluyn: Neukirchener, 1980), pp. 181–82; Ronald E. Clements, *Isaiah 1–39*, New Century Bible Commentary (Grand Rapids: Eerdmans, 1980), pp. 60–66; Otto Kaiser, *Isaiah 1–12*, Old Testament Library, 2d ed. (Philadelphia: Westminster, 1983), pp. 96–109. Isaiah 10:1–4, also introduced by הוֹי, is often combined with 5:8–24 to produce a series of seven woes. At the same time, 5:25–30 is frequently combined with 9:8–21 (Heb., vv.

7–20) because of the refrain in 5:25b, which appears as well in 9:12, 17, 21. Finally, several verses within 5:8–24 are considered to be later interpolations, though commentators often disagree on which ones are to be so labeled. As stated later in this article, a rhetorical analysis of the passage makes these conclusions, based on the methods of form and redaction criticism, highly suspect.

12. The literature on woe oracles is quite extensive, including among others: Claus Westermann, *Basic Forms of Prophetic Speech* (London: Lutterworth, 1967), pp. 190–94; Erhard Gerstenberger, "The Woe-Oracles of the Prophets," *Journal of Biblical Literature* 81 (1962): 249–63; Richard J. Clifford, "The Use of *Hôy* in the Prophets," *Catholic Biblical Quarterly* 28 (1966): 458–64; James G. Williams, "The Alas-Oracles of the Eighth Century Prophets," "*Hebrew Union College Annual* 38 (1967): 75–91; Waldemar Janzen, *Mourning Cry and Woe Oracle* (Berlin: de Gruyter, 1972); Ronald E. Clements, "The Form and Character of Prophetic Woe Oracles," *Semitics* 8 (1982):17–29.

13. Westermann, *Basic Forms of Prophetic Speech*, p. 190.

14. Ibid., pp. 142–61, 169–87.

15. Verse 8, introduced by הוֹי, is an accusation against the wealthy Judean landowners, while judgment on this same group is announced in verses 9–10. In verses 11–12 another accusation appears, while verses 13–17 contain the accompanying announcement of judgment (note לְבֵן, "therefore," at the beginning of v. 13). In the sixth oracle verses 22–23 are accusatory; in verse 24a (introduced by לבֵן) judgment is announced.

16. Clements, *Isaiah* 1–39, pp. 64–65.

17. Kaiser, *Isaiah* 1–12, pp. 96–109.

18. Parunak points out "that more than one pattern may be active simultaneously in a passage" ("Some Axioms for Literary Architecture," p. 10). He adds that these alternate patterns may be concurrent with or embedded in another (pp. 10–12). Parunak also points out that chiasmus is one of the basic structural patterns in oral literature (pp. 7–10; see also his "Oral Typesetting: Some Uses of Biblical Structure," *Biblica* 62 [1981]: 153–68).

19. Kaiser speaks of a "circular composition" in the arrangement of woes, though he sees 10:1–2, which in his scheme is the seventh in the list, as corresponding to 5:8. He notes that both are concerned with "transgressors of the law." He sees this same theme in verse 23, which he places after verse 20, making it fourth in the list (*Isaiah* 1–12, pp. 96–97). The chiasmus is apparent as the text stands; one need not rearrange verses or import passages from other chapters as Kaiser has done.

20. Ibid., p. 100. The incident recorded in 1 Kings 21, though occurring at an earlier date (9th century B.C.) and in a different place (the Northern Kingdom), provides a vivid illustration of how these "land deals" may have worked. For a detailed study of the socio-economic setting of Isaiah 5:8–10, see Eryl Davies, *Prophecy and Ethics* (Sheffield: JSOT, 1981), pp. 65–89.

21. Cf. Kaiser, *Isaiah 1–12*, p. 100. On the importance of the Lord's ownership of the land to Old Testament thought, see Christopher J. H. Wright, *An Eye for an Eye* (Downers Grove, IL: InterVarsity, 1983), pp. 46–62.

22. On the relationship between the judicial system and socio-economic exploitation in ancient Israel, see Davies, *Prophecy and Ethics*, pp. 90–112.

23. In verse 13 the scope expands to include the entire nation (cf. "My people"), though the nobility (the focus of attention in vv. 8–12) may still be singled out for special consideration (cf. כְּבוֹדוֹ, "its [the nation's] glory," which possibly refers to the upper crust of society in contrast to its masses, to which הֲמוֹנוֹ probably refers here).

24. The word הִרְחִיבָה is a prophetic perfect, followed up by two perfects (with *waw* consecutive) carrying a specific future nuance. Cf. E. Kautzsch, ed., *Gesenius' Hebrew Grammar*, 2d English ed. (Oxford: Clarendon, 1910), p. 333 (sec. 112s). In verses 15–16 the *yiqtol* forms (with *waw* consecutive) also have a future sense (note the imperfect תִּשְׁפַּלְנָה in v. 15b; cf. p. 329, sec. 11w). With וַרֵעוּ (perfect with *waw* consecutive) in verse 17 the author returned to the pattern of verse 14.

25. The carousers are not specifically identified as the subject in verse 14b, but הֲדָרָהּ, "its [prob. Jerusalem's] splendor," probably alludes to them (note the contrasting הֲמוֹנָהּ, "Its teeming masses," which follows). The words שְׁאוֹנָהּ, "its uproar," and עָלֵז, "the one who exults," probably refer to the revelry described in verses 11–12 (cf. the use of both roots in 24:8, where drunken revelry is clearly in view).

26. For this same picture of death as having a voracious appetite, see Proverbs 30:15–16 and Habakkuk 2:5. The background for the imagery can be found in Canaanite myth, where deified Death is pictured as one who opens his mouth wide to swallow his hapless victims. See J. C. L. Gibson, *Canaanite Myths and Legends*, 2d ed. (Edinburgh: Clark, 1978), pp. 68–69, for a particularly illustrative text in this regard.

27. The Masoretic text has גֵּרִים, a participle, "resident aliens," in verse 17b (cf. NASB, "strangers"). This reading would make sense

contextually since the גֵּרִים are often mentioned as oppressed elements in society. The picture is that of the oppressed outliving their oppressors. However, tighter parallelism is achieved (cf. כְּבָיִם, "lambs," in v. 17a) if the word is גְּדָיִם, "kids" (this word occurs twice in the construct . . . but the absolute form is used in 1 Sam. 10:3),

28. This writer understands מֵהִים, "fatlings," as a genitive of possession following the construct הָרְבִיּה, "ruins" (which is an adverbial accusative of location here). Attested elsewhere only in Psalm 66:15, מֵה is used of sacrificial animals. Here it is apparently a derogatory reference to the well-fed, rich carousers (cf. Amos 4:1 for similar imagery) who, ironically, are devoured by Sheol as if they were sacrificial animals.

29. See note 11.

30. On the theme of appropriate punishment in these verses, see Patrick D. Miller, Jr., *Sin and Judgment in the Prophets* (Chico, CA: Scholars, 1982), pp. 42–43.

31. On the irony inherent in their arrogant words, see Edwin M. Good, *Irony in the Old Testament* (Philadelphia: Westminster, 1965), pp. 119–20.

32. For some of the literature on the woe oracles, see note 12, Among the proposed backgrounds for the oracle are popular wisdom (Gerstenberger), curse formulae (Westermann), and mourning rites (Chfford, Williams, Janzen).

33. Also see Jeremiah 22:18; 34:5; Amos 5:16.

34. This need not imply that the prophet experienced psychological sorrow over the impending death of the sinners. Ritual mourning was an accepted practice in the biblical world, even to the point of hiring professionals. On this point Clifford writes, "When the prophet hears of impending disaster from Yahweh, he utters a ritual *hôy* in automatic lament, a cry borrowed from the funeral customs of his milieu. The prophet need not feel a psychological drive, but only an 'ontological' one—the situation demands it" ("The Use of *Hôy* in the Prophets," p. 464).

35. Cf. Williams, "The Alas-Oracles of the Eighth Century Prophets," p. 86.

36. The technical term for this device is *hypotyposis* (E. W. Bullinger, *Figures of Speech Used in the Bible* [1898; reprint, Grand Rapids: Baker, 1968], pp. 444–45).

37. Cf. Wildberger, *Jesaja 1–12*, pp. 223–24.

38. Note the appearance of the phrases מֵרָחֹק and מִקְצֵה הָאָרֶץ in both Deuteronomy 28:49 and Isaiah 5:26.

39. The description is, of course, hyperbolic, but also quite realistic in

many respects, as a comparison with Assyrian sculpture (which has its hyperbolic elements as well) indicates. On the sculptural evidence, see Julian Reade, "The Neo-Assyrian Court and Army: Evidence from the Sculptures," *Iraq* 34 (1972):87–112.

40. Public awareness of Assyrian military power and practice would have steadily increased from around 743 B.C. due to increased Assyrian military involvement in the west during the last half of the 8th century B.C. The precise date of origin for Isaiah 5:8–30 is not known. Even if originally proclaimed early in Isaiah's career, it was probably repeated and/or recalled periodically. The description in verses 26–30 would have been especially effective in conjunction with or after Tiglath-pileser's campaign against Damascus and Samaria (ca. 734–732), which reduced the latter to a puppet state, the conquest of Samaria (722), Sargon's Ashdod campaign of 712, and Sennacherib's invasion of Judah (701).

41. Daniel D. Luckenbill, *Ancient Records of Assyria and Babylonia*, 2 vols. (Chicago: University of Chicago Press, 1926–27), 2:27 (par. 56).

42. Ibid., 2:126 (par. 253).

43. Clements, *Isaiah 1–39*, p. 70.

44. Luckenbill, *Ancient Records of Assyria and Babylonia*, 2:94 (par. 171).

45. Ibid., 2:89 (par. 163). Cf. Sennacherib's description of the invading Elamite army (2:126, par. 252): "Like the onset of the locust swarms of the springtime they kept steadily coming on against me to offer battle. With the dust of their feet covering the wide heavens, like a mighty storm with (its) masses of dense clouds, they drew up in battle array."

46. Peter Machinist explores this possibility in "Assyria and Its Image in the First Isaiah," *Journal of the American Oriental Society* 103 (1983):719–37. He concludes that Assyrian propaganda did influence Isaiah's view of Assyria, though he recognizes that general ancient Near Eastern use may account for similarities (note esp. his reservations with respect to the "lion" imagery of Isa. 5:29, pp. 728–29). He discusses possible ways in which Judeans like Isaiah could have become aware of Assyrian propaganda (pp. 728–34).

Chapter 5

1. Joh Lindblom, *A Study on the Immanuel Section in Isaiah vii, 1–ix, 6* (Lund: Gleerup, 1958), p. 15.

2. George Rawlinson, *The Book of the Prophet Isaiah*, Pulpit Commentary (New York: Funk & Wagnalls, n.d.), p. 129.

3. Albert Barnes, *Notes, Critical, Explanatory, and Practical on the Book of the Prophet Isaiah*, 2 vols. (New York: Worthington, 1881), 1:148.

4. Ibid., p. 157.

5. John Skinner, *The Book of the Prophet Isaiah, Chapters I–XXXIX* (Cambridge: Cambridge University Press, 1896), p. 60. Cf. also R. W. Rogers, "Isaiah," in *Abingdon Bible Commentary* (New York: Abingdon, 1929), pp. 243–44; W. Fitch, "Isaiah," in *New Bible Commentary*, ed. F. Davidson (Grand Rapids: Eerdmans, 1953), p. 569; and E. M. Kraeling, "The Immanuel Prophecy, Part 4," *Journal of Biblical Literature* 50 (1931): 277.

6. E. R. Thiele places his accession date at 722 B.C. at the age of 20; see his *The Mysterious Numbers of the Hebrew Kings* (Chicago: University of Chicago Press, 1951), p. 104.

7. Kraeling ably sets forth the three groups of interpretation ("The Immanuel Prophecy," p. 281).

8. Charles R. Brown, "Exegesis of Isaiah VII. 10–17," *Journal of Biblical Literature* 9 (1890): 119.

9. Fitch, "Isaiah," p. 569.

10. George B. Gray, *A Critical and Exegetical Commentary on the Book of Isaiah*, International Critical Commentary (Edinburgh: Clark, 1912) p. 121. Skinner denies that an objective miracle is called for here (*The Book of the Prophet Isaiah, Chapters I–XXXIX*, 60).

11. Barnes, *Notes, Critical, Explanatory, and Practical on the Book of the Prophet Isaiah*, 1:155.

12. Kraeling, "The Immanuel Prophecy," p. 280.

13. J. A. Alexander, *Commentary on the Prophecies of Isaiah*, 2 vols. (Grand Rapids: Zondervan, 1953), 1:167.

14. F. Delitzsch, *Biblical Commentary on the Prophecies of Isaiah*, 2 vols. (reprint, Grand Rapids: Eerdmans, 1949), 1:206.

15. E. J. Young, *Studies in Isaiah* (Grand Rapids: Eerdmans, 1954), p. 159. He concludes, "Isaiah, therefore, because of the tremendous solemnity and importance of the announcement which he was to make, used as much of this ancient formula of announcement as suited his purpose" (ibid., p. 160).

16. Lindblom, *A Study on the Immanuel Section in Isaiah vii, 1–ix. 6*, p. 19. Also see Robert Jamieson, A. R. Fausset, and David Brown, *A Commentary Critical, Experimental and Practical on the Old and New Testaments* (Grand Rapids: Eerdmans, 1948), 3:586.

17. E. W. Hengstenburg, *Christology of the Old Testament*, 4 vols. (reprint, Grand Rapids: Kregel, 1955), 2:44. Young explains it thus: "More natural, however, is the *generic* usage in which the

article serves to designate some particular unknown person" (*Studies in Isaiah*, p. 184).

18. Rogers, "Isaiah," pp. 643–44. For the same approach see Lindblom, *A Study on the Immanuel Section in Isaiah vii, 1–ix.* 18; Carl W. E. Naegelsbach, *The Prophet Isaiah in a Commentary on the Holy Scriptures*, by John Peter Lange (New York: Scribner's Sons, 1878; reprint, Grand Rapids: Zondervan, n.d.), pp. 121, 123; and C. Von Orelli, *The Prophecies of Isaiah*, trans. J. S. Banks (Edinburgh: Clark, 1895), Skinner holds that בְּתוּלָה is not wholly free from ambiguity, while contending that עַלְמָה does not necessary connote virginity (*The Book of the Prophet Isaiah, Chapters I–XXXIX*, p. 56).

19. Gray, *A Critical and Exegetical Commentary on the Book of Isaiah*, pp. 126–27.

20. Cyrus H. Gordon, "Almah in Isaiah 7:14," *Journal of Bible and Religion* 21 (April 1953): 106. Some have overlooked or minimized the fact that Joel 1:8 indicates a בְּתוּלָה has been married and lost her husband. See the interesting observation by William S. LaSor in his "Isaiah 7:14—'Young Woman' or 'Virgin'?" pp. 3–4, especially the larger issues involved at the end of his treatment.

21. J. Gresham Machen, *The Virgin Birth of Christ* (New York: Harper, 1930), p. 288.

22. Alexander, *Commentary on the Prophecies of Isaiah*, p. 170. To avoid some of the difficulties involved here, some take the view that verse 14 refers to Christ, whereas the rest of the passage, that is, verses 15 and 16, relate to Shear-jashub, son of Isaiah (e.g., William Kelly, *An Exposition of the Book of Isaiah* [London: Hammond, 1947], p. 125).

23. Alexander, *Commentary on the Prophecies of Isaiah*, p. 171.

24. Ibid., p. 172.

Chapter 6

1. *Jerome's Commentary on Daniel,* trans. Gleason L. Archer, Jr. (Grand Rapids: Baker, 1958), pp. 140–44 (on Dan. 11:44–45).

2. Leonhard Bertholdt, "Daniel: Aus dem Hebraish-Aramaischen neu übersetzt und erklart, mit einer vollständigen Einleitung und einigen historischen und exegegetischen Excursen," 2 vols. (Erlangen: n.p., 1806).

3. Johann Gottfried Eichhorn, "Daniel," in *Einleitung in das Alte Testament* (Leipzig: n.p., 1780–33).

4. Johann Christoph Doederlein, *Esaias*, 3d ed. (n.p., 1789).

5. Harold Henry Rowley, *Darius the Mede and the Four World Empires in the Book of Daniel* (Cardiff: University of Wales Press,

1935); also see his work *The Aramaic of the Old Testament* (London: Oxford University Press, 1929). It should be added that virtually every argument advanced by Rowley in these and similar writings has been thoroughly refuted by subsequent conservative works, by the discoveries of additional cuneiform records, and by the Aramaic documentation from the Dead Sea Caves.

6. Raymond Hammer, *The Book of Daniel*, Cambridge Bible Commentary (New York: Cambridge University Press, 1976).

7. E.g., J. E. H. Thompson, *Daniel*, The Pulpit Commentary (London: Kegan Paul, Trench, Trübner, 1897); Charles H. H. Wright, *Daniel and His Prophecies* (London: Williams & Norgate, 1906); Robert Dick Wilson, *Studies in the Book of Daniel* (1907; rev. ed., New York: Revell, 1938); Charles Boutflower, *In and Around the Book of Daniel* (1923; Grand Rapids: Zondervan, 1963); Raymond P. Dougherty, *Nabonidus and Belshazzar* (New Haven, CT: Yale University Press, 1929); Edward J. Young, *The Prophecy of Daniel* (Grand Rapids: Eerdmans, 1953); G. Ch. Aalders, *Daniël* (Kampen: J. H. Bok, 1962); D. J. Wiseman et al., *Notes on Some Problems in the Book of Daniel* (London: Tyndale, 1965); H. C. Leupold, *Exposition of Daniel* (1949; rev. ed., Minneapolis: Augsburg, 1969); R. K. Harrison, *Introduction to the Old Testament* (Grand Rapids: Eerdmans, 1969); John F. Walvoord, *Daniel: The Key to Prophetic Interpretation* (Chicago: Moody, 1971); Leon Wood, *A Commentary on Daniel* (Grand Rapids: Zondervan, 1973).

8. Hammer, *The Book of Daniel*, p. 1.

9. Josephus *Contra Apionem* 1.8.

10. The 13 books of the Prophets must have been Joshua, Judges-Ruth, Samuel, Kings, Chronicles, Ezra-Nehemiah, Esther, Isaiah, Jeremiah-Lamentations, Ezekiel, Daniel, the Twelve Minor Prophets, and Canticles. From this it is perfectly evident that the peculiar division of the Masoretic text was a later arrangement, and therefore is of no evidential value whatever as to the possible date for the composition of the Book of Daniel.

11. Hammer, *The Book of Daniel*, p. 4.

12. Dougherty, *Nabonidus and Belshazzar*, pp. 60–68.

13. Ibid., p. 88.

14. Wilson, *Studies in the Book of Daniel;* and John C. Whitcomb, Jr., *Darius the Mede* (Grand Rapids: Eerdmans, 1959).

15. Whitcomb, *Darius the Mede*, pp. 31–42.

16. Aalders, *Daniël*, pp. 16–19,114.

17. William F. Albright, "The Date and Personality of the Chronicler," *Journal of Biblical Literature* 40 (1921): 112–13, n. 19.

18. Wilson, *Studies in the Book of Daniel*, pp. 337–66.

19. W. von Soden points out that in the later stages of the Babylonian dialect of Akkadian, the sibilants s, š, and ṣ often shifted to *l* before dental consonants like t and d. For example the earlier aštur ("I wrote") became altur; the preposition out ištu ("out of") became ultu. On this analogy, the original ethnic designation *Kasdu* or *Kasdim* later became *Kaldu* or *Kaldim*. At that stage, then, *Kasdim* ("Chaldeans") became a homonym of *Kasdim* (plural of the *Kaldu* derived from the Sumerian *Gal.du*) (*Grundriss der Akkadischen Grammatik* [Rome: Pontificium Institutum Biblicum, 1969], p. 31). The latest stage of the Babylonian language, that of the Neo-Babylonian, contemporary with Nebuchadnezzar and Belshazzar, then adopted a policy of archaizing, in an effort to revive the older, classical dialect. Thus it came about that both *Kaldu's* became *Kasdu* and the homonym resemblance continued. (The name *Chaldean* is derived from the Greek form, Χαλδαῖοι which in turn came from *Kaldim*. The Greeks apparently came to know the Chaldeans before the elimination of the secondary *l* in favor of s or š before dentals had taken place.)

20. Hammer, *The Book of Daniel*, pp. 4–5.

21. Robert Dick Wilson's article "The Aramaic of Daniel" appeared in *Biblical and Theological Studies* (New York: Scribner, 1912), as part of the Princeton Seminary Centennial volume. The same material appeared in his book *A Scientific Investigation of the Old Testament* (1926; Chicago: Moody, 1959). Edward J. Young's treatment appears in his *Introduction to the Old Testament* (Grand Rapids: Eerdmans, 1949). Wiseman's *Notes on Some Problems in the Book of Daniel* has an extensive discussion by Kenneth A. Kitchen (pp. 31–79). Harrison deals with this problem in *Introduction to the Old Testament*, pp. 1125–26. The present author has discussed this subject in his *Survey of Old Testament Introduction* (Chicago: Moody, 1974), pp. 386–91.

22. Gleason L. Archer, Jr., "The Aramaic of the Genesis Apocryphon Compared with the Aramaic of Daniel," in *New Perspectives on the Old Testament*, ed. J. Barton Payne (Waco, TX: Word, 1970).

23. E. Y. Kutscher, *Review of Aramaic Documents of the Fifth Century B.C.*, by G. R. Driver (Oxford: Clarendon, 1957).

24. Archer, "The Aramaic of the Genesis Apocryphon," pp. 160–69. In regard to morphology, it is pointed out that the feminine third person pronoun suffix, which is always -*ah* in Daniel and Ezra and the Elephantine papyri, occasionally appears as -*ha'* in the Apocryphon—a form previously known only from Targumic literature. Instead of Daniel's third person plural masculine pronominal suffix, -*hon*, the Apocryphon shows the later Aramaic-*on*. The demonstrative pronoun for "this" appears as *denâ* in

Daniel but as *den* in the Apocryphon. The latter shows a shortened form of *bet* ("house of") which has previously only been known from Talmudic or Rabbinic Aramaic: *bey*. This never appears in Daniel. In regard to verb forms, the later form *yiheh* appears in the Apocryphon rather than the biblical *yihyeh* which appears in Daniel. The feminine third person singular of the perfect tense of weak third-radical verbs appears in the Apocryphon as *-iyat* (hitherto known only from later Aramaic) rather than the *-at* of biblical Aramaic. For example, "it was built" appears as *itbeniyat* rather than Daniel's *hitbenat*. In the matter of vocabulary, the Apocryphon shows a good number of late words, previously known only from Targumic or post-Targumic documents. These occur in such large numbers as to point unmistakably to a much later period than the time of Daniel, Ezra, or the Elephantine papyri.

25. Gleason L. Archer, Jr., "The Hebrew of Daniel Compared with the Qumran Sectarian Documents," in *The Law and the Prophets*, ed. John H. Skilton (Nutley, NJ: Presbyterian and Reformed, 1974), pp. 470–81. The levels of comparison are syntax and morphology (with some distinctive contrasts in regard to word order), postbiblical Hebrew words, postbiblical pronunciation and spelling, and the words used with a postbiblical meaning.

26. Hammer, *The Book of Daniel*, p. 98.

27. Harold W. Hoehner, "Daniel's Seventy Weeks in New Testament Chronology," *Bibliotheca Sacra* 132 (January–March 1974): 47–65. As Hoehner suggests, the number of days from March 5 (the first of Nisan), 444 B.C. to March 30 (the Passover), A.D. 33 is 173,880 days (when 116 days for leap years are included), and that is exactly the number of days in 483 prophetic years (483 years x 360 days = 173,880). This is a slight variation from Anderson's dates of March 14, 445 B.C. to April 6, A.D. 32 (Robert Anderson, *The Coming Prince* [London: Hodder & Stoughton, 1881], pp. 119–29. Cf. Alva J. McClain, *Daniel's Prophecy of the Seventy Weeks* [Grand Rapids: Zondervan, 1969]).

28. Hammer, *The Book of Daniel*, p. 119.

Chapter 7

1. *International Standard Bible Encyclopaedia*, 1939 ed., s.v. "Temple," by W. Shaw Caldecott and James Orr, 5:2935.

2. Carl Friedrich Keil, *The Prophecies of Ezekiel*, 2 vols. (Edinburgh: Clark, 1876, 1885).

3. Patrick Fairbairn, *Ezekiel and the Book of His Prophecies*, 3d ed. (Edinburgh: Clark, 1863), pp. 431–502.

4. W. Shaw Caldecott, ed., *The Tabernacle, Its History and Structure*, quoted by F. W. Grant, *Ezekiel*, The Numerical Bible, vol. 4 (New York: Loizeaux, 1891–1904), pp. 320–21.
5. Ibid., pp. 318–22.
6. Clarence Larkin, *Dispensational Truth*, 4th ed. (Philadelphia: by the author, 1920), pp. 93–94.
7. Ibid.

Chapter 8

1. E. Earle Ellis, "How the New Testament Uses the Old," in *New Testament Interpretation*, ed. I. Howard Marshall (Grand Rapids: Eerdmans, 1977), p. 209. Moisés Silva expresses the same thought: "'Out of Egypt I have called my son' (Hosea 11:1) is applied in Matthew 2:14–15 to what appears to be a *different* and *unrelated* event" ("The New Testament Use of the Old Testament," in *Scripture and Truth*, ed. D. A. Carson and John D. Woodbridge [Grand Rapids: Zondervan, 1983], p. 156 [italics added]).
2. The verb אָהַב ("to love") here conveys the idea of covenant love. This is evident from its close connection with the Exodus event in the second colon. Also in this text אהב denotes more than simple affection. It also describes the Lord's love toward Israel in election (cf. Norman H. Snaith, *The Distinctive Ideas of the Old Testament* [New York: Schocken, 1964, p. 95).
3. Francis Brown, S. R. Driver. and Charles A. Briggs, *A Hebrew and English Lexicon of the Old Testament,* s.v. "בּוּ," p. 102; *Theological Dictionary of the Old Testament*, s.v. "בּוּ," by H. Haag, 2:155.
4. Both Piel imperfects יְדַבְּהוּ and יְקַפְּרוּ are "customary" or "habitual" and thus denote repeated action in past time, hence the translation "kept sacrificing and burning."
5. Robert H. Gundry argues that the connection between Hosea 11:1 and Matthew 2:15 is not the departure into and out of Egypt (Exodus) but "preservation *in* Egypt" (*Matthew: A Commentary on His Literary and Theological Art* [Grand Rapids: Eerdmans, 1982], p. 34). However, the focus of Hosea 11:1–2 is the Exodus from Egypt and the nation's subsequent disobedience; the passage does not describe the preservation of Israel *in* Egypt. Also though the quotation in Matthew 2 occurs before Jesus' actual departure from Egypt (cf. 2:21), it is reasonable to propose that Matthew had in view the entire event of departure into and out of Egypt and thus felt free to quote the passage as early as verse 15 (cf. Raymond E. Brown, *The Birth of Messiah* [Garden City. NY: Doubleday, 1977], pp. 219–20; see also Krister Stendahl, "*Quis et Unde*?: An

Analysis of Matt. 1–2," in *Judentum, Urchristenium: Kirche*, ed., W. Eltester [Berlin: Topelmann, 1960], p.97).

6. For a more complete discussion of the different solutions to the problem consult the writers work, "The Use of Hosea 11:1 in Matthew 2:15" (ThM thesis, Dallas Theological Seminary, 1984), pp. 41–64.

7. R. C. H. Lenski, *An Interpretation of St. Matthew's Gospel* (Minneapolis: Augsburg, 1964), pp. 77–79.

8. J. Barton Payne, *The Theology of the Older Testament* (Grand Rapids: Zondervan, 1962), pp. 269–70, esp. n. 43.

9. Hermann Cremer, *Biblico-Theological Lexicon of New Testament Greek* (Edinburgh: Clark, 1895), s.v "πληρόω," p. 500. Jack Kingsbury notes that the so-called formula quotations indicate that the coming of Jesus means that the time of prophecy has been brought to an end and the time of fulfillment inaugurated ("Form and Message of Matthew," *Interpretation* 29 [1975]: 16).

10. *Theological Dictionary of the New Testament*, s.v. "πληρόω," by Gerhard Delling, 6:295.

11. Bruce M. Metzger, "The Formulas Introducing Quotations of Scripture in the NT and the Mishnah," *Journal of Biblical Literature* 70 (1951): 307.

12. Stanley D. Toussaint, *Behold the King: A Study of Matthew* (Portland, OR: Multnomah, 1980), p. 55.

13. William S. LaSor, "The *Sensus Plenior* and Biblical Interpretation," in *Scripture, Tradition, and Interpretation*, ed. W. Ward Gasque and William S. LaSor (Grand Rapids: Eerdmans, 1978), p. 275.

14. See Rudolph Beirberg, "Does Scripture Have a *Sensus Plenior?*" *Catholic Biblical Quarterly* 10 (1948): 182–95; Raymond E. Brown, *The* Sensus Plenior *of Sacred Scripture* (Baltimore: St. Mary's University, 1955); "The History and Development of the Theory of a *Sensus Plenior*," *Catholic Biblical Quarterly* 15 (1953): 141–62; "The *Sensus Plenior* in the Last Ten Years," *Catholic Biblical Quarterly* 25 (1963): 262–85; Joseph Coppens, "Levels of Meaning in the Bible," in *How Does the Christian Confront the Old Testament?* ed. Pierre Benoit and Roland Murphy (New York: Paulist, 1968), pp. 125–39; Robert H. Krumholtz, "Instrumentality and the *Sensus Plenior*," *Catholic Biblical Quarterly* 20 (1958): 200–205; John J. O'Rourke, "Marginal Notes on the *Sensus Plenior*," *Catholic Biblical Quarterly* 21 (1959): 64–71; Edmund F. Sutchffe, "The Plenary Sense as a Principle of Interpretation," *Biblica* 24 (1953): 333–43; Bruce Vawter, "The Fuller Sense: Some Considerations," *Catholic Biblical Quarterly* 26 (1969): 85–96.

15. In addition to LaSor's proposal, see G. N. Bergado, "The *Sensus*

Plenior as a New Testament Hermeneutical Principle" (MA thesis, Trinity Evangelical Divinity School, May 1969); Donald H. Hagner, "The Old Testament in the New Testament," in *Interpreting the Word of God*, ed. Samuel J. Schultz and Morris Inch (Chicago: Moody, 1976), p. 92; S. Lewis Johnson, *The Old Testament in the New* (Grand Rapids: Zondervan, 1980), p. 50; J. I. Packer, "Biblical Authority Hermeneutics, and Inerrancy" in *Jerusalem and Athens: Critical Discussions on the Theology and Apologetics of Cornelius Van Til*, ed. E. R. Geehan (Nutley, NJ: Presbyterian and Reformed, 197 l), pp. 147–48. Elliott E. Johnson seems to propose a variation of the principle, though he redresses it ("Author's Intention and Biblical Interpretation," in *Hermeneutics, Inerrancy, and the Bible*, ed. Earl D. Radmacher and Robert D. Preus [Grand Rapids: Zondervan, 1984], pp. 407–29). Bruce K. Waltke likewise comes very close to advocating a form of *sensus plenior* in his article, "A Canonical Process Approach to the Psalms," in *Tradition and Testament: Essays in Honor of Charles Lee Feinberg*, ed. John S. Feinberg and Paul D. Feinberg (Chicago: Moody, 1981), pp. 3–18.

16. Brown, *The* Sensus Plenior *of Sacred Scripture*, p. 92.
17. In discussing the role of the instrumentality of the human author, Krumholtz notes that in accord with the principles of instrumental causality the *sensus plenior* would be attributed more properly to God than to the human author (*Sensus Plenior*, p. 205). This would mean the human author is more passive, thus strongly suggesting some kind of mechanical dictation.
18. Walter C. Kaiser, Jr., "A Response to Author's Intention and Biblical Interpretation by Elliott E. Johnson." Paper read at the International Council on Biblical Inerrancy, Chicago, November 1982, p. 1.
19. This seems to be one reason why LaSor chooses two fulfillment texts in Matthew as illustrations of the "fuller sense" (LaSor, "The *Sensus Plenior* and Biblical Interpretation," p. 271).
20. D. A. Carson argues that the "son" language in Hosea 11:1 is part of a messianic matrix that includes such descriptions as Seed of the woman, the elect Son of Abraham, the Prophet like Moses, the Davidic King, and the Messiah; thus "insofar as that matrix points to Jesus the Messiah and insofar as Israel's history looks forward to one who sums it up, then so far also Hosea 11:1 looks forward" ("Matthew," in *The Expositor's Bible Commentary* [Grand Rapids: Zondervan, 1984], 8:92). This point would be more feasible, however, if the "son" terminology were used in the context of Israel's future restoration (cf. Hos. 11:8–11). However, it is used in a text that describes the inception of Israel's history as a people of Yahweh (cf. 11:1–2), a text that is retrospective in its focus.

21. Cf. Packer, "Biblical Authority, Hermeneutics, and Inerrancy," pp. 145–48.
22. LaSor, "The *Sensus Plenior* and Biblical Interpretation," p. 271.
23. Krister Stendahl, *The School of St. Matthew and Its Use of the Old Testament* (Lund: Gleerup, 1954), p. 35; also see H. Benedict Green, *The Gospel according to Matthew*, New Clarendon Bible (Oxford: Oxford University Press, 1975), p. 14. Stendahl's classification has also been adopted by Richard N. Longenecker, *Biblical Exegesis in the Apostolic Period* (Grand Rapids: Eerdmans, 1975), pp. 144–45.
24. Joseph A. Fitzmyer, "The Use of Explicit Old Testament Quotations in Qumran Literature and in the New Testament," *New Testament Studies* 7 (1961):331; every major section in the Dead Sea Scrolls Commentary on Habakkuk begins with either פשרו על or פשר הדבר, which in the Qumran community means "its prophetic interpretation" or "the interpretation of the prophetic word."
25. The Qumran Habakkuk commentary, column 2:10–12 reads, "Behold, I am raising up the Chaldeans . . . its prophetic meaning concerns the Kittim." Maurya Horgan notes that the Kittim are surely to be identified with the Romans and that the period to which the commentary refers is the Roman conquest in 63 B.C. (cf. *Pesharim: Qumran Interpretations of Biblical Books*, Catholic Biblical Monograph Series, no. 8 [Washington: Catholic Biblical Association of America, 1979], pp. 8, 26).
26. Brown, *The Birth of Messiah*, p. 102, n, 13,
27. W. D. Davies, *The Setting of the Sermon on the Mount* (Cambridge: University Press, 1964), pp, 209–10; see also David Hill, *The Gospel of Matthew*, New Century Bible Commentary (Grand Rapids, Eerdmans, l981), p. 36.
28. Cf. Brown, *The Birth of Messiah*, pp. 560–61.
29. In his book *The Old Testament in the New* S. Lewis Johnson proposes that the New Testament writers took into account the original intent of the Old Testament passages when they quoted those passages. He attempts to show that any approach that distorts the meaning of the Old Testament context runs the risk of denying inspiration.
30. Fitzmyer finds only seven places in which the original context was considered by the Qumran community ("The Use of Explicit Old Testament Quotations in Qumran Literature and in the New Testament," pp. 297–333), Elsewhere the community either modernized, accommodated, or applied the texts eschatologically (i.e., considered them strictly predictive).
31. In Gundry's controversial commentary on Matthew he proposed that Matthew is a Gospel written in the Jewish tradition of "midrash

and haggadah." The connection, however, that he makes between Matthew 2:15 and Hosea 11:1 is literal and historical. Even though his "preservation" motif is questionable (see n. 5), he feels the meaning of Hosea 11:1 is legitimately applied in the Matthean setting; hence Matthew's hermeneutic does not violate the contextual integrity of the Hosea passage. Thus the problem with Gundry is not his view of how Matthew used the Old Testament specifically (the problem with Stendahl) but his view of Matthew's alteration of the dominical tradition which thus results in a different picture of the Matthean tradition.

32. For the best survey of literature on the subject of typology, see Richard M. Davidson, *Typology In Scripture: A Study of Hermeneutical* ΤΥΠΟΣ *Structures*, Andrews University Seminary Doctoral Dissertation Series, no. 2 (Berrien Springs, MI: Andrews University Press, 1981), pp. 15–114. For a helpful discussion of modern definitions of "typology" see D. L. Baker, *Two Testaments, One Bible: A Study of Some Modern Solutions to the Theological Problem of the Relationship between the Old and New Testament* (Downers Grove, IL: InterVarsity, 1976), pp. 242–43.

33. C. T. Fritsch, "Biblical typology," *Bibliotheca Sacra* 104 (1947):214–22 (italics added); also see Leonard Goppelt, *Typos: The Typological Interpretation of the New*, trans. Donald H. Madvig (Grand Rapids: Eerdmans, 1982), pp. 17–18.

34. See A. B. Bruce, "Matthew," in *The Expositor's Greek Testament*, ed. W. Robertson Nicoll, 5 vols. (reprint, Grand Rapids: Eerdmans, 1979), 1:75; William Hendriksen, *Exposition of the Gospel according to Matthew* (Grand Rapids: Baker), 1973), pp. 178–79; Alfred Plummer, *An Exegetical Commentary on the Gospel according to Matthew* (reprint, Grand Rapids: Eerdmans, 1953), p. 19.

35. Brown, *The* Sensus Plenior *of Sacred Scripture*, p. 118.

36. K. J. Woolcombe, "The Biblical Origins and Patristic Development of Typology," in *Essays on Typology*, Studies in Biblical Theology, no. 22, ed. Geoffrey W. H. Lampe and Kenneth J. Woolcombe (Naperville, IL: Allenson, 1957), pp. 39–40.

37. Hans W. Wolff likewise develops the idea of typology as the "analogy" between the Old and New Testaments ("The Hermeneutics of the Old Testament," in *Essays on Old Testament Interpretation*, ed. Claus Westermann [Atlanta: Knox, 1963], pp. 167–81). Also see Gerhard von Rad, *Old Testament Theology*, trans. D. M. G. Stalker, 2 vols. (New York: Harper & Row, 1962), 2:363; he uses the term "structural analogies."

38. This writer does not deny a prefiguration typology in places where the Old Testament writer understood some aspect of a latent

antitype (see, e.g., Davidson, who suggests that Exodus 25:40 is an example of prefiguration; *Typology in Scripture*, pp. 367–88). However, in places where the New Testament author clearly draws a correspondence, it is preferable to speak of analogy rather than type. This seems to be the case with Matthew's use of Hosea 11:1.

39. W. F. Albright and C. S. Mann, *Matthew*, Anchor Bible (Garden City, NY: Doubleday, 1971), p. lxii (italics added). C. H. Dodd argues that the single verses in Old Testament quotations in the New were frequently pointers to the entire context (*According to the Scriptures: The Substructure of New Testament Theology* [London: Misbet, 1952], p. 126).

40. Davies sees Jesus as the new Moses who inaugurates a new exodus, Moses was the key figure in the Exodus from Egypt, the crossing of the Red Sea, the journey through the wilderness, and the reception of the Law. According to Davies, in a similar fashion Matthew portrayed Jesus as the central figure in the new exodus (Matt. 2), the baptism (Matt. 3), the temptation in the wilderness (Matt. 4), and the inauguration of New Covenant law (Matt. 5–7) (*The Setting of the Sermon on the Mount*, p. 78).

41. Cf. Dietrich Ritschl, "God's Conversion," *Interpretation* 15 (1961):297.

42. This view is quite compatible with the proposed nuance of πληρόω as "to complete" or "to establish" (see n. 9). Cf. Louis A. Barbieri, Jr., Matthew," in *The Bible Knowledge Commentary, New Testament*, ed. John F. Walvoord and Roy B. Zuck (Wheaton, IL: Victor, 1983), pp. 22–23.

43. Richard N. Longenecker, "Can We Reproduce the Exegesis of the New Testament?" *Tyndale Bulletin* 21 (1970): 3–38.

Chapter 9

1. To define and evaluate each of these views fully would require another article the length of this one. Those who desire this may consult this writer's "Cross-Bearing in Mark 8" (Th.M. thesis, Dallas Theological Seminary, 1982), pp. 4–23.

2. For example "Mark undoubtedly means actual martyrdom" (John Knox, "The Gospel according to St. Luke," in *The Interpreter's Bible*, ed. George A. Buttrick, 12 vols. [New York: Abingdon], 8 [1952]: 170); and Manson's comment that to "take up his cross" meant "the voluntary acceptance of martyrdom a the hands of the Roman Empire" (T. W. Manson, *The Sayings of Jesus as Recorded in the Gospels according to St. Matthew and St. Luke Arranged with Introduction and Commentary* [Grand Rapids: Ecrdmans, 1979], p. 131). Earnest Best cites some German works holding

this view (*Following Jesus: Discipleship in the Gospel of Mark* [Sheffield: JSNT, 1981], p. 50, n. 67). On pp. 38–39 he ably summarizes its major weaknesses.

3. Examples are Willoughby C. Allen, *A Critical and Exegetical Commentary on the Gospel according to S. Matthew*, 3d ed., International Critical Commentary (Edinburgh: Clark, 1912), pp. 111, 182; F. F. Bruce, *New Testament History* (Garden City, NY: Doubleday, 1972), p. 187; C. E. B. Cranfield, *The Gospel according to Saint Mark*, Cambridge Greek Testament Commentary (Cambridge: University Press, 1979), p. 282; Donald R. Fletcher, "Condemned to Die: The Legion on Cross-bearing: What Does it Mean?" *Interpretation* 18 (1964):163–64; Norval Geldenhuys, *Commentary on the Gospel of Luke*, New International Commentary on the New Testament (Grand Rapids: Eerdmans, 1951), p. 398 (on Luke 14:27; however, on Luke 9:23 Geldenhuys supports the suffering view); William L. Lane, *The Gospel according to Mark*, New International Commentary on the New Testament (Grand Rapids: Eerdmans, 1974), p. 308; John Peter Lange, *The Gospel according to Matthew*, trans. Phillip Schaff, *A Commentary on the Holy Scriptures,* vol. 8 (reprint, Grand Rapids: Zondervan, 1978), p. 303; Gilmour S. MacLean, "The Gospel according to St. Luke," in *The Interpreter's Bible*, 8 (1952):170; I. Howard Marshall, *The Gospel of Luke: A Commentary on the Greek Text*, New International Greek Testament Commentary (Grand Rapids: Eerdmans, 1978), pp. 372–73 (on p. 373 he also supports the self-denial view); Leon Morris, *The Cross in the New Testament* (Grand Rapids: Eerdmans, 1965), p. 26 (Morris supports several views); J. Oswald Sanders, *Bible Studies in Matthew's Gospel* (Grand Rapids: Zondervan, 1973), p. 62; R. V. G. Tasker, *The Gospel according to St. Matthew*, Tyndale New Testament Commentaries (Grand Rapids: Eerdmans, 1977), p. 109. Also note the *Theological Dictionary of the New Testament*, s.v. "σταυρός," by Johannes Schneider, 7 (1971):578, item b.

4. Marshall, *The Gospel of Luke*, p. 373. However, Hengel has observed, "It is striking that the metaphorical terminology is limited to the Latin sphere, whereas in the Greek world the cross is never, so far as I can see, used in a metaphorical sense. Presumably the word was too offensive for it to be used as a metaphor by the Greeks" (Martin Hengel, *Crucifixion in the Ancient World and the Folly of the Cross* [Philadelphia: Fortress, 1977], p. 68). Thus an interpretation based on the saying as a metaphor seems unlikely.

5. Sanders, *Bible Studies in Matthew's Gospel*, p. 62. Also see *Theological Dictionary of the New Testament*, s.v. "σταυρὸς," by

Johannes Schneider, 7 (1971): 579. Buttrick is poetic: "The cross is the plucking off of poor buds that one fine bud may come to flower; it is the pruning of the tree that there may be an abundant harvest" (George A. Buttrick, "The Gospel according to St. Matthew," in *The Interpreter's Bible*, 7 (1951): 374, see also p. 455; cf. David Hill, *The Gospel of Matthew*, New Century Bible Commentary (Grand Rapids: Eerdmans, 1981), p. 195; and Leon Morris, *The Gospel according to St. Luke*, Tyndale New Testament Commentaries (Grand Rapids: Eerdmans, 1974), p. 170.

6. Perhaps the best-known modern proponent of this view is Dietrich Bonhoeffer, who wrote, "the cross (for a disciple) means rejection and shame as well as suffering," and "if we refuse to take up our cross and submit to suffering and rejection at the hands of men, we forfeit our fellowship with Christ and have ceased to follow Him." Indeed "the cross is triumph over suffering" (*The Cost of Discipleship*, trans. R. H. Fuller, rev. ed. [London: SCM, 1959], pp. 77–81). Bultmann has suggested that σταυρός ("cross") might have been "a traditional metaphor for suffering and sacrifice" (cited in *Theological Dictionary of the New Testament*, s.v. "σταυρός," by Johannes Schneider, 7 [1971]: 578, n. 51). Colin Brown says, "for Jesus the inevitable, therefore, those who associate with Him as the Christ are liable to the same facts" (*New International Dictionary of New Testament Theology*, s.v. "Cross" 1 [1971]: 404). Lane presents an interesting theological speculation when he states "suffering with the Messiah is the condition of glorification with Him" (Lane, *The Gospel according to Mark*, p. 308). Hendriksen sees the disciples' cross as a "voluntary and decisive accepting of pain, shame and persecution" (William Hendriksen, *Exposition of the Gospel according to Mark*, New Testament Commentary [Grand Rapids: Baker, 1975], p. 330). Other supporters of the suffering view are Albert Barnes, *Barnes' Notes on the New Testament* (Grand Rapids: Kregel, 1962), p. 51. Calvin, *Institutes of the Christian Religion*, trans. Fred Lewis Battles, 2 vols. (Philadelphia: Westminster, 1960), 3.8.1–2 (1:765–67); Fletcher, "Condemned to Die," p. 159; Geidenhuys, *Commentary on the Gospel of Luke*, p. 276; R. C. H. Lenski, *The Interpretation of Dictionary of New Testament Theology*, s.v. "Cross," by Burghard Siede, 1:389–91; Ray Stedman, *The Servant Who Rules* (Waco, TX: Word, 1976), p. 215; Tertullian, "On Idolatry," in *The Anti-Nicene Fathers*, ed. Alexander Roberts and James Donaldson (Grand Rapids: Eerdmans), 3 (1976): 68. Luther commented, "In a word, a Christian, just because he is a Christian, . . . must suffer either at the hands of men or from the devil himself, who plagues

and terrifies him with tribulation, persecution, poverty, and sickness, or within the heart, with his poisonous darts" (cited in Ewald M. Plass, *What Luther Says: An Anthology*, 3 vols. [St. Louis: Concordia, 1959], 1:229).

7. *Theological Dictionary of the New Testament*, s.v. "σταυρός," by Johannes Schneider, 7 (1971): 580.

8. Sherman E. Johnson, *A Commentary on the Gospel according to St. Mark*, Harper's New Testament Commentaries (New York: Harper & Brothers, 1960), p. 151.

9. *Theological Dictionary of the New Testament*, s.v. "σταυρός," by Johannes Schneider, 7 (1971): 578.

10. Ibid., p. 578. n. 48.

11. Ibid., p. 578, n. 49.

12. Ibid., p. 579.

13. *The Midrash Rabbah* 56:3 (*Genesis*, vol. 1, trans. H. Freedman and Maurice Simon, 10 vols. [Oxford: Oxford University Press, n.d.], p. 493). This translation is somewhat different from the one noted by Brandenburger: "Abraham took the wood for sacrifice and laid it on his son Isaac, like one who bears the cross on his shoulders" (*New International Dictionary of New Testament Theology*, s.v. "Cross," by Egon Brandenburger, 1 [1974]: 403). Cf. Marshall, *The Gospel of Luke*, p. 374, and Gustaf Dalman, *Jesus-Jeshua Studies in the Gospels*, trans. Paul P. Levertoff (London: S.P.C.K., 1929). pp. 191–92.

14. Bonhoeffer, *The Cost of Discipleship*, p. 76. Bonhoeffer's interpretation, however, is the suffering view.

15. *Theological Dictionary of the New Testament*, s.v. "σταυρός," by Johannes Schneider, 7 (1971): 578, item c.

16. Marshall, *The Gospel of Luke*, p. 373: *New International Dictionary of New Testament Theology*, s.v. "Cross," by Egon Brandenburger, 1 (1975):403.

17. A. B. Bruce, *The Training of the Twelve* (reprint, Grand Rapids: Kregel, 1974), p. 183. However, Bruce's intrepetation of cross-bearing represents "troubles"; thus it is a minor variation of the suffering view.

18. Hans-Ruedi Weber, *The Cross: Tradition and Interpretation*, trans. Elke Jessett (Grand Rapids: Eerdmans, 1980), p. 123. Chrysostom, commenting on Matthew 16:24, said, "it will be impossible for thee even to be saved, unless thou thyself too be continually prepared for death" (Chrysostom, "Homily LV on Matt. 16:24," in *Nicene and Post-Nicene Fathers*, ed. Philip Schaff [reprint, Grand Rapids: Eerdmans, 1978], 10:338). Morris comments that "salvation comes from faith . . . an attitude of wholehearted trust" as seen in

the cross-bearing invitation (*The Cross in the New Testament*, p. 102).

19. Morris, *The Cross in the New Testament*, p. 393.
20. J. Gwyn Griffiths, "The Disciple's Cross," *New Testament Studies* 16 (July 1970): 364.
21. Morris, *The Cross in the New Testament*, p. 393.
22. Matthew 16:21 and Mark 8:31 are quite forceful on the central issue of being submissive to the Father's will through the use of δεις, "it is necessary, one must, one has to" (Walter Bauer, William F. Arndt, and F. Wilbur Gingrich, *A Greek-English Lexicon of the New Testament and Other Early Christian Literature* [Chicago: University of Chicago Press, 1957], p. 171). This term refers to "a necessity beyond human comprehension, grounded in the will of God" (Cranfield, *The Gospel according to Saint Mark*, p. 272). Cranfield suggests that δεῖ here probably refers to Scriptures such as Psalms 22; 118:10, 13, 18, 22; Isaiah 52:13–53:12; Daniel 7:21, 25; and Zechariah 13:7. However, Bennett seeks to refute this view and understands δεῖ as "a circumlocution which carried the weight of 'God has willed it'" (W. J. Bennett, Jr., "The Son of Man Must . . ." *Novum Testamentum* 17 [April 1975]:128). He further links δεῖ with γέγραπται in Mark 9:12 as being synonymous circumlocutions for "God wills it," as part of a general "eschatological drama" (ibid., pp. 128–29). In either event the divine necessity is clear enough, and Jesus' concern is not that Peter is dissuading Him from suffering, but that Peter was seeking to dissuade Him from obeying the Father's will.
23. Nineham says, "The blistering severity of Jesus' reply is evidence enough that what is at stake is a matter of quite central importance" (D. E. Nineham, *The Gospel of St. Mark,* Pelican New Testament Commentaries [New York: Penguin, 1977], p. 225).
24. The question of whether cross-bearing is soteriological or not is of great importance. The context in Mark seems to favor quite strongly a post-salvation situation, the view held by this author. For a helpful argument that the verb ἀκολουθέω does not connote salvation, and that not every μάθητης is a believer, see David Rae Kelly, "The Relation between Akoloutheō and Discipleship in Luke's Gospel" (Th.M. thesis, Dallas Theological Seminary, May 1979). DeBoer holds that in Mark "an equation of discipleship and salvation seems impossible" (Donald R. DeBoer, "Salvation and Discipleship in Mark" [Th.M. thesis, Dallas Theological Seminary, July 1979]), p. 28.
25. *Theological Dictionary of the New Testament*, s.v. "ὀπίσω," by Heinrich Seesemann, 5 (1967): 291.

26. Bauer, Arndt, and Gingrich, *A Greek-English Lexicon of the New Testament and Other Early Christian Literature*, p. 30. However, the United Bible Societies text here uses ἀκολουθέω. Neither reading affects the interpretation of cross-bearing. When it refers to individuals, it "is always the call to decisive and intimate discipleship of the earthly Jesus" (*Theological Dictionary of the New Testament*, s.v. "ἀκολουθέω," by Gerhard Kittel, 1 [1964]: 210–15, esp. p. 214). In contrast Lane sees this term as a reference "the common commitment to Jesus which distinguishes all Christians from those who fail to recognize Him as God's appointed Savior" (Lane, *The Gospel according to Mark*, p. 307).

27. Bauer, Arndt, and Gingrich, *A Greek-English Lexicon of the New Testament and Other Early Christian Literature*, p. 80.

28. Such an attempt would ultimately be futile unless one were first regenerated. The verse ἀπαρνησάσθω ("deny") and ἀράτω ("take up") are both aorist imperatives and probably are best understood as ingressive aorists.

29. Proponents of the submission view are practically nonexistent. One who comes close is Taylor who sees "to take up your cross" as meaning "to accept the last consequences of obedience . . . the cross as an instrument of death" (Vincent Taylor, *The Gospel according to Mark* [Grand Rapids: Baker, 1981], p. 381). He thus holds to a combination of the obedience and martyrdom views. It should be noted here that the submission view should not be understood to mean that the believer will not suffer for his faith in Christ. The Scriptures make this clear. Jesus is not advocating some type of asceticism or saying that enduring pain, grief, suffering, or even death are the way to follow Him. One's cross is not essentially any of these. A disciple is one who has ceased rebelling against the rule of the King and who is actively and continually submitting himself to His rule.
    F. J. Taylor makes an almost unprecedented statement when, after describing cross-bearing as an act of suffering, humility, and shame (he thus holds to the suffering views), he says, "to the Jew it was the public demonstration of servitude to the Roman overlord" (*A Theological Word Book of the Bible*, s.v. "Cross," by F. J. Taylor, p. 57, n. 23). This observation supports the submission interpretation. The only obedience proponent found by this student is J. Dwight Pentecost. He writes, "An individual's cross is the revealed will of God for him" (*The Words and Works of Jesus Christ* [Grand Rapids: Zondervan, 1981], p. 196) and to take up one's cross is to "accept God's will" for his life (ibid., p. 272). Pentecost stands alone (among scores of interpreters surveyed) in holding to the submission-to-

God's will view and in never mixing in even a little of the suffering or self-denial views. Some would add Lane to this list, for on Mark 8:34 he urges "a sustained willingness to say 'No' to oneself in order to be able to say 'Yes' to God" (Lane, *The Gospel according to Mark*, p. 307). This certainly sounds like the submission view of cross-bearing, and it would be if Lane were describing cross-bearing, but he is not. The quotation above is a description of "the central thought in self-denial." On the next page Lane describes cross-bearing as a "commitment" which "permitted no turning back, and if necessary, a willingness to submit to the cross in pursuance of the will of God" (ibid., p. 308). Thus Lane's interpretation of cross-bearing is actually potential martyrdom, or the commitment necessary to fulfill denying self.

30. Morris, *The Cross in the New Testament*, p. 293.
31. G. Campbell Morgan, *The Bible and the Cross* (New York: Revell, 1909), p. 93.
32. John Murray, *Redemption, Accomplished and Applied* (Grand Rapids: Eerdmans, 1955), p. 19. For a discussion of the righteousness of Christ being composed of passive obedience and active obedience see Charles Hodge, *Systematic Theology*, 3 vols. (reprint, Grand Rapids: Eerdmans, 1979), pp. 142–43.
33. *Encyclopedia of Christianity*, s.v. "Atonement," by John Murray, 1:467.
34. *Theological Dictionary of the New Testament*, s.v. "σταυρός," by Johannes Schneider, 7 (1971):575.
35. Many writers seek to understand this event in terms of similar pagan or even Jewish analogies. For an excellent refutation of these interpretations see Martin Hengel, *The Atonement*, trans. John Bowden (Philadelphia: Fortress, 1981).
36. Brooke Foss Westcott, *The Epistle to the Hebrews* (1892; reprint, Grand Rapids: Eerdmans, n.d.), p. 128. F. F. Bruce comments: "We know the sense in which the words are true of us; we learn to be obedient because of the unpleasant consequences which follow disobedience. It was not so with Him: He set out from the start on the path of obedience to God, and learned by the sufferings which came His way in consequence just what obedience to God involved in practice in the conditions of human life on earth" (*The Epistle to the Hebrews*, New International Commentary on the New Testament [Grand Rapids: Eerdmans, 1964], p. 103).
37. Calvin, *Institutes of the Christian Religion*, 3.8.2 (1:766–67).
38. Hengel, *Crucifixion in the Ancient World and the Folly of the Cross*, pp. 22–23. For a full listing of classical sources consulted see Green, "Cross-Bearing in Mark 8," pp. 62–65.

39. Ibid., p. 23.
40. *Theological Dictionary of the New Testament*, s.v. "σταυρός," by Johannes Schneider, 7 (1971):573.
41. Hengel, *Crucifixion in the Ancient World*, p. 76.
42. Plutarch *Moralia* 554B.
43. Chariton, cited by Hengel, *Crucifixion in the Ancient World*, p. 82 (italics added).
44. Hengel, *Crucifixion in the Ancient World*, p. 82.
45. The *crux* was the foremost of the Roman *summa supplicia* (supreme penalties). The other two were *crematio* (burning) and *decollatio* (decapitation) (Hengel, *Crucifixion in the Ancient World*, p. 23). There was also death by the beasts as well as other forms, often depending on the local situation.
46. F. F. Bruce, *New Testament History* (Garden City, NY: Doubleday, 1971), p. 201.
47. Hengel, *Crucifixion in the Ancient World*, p. 83. Hengel also gives a specific listing of crimes punished by crucifixion: "desertion to the enemy, the betraying of secrets, incitement to rebellion, murder, prophecy about the welfare of rulers (*de salute dominorum*), nocturnal impiety (*sacra impia nocturna*), magic (*ars magica*), serious cases of falsification of wills, etc." (ibid.).
48. Ibid., p. 88. In general the crucifixion of a Roman citizen was prohibited. Though a few exceptions occurred, they always were met with public indignation (*International Standard Bible Encyclopedia*, s.v. "Cross; Crucify," by D. G. Burke, 1 [1979]: 828). For a stirring statement of the Roman citizen's attitude on crucifixion consider Cicero. "Even if we are threatened with death, we may die free men. But the executioner, the veiling of the head, and the very word 'cross' should be far removed not only from the person of a Roman citizen but from his thoughts, his eyes, and ears. For it is not only the actual occurrence of these things or the endurance of them, but liability to them, the expectation, nay, the mere mention of them, that is unworthy of a Roman citizen and a free man" (Cicero *In Defense of Rabirius* 5.16, trans. H. Grose Hodge in Cicero, *The Speeches*, Loeb Classical Library [New York: Putnam's Sons, 1927]).
49. Tacitus *The Annals* 14.42–45. See also Seneca the Elder *Controversiae* 7.6, which illustrates the submission-rebellion theme present in crucifixion.
50. Hengel, *Crucifixion in the Ancient World*, p. 49.
51. *Theological Dictionary of the New Testament*, s.v. "σταυρός," by Johannes Schneider, 7 (1971): 573.
52. E. Benz, "Der gekreuzigte Gerecthe bie Plato, im NT v. in d. Alten Kirche," *AA Mainz* (1950):1055, cited in *Theological*

Dictionary of the New Testament, s.v. "σταυρός," by Johannes Schneider, 7 (1971): 574, n. 21.

53. *New International Dictionary of New Testament Theology*, s.v. "Cross," by Egon Brandenburger, 1 (1975): 392.

54. Ibid.

55. Hengel, *Crucifixion in the Ancient World*, p. 87.

56. *Theological Dictionary of the New Testament*, s.v. "σταυρός," by Johannes Schneider, 7 (1971): 574.

57. Ibid., p. 573. For an example of this see Dio *Roman History* 54.3.7. Sometimes that tablet was carried by a herald who preceded the offender.

58. For a detailed description of an actual crucified man see J. H. Charlesworth, "Jesus and Jehohanan: An Archaeological Note on Crucifixion," *Expository Times* 74 (February 1973): 147–50; and N. Haas, "Anthropological Observations on the Skeletal Remains from Giv'at Hamiutar," *Israel Exploration Journal* 20 (1970): 38–59.

59. Most encyclopedias list the types of crosses employed. Hengel has an important observation: "In view of the evidence from antiquity, it is incomprehensible that some scholars could have stated recently that crucifixion was 'by nature a bloodless form of execution'" (Hengel, *Crucifixion in the Ancient Word*, p. 31). For a description of the medical cause of death, see *Zondervan Pictorial Encyclopedia of the Bible*, s.v. "Crucifixion," by H. L. Drumwright, 1:1041.

60. See Hengel, *Crucifixion in the Ancient World*, p. 84. Also see 1 Corinthians 1:23 and Galatians 5:11.

61. Ibid. (citation of conclusion recorded by Y. Yadin).

62. *New International Dictionary of New Testament Theology*, s.v. "Cross," by Egon Brandenburger, 1 (1975):403.

63. Fletcher states that "cross-bearing was not a Jewish metaphor" ("Condemned to Die," p. 162). Dalmon notes that "the figurative application of this expression is in Rabbinic literature without example" (*Jesus-Jeshua Studies in the Gospels*, p. 191). However, a rabbinic example does exist (the Abrahamic-parallel view).

64. Harold W. Hoehner, *Chronological Aspects of the Life of Christ* (Grand Rapids: Zondervan, 1977), p. 143. The revolt at Sepphoris has been made well known largely through Barclay's commentary on Luke 9:23–27. He incorrectly says that Jesus was 11 years old when this happened: actually he was one year old (William Barclay, *The Gospel of Luke* [Philadelphia: Westminster, 1956], p. 122).

65. *Student Map Manual and Historical Geography of the Bible Lands*, map 13–5. Four miles is a straight line distance on a "line of communication" shown on this map. The distance is also given as

seven miles, apparently from a reference in *The Macmillan Bible Atlas* (New York: Macmillan, 1968), p. 142.

66. See Josephus *The Antiquities of the Jews* 17.10.5–10 and idem *The Jewish War* 2.4.1–2. Varus was in Syria from 6 B.C. to 4 B.C. and died in A.D. 9 in Germany.

67. Hengel, *Crucifixion in the Ancient World*, p. 85.

68. J. J. Blinzler, *Der Prozess Jesu* (1960):269, cited in *Theological Dictionary of the New Testament*, s.v. "σταυρός," by Johannes Schneider, 7 (1971): 574, n. 22.

69. See Matthew 27:48 and Luke 23:36, which record one of the soldiers offering Jesus the drink.

Chapter 10

1. Robert H. Stein, "Wine-Drinking in New Testament Times," *Christianity Today*, June 20, 1975, p. 19. Cf. Leon Morris, *The Gospel according to John* (Grand Rapids: Eerdmans, 1971), p. 179, footnote.

2. Morris, *The Gospel according to John*, p. 179.

3. Henry George Liddell and Robert Scott, *A Greek-English Lexicon* (Oxford: Clarendon, 1958), p. 363.

4. Frederick Louis Godet, *Commentary on the Gospel of John*, 2 vols. (1893; reprint, Grand Rapids: Zondervan, n.d.), 1:347.

5. Walter Bauer, William F. Arndt, and F. Wilbur Gingrich, *A Greek-English Lexicon of the New Testament and Other Early Christian Literature* (Chicago: University of Chicago Press, 1957), p. 500.

6. B. F. Westcott, *The Gospel according to St. John* (1881; reprint, Grand Rapids: Eerdmans, 1954), p. 36.

Chapter 11

1. Charles R. Smith, "The Unfruitful Branches in John 15," *Grace Journal* 9 (Spring 1968): 10.

2. J. C. Ryle, *Expository Thoughts on the Gospels,* 4 vols. (Grand Rapids: Zondervan, n.d.), 4:334.

3. J. Carl Laney, "Abiding Is Believing: The Analogy of the Vine in John 15:1–6," *Bibliotheca Sacra* 146 (January–March 1989): 64.

4. Six of the 16 occurrences refer to the Father being in the Son. They are 10:38; 14:10 (twice), 11; and 17:21, 23. And one verse (14:30) speaks of Satan's having nothing "in Me," that is, having no true fellowship with Christ.

5. Walter Bauer, William F. Arndt, and F. Wilbur Gingrich, *A Greek-English Lexicon of the New Testament and Other Early Christian Literature*, 2d ed., rev. F. Wilbur Gingrich and Frederick W. Danker (Chicago: University of Chicago Press, 1979), p. 259.

6. *The New International Dictionary of New Testament Theology,* s.v. "Prepositions and Theology in the Greek New Testament," by M. J. Harris, 3:1191.

7. In John 14:10 "in Me" refers to a close working relationship between Christ and the Father, a unity of purpose.

8. In 14:20 the Lord said that "in that day" they would know that He was in them and they were in Him ("you in Me and I in you"). This means that when they would see Him in His resurrected state, they would know again the fellowship they had with Him before. "That day" could refer to either the coming of the Holy Spirit at Pentecost or the appearances of the resurrected Christ to His disciples. The previous verse seems to connect it with the resurrection appearances. This is confirmed in 16:16, where He also spoke of the fact that in a little while they would no longer behold Him and then in a little while they would see Him, a reference to His appearance in resurrection.

The meaning then is that, when they would see Christ in resurrection, they would understand fully some things they did not fully understand before. The objective knowledge of the resurrected Christ would bring about this clear perception. At that time they would see clearly that Christ had been operating in complete unity of purpose with the Father and that they were in complete unity of purpose with Him. Apparently they would know something they did not know before. They were already regenerate, but there was something they either did not know at all or knew only imperfectly. What would bring about the change? The New Testament does not say, but later John stated that before the resurrection the disciples did not understand that He had to rise from the dead (John 20:9). Apparently seeing Christ resurrected brought a flood of understanding concerning the Old Testament predictions and Christ's unity of purpose with and obedience to the Father. The resurrection removed doubts about who Christ is and resulted in a change that lasted the rest of their lives. They committed themselves fully to follow Him forever. That commitment brought about by their seeing Christ in His resurrection on "that day" resulted in their total unity of purpose and obedience to Him. That is when they knew the experience of unity and fellowship, "you in Me and I in you," with their resurrected Lord.

9. Bauer, Arndt, and Gingrich, *A Greek-English Lexicon of the New Testament and Other Early Christian Literature,* p. 259.

10. *Webster's Ninth New Collegiate Dictionary* (Springfield, MA: Merriam-Webster, 1987), p. 44.

11. For example Hauck says it means "to stay in a place," figuratively

"to remain in a sphere," "to stand against opposition, to endure, to hold fast" (*Theological Dictionary of the New Testament*, s.v. μένω, by F. Hauck, 4:574–88). The word is used of the permanence of God in contrast to human mutability. God's counsel "endures" (Rom. 9:11), His Word endures (1 Pet. 1:23, 25), the New Covenant endures (2 Cor. 3:11), and faith, hope, and love endure (1 Cor. 13:13). Paul used μένω of the perseverance of believers in the faith (1 Tim. 2:15). If they endure, they will reign with Him. But if they are faithless, He "remains" faithful (2 Tim. 2:12–13). Munzer says μένω "means to remain, e.g., to stay in a place (Luke 19:5), or with someone (Luke 24:29; Matt. 26:38); to continue to exist for a specific time (Matt. 11:23); to live (John 1:38); or metaphorically to hold fast, or remain steadfast, e.g., in a teaching (2 Tim. 3:14; 2 John 9), in fellowship with (John 14:10), in the unmarried state (1 Cor. 7:40), to stand firm, pass the test, e.g., when one's works are judged (1 Cor. 3:14); to live on, and not to have died (1 Cor. 15:6)" (*The New International Dictionary of New Testament Theology*, s.v. "Remain," by Karlfried Munzer, 3:224).

12. John used μένω frequently, 66 of the 118 times it occurs in the New Testament (40 in John, 23 in 1 John, and 3 in 2 John).

13. Edwin A. Blum, "John," in *The Bible Knowledge Commentary, New Testament*, ed. John F. Walvoord and Roy B. Zuck (Wheaton, IL: Victor, 1983), p. 325.

14. "Abiding in Christ is the same as bearing fruit (John 15:5). If there is no fruit, it is a sign that the fellowship has already been interrupted (John 15:6; 1 John 3:6)" (Munzer, "Remain," p. 226).

15. *The International Standard Bible Encyclopedia*, s.v. "Vine," by R. K. Harrison, 4 (1988): 986.

16. Laney, "Abiding Is Believing: The Analogy of the Vine in John 15:1–6," p. 59.

17. Harrison, "Vine," p. 986. Harrison states that αἴρει in John 15:2 is from αἴρω, "to lift," not from αἱρέω, "to catch, take away."

18. Laney, "Abiding Is Believing: The Analogy of the Vine in John 15:1–6," p. 61.

19. Ibid., p. 64. Laney calls it being in the sphere of Christ and under His influence.

20. Ibid.

21. Lewis Sperry Chafer, *Systematic Theology*, 8 vols. (Dallas, TX: Dallas Seminary Press, 1948; reprint [8 vols. in 4], Grand Rapids: Kregel, 1992), 7:4.

22. Laney, "Abiding Is Believing: The Analogy of the Vine in John 15:1–6," p. 61.

23. A metonym is a figure of speech in which the name of one thing is

used for that of another of which it is an attribute or with which it is associated.

Chapter 12

1. In light of the chronological and other difficulties, de Vaux says that "it is not possible to write a well-ordered history of the period of the Judges" (Roland de Vaux, *The Early History of Israel*, trans. David Smith [Philadelphia: Westminster, 1978], p. 693).
2. Edwin R. Thiele, *The Mysterious Numbers of the Hebrew Kings* (Grand Rapids: Eerdmans, 1965).
3. Peter R. Ackroyd, *Exile and Restoration* (Philadelphia: Westminster, 1968), esp. pp. 17–38.
4. For a recent resume see Edwin M. Yamauchi, "The Archaeological Background of Nehemiah," *Bibliotheca Sacra* 137 (October–December 1980): 292–95.
5. See, for example, John Bright, *A History of Israel* (Philadelphia: Westminster, 1972), pp. 190–91; John H. Hayes and J. Maxwell Miller, *Israelite and Judaean History* (Philadelphia: Westminster, 1977), pp. 682–83; and Leon Wood, *A Survey of Israel's History* (Grand Rapid: Zondervan, 1970), p. 260.
6. This date is defended on pages 129-30.
7. See pages 130-31.
8. Many scholars reject the figures given because of their alleged artificiality. It is true that there are many instances of 20–, 40–, and even 80–year periods, but this need not indicate artificiality. There may, rather, be approximations (rounded figures) similar to that assigned to David's reign. First Kings 2:11 says he reigned 40 years whereas 2 Samuel 5:4–5 gives a total of 40 and one-half years. The 40 is obviously a round number. Moreover, the number 40 and its multiples is a frequently recurring biblical number with clearly symbolical import (see Gen. 7:4. 12; 25:20; 26:34; Ex. 16:35; 24:18; 34:28; 1 Sam. 17:16; Ezek. 4:6; 29:11; 41:2; Jonah 3:4; Matt. 4:2). Besides, if these numbers 20, 40, and 80 are artificial in Judges, why are there also the numbers 6, 7, 8, 10, 18, and others?
9. A comprehensive statement of the problem and the various attempts to resolve it may be found as long ago as 1868 in C. F. Keil and Franz Delitzsch, *Biblical Commentary on the Old Testament: Joshua, Judges, Ruth* (1868; reprint, Grand Rapids: Eerdmans, 1960), pp. 276–92.
10. Judges 10:7 says that Yahweh gave Israel over to the Philistines and the Ammonites "who that year shattered and crushed them" (NIV). The antecedent of "who" (*waw* consecutive in Hebrew) can

be either the Ammonites or both the Ammonites and Philistines. Since the subject of verse 7 is compound, one logically assumes that the "they" of verse 8 is also compound. In support of this see G. F. Moore, *A Critical and Exegetical Commentary on Judges* (New York: Scribner's Sons, 1895), p. 277.

11. The United Bible Societies Greek Text cites in support of the Textus Receptus only D, E, P, פ, and some 19 uncials and minuscules (*The Greek New Testament*, ed. Kurt Aland et al., 3d ed. [New York: American Bible Society, 1975], p. 466). In support of Westcott and Hort are p⁷⁴, א, A, B, C, and a few minuscules.

12. The crucial difference between the two readings concerns the phrase "about 450 years." The Textus Receptus requires that the 450 years follow the conquest of Canaan whereas the Westcott and Hort reading requires that it precede and include the time of conquest.

13. This NIV translation is not in the Greek text, which reads literally, "gave their land as an inheritance for about 450 years." "All this" is, however, an appropriate rendition for it introduces a concluding statement summarizing all of God's dealings with His people, beginning with verse 17.

14. See, for example, R. C. H. Lenski, *The Interpretation of the Acts of the Apostles* (Minneapolis: Augsburg, 1961), p. 519. He argues that the total of 450 years comes from the 400 of the sojourn plus 40 in the wilderness plus 10 of conquest. The problem with this is that it requires a 400–year sojourn rather than the 430–year period clearly indicated in Exodus 12:40. It does no good for Lenski to cite Stephen's reference to 400 years in Acts 7:6 since Stephen is only quoting Genesis 15:13, a passage which is certainly using "hundred" for century as Genesis 15:16 ("fourth generation") clearly suggests. See H. H. Rowley, *From Joseph to Joshua* (London: Oxford University Press, 1950), pp. 69–70.

15. This is seldom if ever noted by the commentators. Bruce says, "It [Acts 13:20] is best explained as covering the 400 years' sojourning, . . . the 40 years in the wilderness, and the time that elapsed between the entry into Canaan and the distribution of the land in Josh. xiv" (*The Acts of the Apostles* [London: Tyndale, 1951], p. 264). But the Greek sentence clearly begins with verse 17, which describes God's election of the fathers. Unless qualified, the term "fathers" always refers to the patriarchs. It is arbitrary to commence the 450 years with the beginning of the sojourn.

16. This is immediately evident from the fact that 1 Kings 6:1 allots only 480 years from the Exodus to the fourth year of Solomon. If the period of the judges is 450 years, the total span from the Exodus

to the temple would be closer to 618 years (40 years wandering + 10 years conquest + 450 years of judges + 34 years of Samuel + 40 years of Saul + 40 years of David + 4 years of Solomon). It is this consideration that forces many scholars to opt for the Westcott and Hort text and place the 450 years before the period of the judges. This concession is made by Bruce (*Acts*, p. 264).

17. The expression "young man" translates the Hebrew נַעַר, which means either a "youth" (usually a boy or lad) or "a personal valet or servant" (Francis Brown, S. R. Driver, and C. A. Briggs, *A Hebrew and English Lexicon of the Old Testament* ([Oxford: Clarendon Press, 1972], pp. 654–55). The latter is almost certainly the meaning in Exodus 33:11 since it appears to be epexegetical to מְשָׁרְתוֹ ("his assistant").

18. It is frequently pointed out that the Conquest was completed by the time Caleb requested his inheritance; and since this was about 1400 B.C. when Caleb was 85 years of age (Josh. 14:7–10), the era of the judges must have begun shortly after 1400. But the assumption that Othniel, the first judge and nephew of Caleb, began his tenure immediately after the disposition of Caleb's inheritance is extremely tenuous. As was mentioned above, the "cycle of sin" which marked the initiation of the period of the Judges did not begin until Joshua and even his younger contemporaries had died. Moreover, there appear to be hints in Joshua 14–24 of the passing of considerable time between the granting of Caleb's request and Joshua's death (see 18:1–7; 22:1–3; 24:29–31).

19. The notoriously difficult text of 1 Samuel 13:1 reads, according to the Masoretic text, "Saul was ____ years old when he became king, and he reigned over Israel for two years." An alternate (and necessary) translation of the second clause is "and when he had reigned over Israel for two years. . . ." There is a problem with the form of the noun here (שְׁתֵּי שָׁנִים for the expected שְׁנָתַיִם), which may explain the NIV "forty-two years." However, the plural is also attested with the number two (cf. E. Kautzsch, ed., *Gesenius' Hebrew Grammar*, 2d English ed. [Oxford: Clarendon, 1910], p. 433, 134e). Both Josephus (*The Antiquities of the Jews* 6.14.9) and Paul indicate 40 years, perhaps a rounding off of 42. For the lacuna in the Masoretic text a few Septuagint minuscules supply "30," a reasonable conjecture but only a conjecture. With these suggestions in view one may translate the verse, "Saul was 30 years old when he became king, and when he had reigned over Israel two years. . . ."

20. Many scholars argue that Ishvi of 1 Samuel 14:49 is none other

than Ish-bosheth (so H. W. Hertzberg, *I and II Samuel* [Philadelphia: Westminster 1976], p. 120). The original יִשְׁוִי (Septuagint יִשְׁוִי) going to the later אֶשְׁבַּעַל (= אִישׁ בֹּשֶׁת). It is much more likely, however, that Ishvi is the same as the Abinadab of 1 Chronicles 10:2, for the list of sons there is identical to that of 1 Samuel 14:49 if this equation is made. Otherwise one cannot identify Abinadab. In addition in both 1 Chronicles 8:33 and 9:39 Esh-baal (Ish-bosheth) is listed with the other three sons, including Abinadab but not Ishvi. The implication is clear—Ish-bosheth was born after Saul became king.

21. This apparently arbitrary date is the result of a chronological reconstruction far too complex to be dealt with here in detail. It must suffice to say that the battle of Ebenezer, which ended the 40-year oppression by the Philistines (1 Sam. 7:12–14), must be dated at 1084 B.C. because the oppression had begun in 1124 as has already been shown. Meanwhile the ark of Yahweh had remained at Kiriath-jearim for 20 years, right to the time of the battle of 1084 (1 Sam. 7:2–3). And of course the ark was taken to Kiriath-jearim in the very year Shiloh was destroyed and Eli died (1 Sam. 4:11, 18; cf. 6:1). Finally it seems that Samuel's recognition as a prophet surely preceded the taking of the ark by the Philistines, an event which occurred in 1104 on the basis of the foregoing argument.

22. This date is based on the fact that Jephthah's judgeship began three hundred years after the conquest of the Transjordan (Judg. 11:26), or in 1106, and 18 years after the beginning of the Ammonite oppression (10:8). This means that the Ammonite (and Philistine) oppression commenced in 1124.

23. If Samson did not die before the battle of Ebenezer, then the statement in 1 Samuel 7:13 that "the Philistines were subdued and came no more within the border of Israel" is inaccurate since they came at least as far as the Valley of Sorek to arrest Samson (Judg. 16:4–5).

24. This is the conclusion of practically all conservative scholars, though insufficient attention has been paid by them to Paul's obvious consideration of the formula of judgeship. The apostle adopted the formula as his organizing principle rather than the literary limits of the Book of Judges alone.

25. See note 2 above.

26. For excellent studies see J. Barton Payne, "The Validity of Numbers in Chronicles," *Bibliotheca Sacra* 136 (July–September 1979): 214–18; and J. W. Wenham, "Large Numbers in the Old Testament," *Tyndale Bulletin* 18 (1967): 19–53.

27. In the so-called "Six-day War" of 1967, Israel mustered an army

of 60,000 regulars and 204,000 reservists in a nation of fewer than three million people. At the same ratio of military to total population, Old Testament Israel and Judah must have had a population of at least 12 million. See *Lightning Out of Israel* (New York: Associated Press, 1967), p. 51.

28. In an unvocalized text there would be no difference between '*alp* meaning "thousand" and '*alp* meaning "chieftain" or "commander." As Payne shows, "chieftain" is no doubt often intended where the Masoretic text has "thousand" ("The Validity of Numbers," pp. 214–18). So Abijah, then, had four hundred '*alluph's* ("chosen men"), while Jeroboam had eight hundred, some five hundred of whom were slain. '*Alluph* is derived from '*alaph* I, "be linked with" or "be familiar with." See Ludwig Koehler and Walter Baumgartner, eds., *Lexicon in Veteris Testament Libros* (Leiden: Brill, 1953), p. 52.

29. T. Jacobsen, *The Sumerian King List* (Chicago: University of Chicago Press, 1939), esp. pp. 158–64.

30. For examples of these texts which mention kings on the list who appear to be generations apart but are actually contemporary, see Jacobsen, *The Sumerian King List*, pp. 178–90.

Chapter 13

1. Walter Lüthi, *The Letter to the Romans: An Exposition*, trans. Kurt Schoenenberger (Richmond, VA: Knox, 1961), p. 19.

2. There is nothing unusual about the Hebrew adjectives זר and נכריה translated "strange" in the KJV, except perhaps their emphatic position. That is their meaning. The NASB has "unusual" and "extraordinary."

3. Martin prefers to define the subjects: "the Greek religious type, man without special revelation," but the sense is the same (James P. Martin, "The Kerygma of Romans," *Interpretation* 25 [July 1971]: 311.

4. Natural revelation exists, but its light is not fully appropriated because of human sin. *Notitia* and *assensus*, two of the basic elements of faith, may be present as a result of God's revelation of Himself in nature, but the vital element of faith, *fiducia*, is never given through natural revelation. In its place is the rebellion of suppression. Cf. John Calvin, *Institutes of the Christian Religion*, ed. John T. McNeill, trans. Ford Lewis Battles, 2 vols. (Philadelphia: Westminster, 1960); T. H. L. Parker, *Calvin's Doctrine of the Knowledge of God* (Grand Rapids: Eerdmans, 1959); Edward A. Dowey, Jr., *The Knowledge of God in Calvin's Theology* (New York: Columbia University Press, 1965). An article

of some worth by Gerald J. Postema is "Calvin's Alleged Rejection of Natural Revelation," *Scottish Journal of Theology* 24 (November 1971): 423–34.

5. Godet thinks there is more than vigor here; there is a feeling of indignation. He writes, "The verses have something of that παραξυσμός, that exasperation of heart, of which the author of the Acts speaks (17:16) when describing Paul's impressions during his stay at Athens" (F. Godet, *Commentary on the Epistle to the Romans*, trans. A. Cusin, 2 vols. [Edinburgh: Clark, 1881], 1:177).

6. The Byzantine text and some of the leading representatives of the Western text have a καί (KJV, "also") following διό. If this were genuine, it would suggest the harmony of the nature of the punishment and the offense. Godet has put it well, "They sinned, wherefore God punished them; they sinned by degrading God, wherefore also God degraded them" (ibid.). Zahn seems to incline toward its genuineness, too (Theodor Zahn, *Der Brief des Paulus an die Römer* [Leipzig: 1910], p. 96).

7. C . M. J. Lagrange, *Saint Paul Épitre aux Romains*, 4th ed. (Paris: Gabalda 1930), p. 28. He remarks that the term's threefold occurrence is not climactic, but is a kind of refrain.

8. Cf. Heinrich August Wilhelm Meyer, *Critical and Exegetical Handbook to the Epistle to the Romans*, trans. John C. Moore, 2 vols. (Edinburgh: Clark, 1881), p. 86.

9. Godet, *Commentary on the Epistle to the Romans*, 1:177–78.

10. The clause may be translated, "'he stripped (them) of his own foresight."

11. The words may be rendered, "he delivers him over for further suffering."

12. Meyer, *Critical and Exegetical Handbook to the Epistle to the Romans*, 1:86.

13. John Murray, *The Epistle to the Romans*, 2 vols. (Grand Rapids: Eerdmans, 1959), p. 44.

14. Charles Hodge, *Commentary on the Epistle to the Romans* (Philadelphia: Westminster, 1886), p. 40.

15. Cf. Otto Michel, *Der Brief an die Römer*, 11th ed. (Göttengen: Vanderhoeck & Ruprecht, 1955), p. 58; and Zahn, *Der Brief des Paulus an die Römer*, pp. 96-97. Both point out that Paul's expression must not be weakened, but neither develops the question theologically.

16. Schlatter points out that παρέδωκεν is the usual word for the sentence of a judge (Adolf von Schlatter, *Gottes Gerechtigkeit* [Stuttgart: Calwer, 1959]), p. 66).

17. Murray, *The Epistle to the Romans,* 1:44–45.

18. *Theological Dictionary of the New Testament*, s.v. "δίδωμι et al.," by Friedrich Buchsel, 2:170. The positive force is present in each occurrence.
19. Hodge, *Commentary on the Epistle to the Romans*, p. 45.
20. "Homosexuality," *Time*, October 24, 1969, p. 82.
21. Of course the truth of the matter is that homosexuality is a perversion of the created order (C. K. Barrett, *A Commentary on the Epistle to the Romans* [New York: Harper, 1957], p. 39).
22. "The Homosexual: Newly Visible, Newly Understood," *Time*, October 31,1969, p. 65.
23. Cf. I. E. Howard, "The Fever Chart of a Sick Society," *Christian Economics*, April 6, 1965, p. 4. Howard's brief article is very suggestive, and the writer is deeply indebted to it.
24. Ibid.
25. Hodge, *Commentary on the Epistle to the Romans*, p. 45.
26. Cf. Barrett, *A Commentary on the Epistle to the Romans*, 38. He writes, "God's judgment has already broken forth; only He has consigned sinners not to hell but to sin—if indeed these be alternatives."
27. Cf. "Doctrinal Changes at Fuller," *Christianity Today*, May 7, 1971, pp. 39–40.
28. The twofold use of the adjective αἰώνιον ("'everlasting") with κόλασιν ("eternal") and ζωήν ("life") indicates that the punishment for sin is just as long as the life God gives the faithful. Both are eternal. Many other passages express the same truth.
29. Cf. Augustus Hopkins Strong, *Systematic Theology*, rev. ed., 3 vols. (Philadelphia: Judson, 1907), pp. 1052–53.
30. Cf. M. D. Hooker, "Adam in Romans 1," *New Testament Studies* 6 (July 1960): 301.

Chapter 14

1. R. C. H. Lenski, *The Interpretation of St. Paul's Epistle to the Romans* (Minneapolis: Augsburg, 1961), p. 550.
2. Thomas Watson, *All Things for Good* (1663; reprint, Edinburgh: Banner of Truth, 1986), p. 10.
3. Source unidentified.
4. John A. Witmer, "Romans," in *The Bible Knowledge Commentary, New Testament*, ed. John F. Walvoord and Roy B. Zuck (Wheaton, IL: Victor, 1983), p. 473.
5. J. N. Darby, *The "Holy Scriptures," A New Translation* (reprint, Kingston-on-Thames: Stow Hill Bible & Tract Depot, 1949); Gerrit Verkuyl, ed., *The Modern Language Bible: The New Berkeley Version* (Grand Rapids: Zondervan, 1969); *The Twentieth Century*

New Testament: A Translation into Modern English (reprint, Chicago: Moody, n.d.).

6. Frederic Louis Godet, *Commentary on Romans* (1883; reprint, Grand Rapids: Kregel, 1977), p. 322 (italics his).

7. H. A. W. Meyer, *Critical and Exegetical Hand-Book to the Epistle to the Romans* (1883; reprint, Winona Lake, IN: Alpha, 1979), p. 333.

8. Most English versions translate the particle as "and"; several omit the particle entirely.

9. J. B. Rotherham, *The Emphasized New Testament* (reprint, Grand Rapids: Kregel, 1959).

10. Lenski, *The Interpretation of St. Paul's Epistle to the Romans,* p. 550.

11. William Hendriksen, *Exposition of Paul's Epistle to the Romans,* New Testament Commentary (Grand Rapids: Baker, 1980), pp. 278–79 (italics his).

12. Lenski, *The Interpretation of St. Paul's Epistle to the Romans,* p. 551.

13. "A neuter plural subject regularly takes a singular verb" (H. E. Dana and Julius R. Mantey, *A Manual Grammar of the Greek New Testament* [reprint, New York: Macmillan, 1967], p. 165).

14. James D. G. Dunn, *Romans 1–8,* Word Biblical Commentary (Dallas, TX: Word, 1988), p. 481. See the literature cited. See also *The New International Dictionary of New Testament Theology,* s.v. "Work, Do, Accomplish," by Hans-Christoph Hahn, 3:1152 and the references cited.

15. See United Bible Societies, *The Greek New Testament,* 3d ed. (New York: American Bible Society, 1975).

16. Hendriksen, *Exposition of Paul's Epistle to the Romans,* p. 279.

17. J. B. Rotherham, *The Emphasized New Testament; The Twentieth Century New Testament; The New Berkeley Version; The New Testament of the Jerusalem Bible;* the *New American Standard Bible;* and the *Revised Standard Version.*

18. William Barclay, *The New Testament: A New Translation* (Cleveland: Foundation, 1976), p. 324.

19. Hendriksen, *Exposition of Paul's Epistle to the Romans,* pp. 279–80.

20. *Theological Dictionary of the New Testament,* s.v. "ἀγαθὸς," by Walter Grundmann, 1:17.

21. Watson, *All Things for Good,* p. 11.

22. Dunn, *Romans 1–8,* p. 481.

23. Lenski, *The Interpretation of St. Paul's Epistle to the Romans,* p. 551.

24. Watson, *All Things for Good,* p. 66.
25. Lenski, *The Interpretation of St. Paul's Epistle to the Romans,* p. 550.
26. C. F. Hogg and W. E. Vine, *The Epistles of Paul the Apostle to the Thessalonians* (reprint, Grand Rapids: Kregel, 1959), p. 105.
27. John Murray, *The Epistle to the Romans,* New International Commentary (Grand Rapids: Eerdmans, 1959), p. 314.
28. *Theological Dictionary of the New Testament,* s.v. "ἀγαράω," by Ethelbert Stauffer, 1:50.
29. Lenski, *The Interpretation of St. Paul's Epistle to the Romans,* pp. 553–54.
30. Ibid., p. 555.
31. William Kelly, *Notes on the Epistle of Paul the Apostle to the Romans* (London: Morrish, 1873; reprint, n.d.), p. 153.
32. Meyer, *Critical and Exegetical Hand-Book to the Epistle to the Romans,* p. 335.
33. *Theological Dictionary of the New Testament,* s.v. "προνοέω, πρόνοια," by J. Behm, 4:1016.
34. Murray, *The Epistle to the Romans,* p. 318.
35. Dunn, *Romans 1–8,* p. 483.
36. Kenneth S. Wuest, *Romans in the Greek New Testament for the English Reader* (Grand Rapids: Eerdmans, 1955), p. 145.
37. W. E. Vine, *An Expository Dictionary of New Testament Words,* 2 vols. in 1 (Westwood, NJ: Revell, 1940), 2:247.
38. Hendriksen, *Exposition of Paul's Epistle to the Romans,* p. 283 (italics his).
39. Lenski, *The Interpretation of St. Paul's Epistle to the Romans,* p. 561.
40. Dunn, *Romans 1–8,* p. 483.
41. R. Govett, *The Righteousness of God, The Salvation of the Believer: or, The Argument of the Romans* (Norwich: Fletcher and Son, 1891; reprint, Miami Springs, FL: Conley and Schoettle, 1981, under the title *Govett on Romans*), p. 368.
42. Vine, *An Expository Dictionary of New Testament Words,* 2:104.

Chapter 15

1. G. G. Findlay, "The First Epistle of Paul to the Corinthians," in *The Expositor's Greek New Testament,* 5 vols. (Grand Rapids: Eerdmans, n.d.), 2:870; Archibald Robertson and Alfred Plummer, *A Critical and Exegetical Commentary on the First Epistle of St Paul to the Corinthians,* International Critical Commentary (Edinburgh: Clark, n.d.), p. 228; F. W. Grosheide, *The First Epistle to the Corinthians,* New International Commentary on the New Testament (Grand Rapids: Eerdmans, 1953), p. 248.

2. Charles J. Ellicott, *St. Paul's First Epistle to the Corinthians: With a Critical and Grammatical Commentary* (Minneapolis: James Family, 1978), p. 199; Robertson and Plummer, *A Critical and Exegetical Commentary on the First Epistle of St Paul to the Corinthians,* p. 228; W. Harold Mare, "1 Corinthians," in *The Expositor's Bible Commentary,* 12 vols. (Grand Rapids: Zondervan, 1976), 10:254. All these commentators see Paul introducing this topic on his own.

3. Findlay, "The First Epistle of Paul to the Corinthians," 2:871.

4. Robertson and Plummer, *A Critical and Exegetical Commentary on the First Epistle of St Paul to the Corinthians,* p. 228, first footnote.

5. See 1 Corinthians 1:4–9 and other Pauline introductions. The term used to describe such introductions is *Captatio Benevolentiae.*

6. Walter Bauer, William F. Arndt, and F. Wilbur Gingrich, A *Greek-English Lexicon of the New Testament and Other Early Christian Literature,* 2d ed., rev. F. Wilbur Gingrich and Frederick W. Danker (Chicago: University of Chicago Press, 1979), p. 423.

7. Ellicott, *St. Paul's First Epistle to the Corinthians,* p. 199; Robert G. Gromacki, *Called to Be Saints* (Grand Rapids: Baker, 1977), p. 133; Leon Morris, *The First Epistle of Paul to the Corinthians,* Tyndale New Testament Commentaries (Grand Rapids: Eerdmans, 1958), p. 151; Findlay, "The First Epistle of Paul to the Corinthians," 2:871.

8. Frederick Louis Godet, *Commentary on First Corinthians* (Grand Rapids: Kregel, 1977), p. 615.

9. Bauer, Arndt, and Gingrich, *A Greek-English Lexicon of the New Testament and Other Early Christian Literature,* p. 615.

10. Gordon D. Fee, *The First Epistle to the Corinthians,* New International Commentary on the New Testament (Grand Rapids: Eerdmans, 1987), pp. 491–92.

11. F. Blass and A. Debrunner, *A Greek Grammar of the New Testament and Other Early Christian Literature* (Chicago: University of Chicago Press, 1961), p. 262.

12. Bauer, Arndt, and Gingrich, *A Greek-English Lexicon of the New Testament and Other Early Christian Literature,* p. 171; Ellicott, *St. Paul's First Epistle to the Corinthians,* p. 199.

13. Bruce K. Waltke, "1 Corinthians 11:2–16: An Interpretation," *Bibliotheca Sacra* 135 (January–March 1978): 48.

14. Robertson and Plummer, *A Critical and Exegetical Commentary on the First Epistle of St Paul to the Corinthians,* p. 229; Findlay, "The First Epistle of Paul to the Corinthians."

15. See F. F. Bruce, *1 and 2 Corinthians,* New Century Bible

Commentary (Grand Rapids: Eerdmans, 1971), p. 103; C. K. Barrett, *The First Epistle to the Corinthians* (New York: Harper & Row, 1968), p. 248; Fee, *The First Epistle to the Corinthians*, p. 502, n. 42.

16. *Evangelical Dictionary of Theology*, s.v. "Arianism," by V. L. Walter, pp. 74–75.

17. John F. Walvoord, *Jesus Christ Our Lord* (Chicago: Moody, 1969), pp. 42–46.

18. For further support of this view see David K. Lowery, "The Headcovering and Lord's Supper in 1 Corinthians 11:2–34," *Bibliotheca Sacra* 143 (April–June 1986): 157.

19. Morris, *The First Epistle of Paul to the Corinthians*, p. 152; Bruce, *1 and 2 Corinthians*, p. 103.

20. Barrett, *A Commentary on the First Epistle to the Corinthians*, p. 250; Godet, *Commentary on First Corinthians*, p. 540.

21. Waltke, "1 Corinthians 11:2–16: An Interpretation," p. 49; Hurley, *Man and Woman in Biblical Perspective*, pp. 269–71; *New International Dictionary of New Testament Theology*, s.v. "Head," by Colin Brown, 2:160.

22. Robertson and Plummer, *A Critical and Exegetical Commentary on the First Epistle of St Paul to the Corinthians*, p. 229.

23. Waltke, "1 Corinthians 11:2–16: An Interpretation," p. 49; Hurley, *Man and Woman in Biblical Perspective*, pp. 269–71; *New International Dictionary of New Testament Theology*, s.v. "Head," by Colin Brown, 2:160.

24. Charles Talbert, *Reading Corinthians* (New York: Crossroad, 1987), p. 67.

25. David K. Lowery, "1 Corinthians," in *The Bible Knowledge Commentary*, *New Testament*, ed. John F. Walvoord and Roy B. Zuck, (Wheaton, IL: Victor, 1983), p. 529.

26. Hurley, *Man and Woman in Biblical Perspective*, pp. 254–71; *New International Dictionary of New Testament Theology*, s.v. "Head," by Colin Brown, 2:160.

27. Waltke, "1 Corinthians 11:2–16: An Interpretation," p. 46; Findlay, "The First Epistle of Paul to the Corinthians," 2:870; Morris, *The First Epistle of Paul to the Corinthians*, p. 151.

28. For an elaboration of this point see Talbert, *Reading Corinthians*, pp. 66–72.

29. *New International Dictionary of New Testament Theology*, s.v. "Hide, Conceal," by Wilhelm Mundle, 2:212; Bauer, Arndt, and Gingrich, *A Greek-English Lexicon of the New Testament and Other Early Christian Literature*, pp. 29, 411.

30. Robertson and Plummer, *A Critical and Exegetical Commentary*

on the First Epistle of St Paul to the Corinthians, p. 229; Waltke, "1 Corinthians 11:2–16: An Interpretation," p. 49; *New International Dictionary of New Testament Theology,* s.v. "Head," by Colin Brown, 2:160.

31. Blass and Debrunner, *A Greek Grammar of the New Testament and Other Early Christian Literature,* p. 294.

32. Waltke, "1 Corinthians 11:2–16: An Interpretation," p. 50; Findlay, "The First Epistle of Paul to the Corinthians," 2:872; *New International Dictionary of New Testament Theology,* s.v. "Head," by Colin Brown, 2:160.

33. Daniel B. Wallace, unpublished "Grammar Notes on the New Testament," p. 150.

34. Hurley, *Man and Woman in Biblical Perspective,* p. 180.

35. Grosheide, *The First Epistle to the Corinthians;* Godet, *Commentary on First Corinthians,* p. 541.

36. Charles C. Ryrie, *The Ryrie Study Bible* (Chicago: Moody, 1978), p. 1741.

37. This understanding has been adopted in a number of recent studies, including Hurley, *Man and Woman in Biblical Perspective,* pp. 188–89, and D. A. Carson, *Showing the Spirit: A Theological Exposition of 1 Corinthians 12–14* (Grand Rapids: Baker, 1987), pp. 129–30.

38. See Hurley's outline of the passage (*Man and Woman in Biblical Perspective,* pp. 188–89).

39. For further discussion of this issue see H. Wayne House, *The Role of Women in the Ministry Today* (Nashville: Nelson, 1990).

40. For a further elaboration of this view see Wayne C. Grudem, *The Gift of Prophecy in the New Testament and Today* (Westchester, IL: Crossway, 1988).

41. Barrett, *The First Epistle to the Corinthians,* p. 252.

42. Robertson and Plummer, *A Critical and Exegetical Commentary on the First Epistle of St Paul to the Corinthians,* p. 231; Findlay, "The First Epistle of Paul to the Corinthians," 2:873; Godet, *Commentary on First Corinthians,* p. 547.

43. Godet, *Commentary on First Corinthians,* p. 548; Hurley, *Man and Woman in Biblical Perspective,* p. 174; Robertson and Plummer, *A Critical and Exegetical Commentary on the First Epistle of St Paul to the Corinthians,* p. 231.

44. Bauer, Arndt, and Gingrich, *A Greek-English Lexicon of the New Testament and Other Early Christian Literature,* p. 222; Ellicott, *St. Paul's First Epistle to the Corinthians: With a Critical and Grammatical Commentary,* p. 203; Findlay, "The First Epistle of Paul to the Corinthians," 2:873.

45. Hurley, *Man and Woman in Biblical Perspective*, p. 174.
46. Waltke, "1 Corinthians 11:2–16: An Interpretation," p. 51.
47. Ellicott, *St. Paul's First Epistle to the Corinthians: With a Critical and Grammatical Commentary,* p. 203.
48. Findlay, "The First Epistle of Paul to the Corinthians," 2:873.
49. Fee, *The First Epistle to the Corinthians*, p. 514.
50. Ibid.
51. Waltke, "1 Corinthians 11:2–16: An Interpretation," p. 52; Robertson and Plummer, *A Critical and Exegetical Commentary on the First Epistle of St Paul to the Corinthians*, p. 231; Findlay, "The First Epistle of Paul to the Corinthians," 2:874; Grosheide, *The First Epistle to the Corinthians*, p. 256.
52. Ellicott, *St. Paul's First Epistle to the Corinthians: With a Critical and Grammatical Commentary*, p. 204.
53. Barrett, *The First Epistle to the Corinthians*, pp. 252–53; Godet, *Commentary on First Corinthians*, p. 549.
54. F. W. Grosheide, *The First Epistle to the Corinthians*, p. 256.
55. The meaning of עֵזֶר כְּנֶגְדּוֹ in Genesis 2:18 is conveyed by "corresponding completer." The woman fits the man and completes him in his desperate situation. See the exposition of this point in Allen Ross, *Creation and Blessing: A Guide to the Study and Exposition of Genesis* (Grand Rapids: Baker, 1988), pp. 126–27.
56. Waltke, "1 Corinthians 11:2–16: An Interpretation," p. 53; Bruce, *1 and 2 Corinthians,* p. 106.
57. Lowery, "1 Corinthians," p. 529; Findlay, "The First Epistle of Paul to the Corinthians," 2:874.
58. See Fee, *The First Epistle to the Corinthians*, p. 518, for a discussion of this common occurrence in Paul's writings.
59. Findlay, "The First Epistle of Paul to the Corinthians," 2:874.
60. Bauer, Arndt, and Gingrich, *A Greek-English Lexicon of the New Testament and Other Early Christian Literature*, p. 277.
61. Hurley, *Man and Woman in Biblical Perspective*, pp. 176–77; Barrett, *1 Corinthians*, pp. 254–58; *New International Dictionary of New Testament Theology*, s.v. "Head," by Colin Brown, 2:161; Morna D. Hooker, "Authority on Her Head: An Examination of 1 Cor. XI. 10," *New Testament Studies* 10 (1964): 410.
62. Talbert, *Reading Corinthians*, p. 69.
63. Bauer, Arndt, and Gingrich, *A Greek-English Lexicon of the New Testament and Other Early Christian Literature*, p. 7.
64. Ibid., p. 8.
65. Ibid., p. 7.
66. Waltke, "1 Corinthians 11:2–16: An Interpretation," p. 53; Bruce, *1 and 2 Corinthians*, p. 106.

67. Robertson and Plummer, *A Critical and Exegetical Commentary on the First Epistle of St Paul to the Corinthians,* p. 233.
68. Hurley, *Man and Woman in Biblical Perspective,* pp. 269–71.
69. W. F. Moulton and A. S. Geden, *A Concordance to the Greek New Testament* (Edinburgh: Clark, 1978), pp. 9–10.
70. Waltke, "1 Corinthians 11:2–16: An Interpretation," p. 53.
71. Robertson and Plummer, *A Critical and Exegetical Commentary on the First Epistle of St Paul to the Corinthians,* p. 233.
72. See Fee's excellent discussion of the Corinthians' perspective on marriage as colored by their errant view of having arrived at an angelic state (*The First Epistle to the Corinthians,* pp. 266–357).
73. Ellicott, *St. Paul's First Epistle to the Corinthians: With a Critical and Grammatical Commentary,* p. 206; Robertson and Plummer, *A Critical and Exegetical Commentary on the First Epistle of St Paul to the Corinthians,* p. 234.
74. For the use of ὥσπερ γὰρ (v. 12) to introduce an illustration see Blass and Debrunner, *A Greek Grammar of the New Testament and Other Early Christian Literature,* p. 236.
75. E. W. Bullinger, *Figures of Speech Used in the Bible* (reprint; Grand Rapids: Baker, 1968), p. 137.
76. Blass and Debrunner, *A Greek Grammar of the New Testament and Other Early Christian Literature,* p. 262.
77. Robertson and Plummer, *A Critical and Exegetical Commentary on the First Epistle of St Paul to the Corinthians;* Findlay, "The First Epistle of Paul to the Corinthians," 2:875.
78. Bauer, Arndt, and Gingrich, *A Greek-English Lexicon of the New Testament and Other Early Christian Literature,* p. 699; James Hope Moulton and George Milligan, *The Vocabulary of the Greek New Testament* (Grand Rapids: Eerdmans, 1930), p. 534.
79. Blass and Debrunner, *A Greek Grammar of the New Testament and Other Early Christian Literature,* p. 262.
80. Findlay, "The First Epistle of Paul to the Corinthians," 2:875.
81. Grosheide, *The First Epistle to the Corinthians,* p. 260.
82. Godet, *Commentary on First Corinthians,* p. 556.
83. E.g., the Spartan warriors (Findlay, "The First Epistle of Paul to the Corinthians," 2:875).
84. Bauer, Arndt, and Gingrich, *A Greek-English Lexicon of the New Testament and Other Early Christian Literature,* p. 869.
85. Fee, *The First Epistle to the Corinthians,* p. 527.
86. Robertson and Plummer, *A Critical and Exegetical Commentary on the First Epistle of St Paul to the Corinthians,* p. 235; Morris, *The First Epistle of Paul to the Corinthians,* p. 135; Lowery, "1 Corinthians," p. 530.

87. *New International Dictionary of New Testament Theology*, s.v. "Head," by Colin Brown, 2:162.
88. Godet, *Commentary on First Corinthians*, p. 557; Hurley, *Man and Woman in Biblical Perspective*, p. 179.
89. *New International Dictionary of New Testament Theology*, s.v. "Head," by Colin Brown, 2:162.
90. Hurley, *Man and Woman in Biblical Perspective*, pp. 254–71.
91. Henry Alford, *Alford's Greek Testament: An Exegetical and Critical Commentary*, 4 vols. (reprint; Grand Rapids: Baker, 1980), 2:568; also see Ellicott, *St. Paul's First Epistle to the Corinthians: With a Critical and Grammatical Commentary*, p. 208.
92. Blass and Debrunner, *A Greek Grammar of the New Testament and Other Early Christian Literature*, p. 189.
93. Bauer, Arndt, and Gingrich, *A Greek-English Lexicon of the New Testament and other Early Christian Literature*, p. 860; Moulton and Milligan, *The Vocabulary of the Greek New Testament*, pp. 670–71.
94. Findlay, "The First Epistle of Paul to the Corinthians," 2:876.
95. Grosheide, *The First Epistle to the Corinthians*, p. 261.
96. Robertson and Plummer, *A Critical and Exegetical Commentary on the First Epistle of St Paul to the Corinthians*, p. 235; Findlay, "The First Epistle of Paul to the Corinthians," 2:876; Godet, *Commentary on First Corinthians*, p. 559; Barrett, *The First Epistle to the Corinthians*, p. 258; Waltke, "1 Corinthians 11:2–16: An Interpretation," p. 55; Ellicott, *St. Paul's First Epistle to the Corinthians: With a Critical and Grammatical Commentary*, p. 209.
97. Fee, *The First Epistle to the Corinthians*, p. 512.
98. Rick Simmons, "The Teaching of 1 Corinthians 11:2–16 and 14:34–36 on the Role of Women in Public Worship," unpublished paper, Summer 1990.
99. Ibid., p. 18.
100. Ibid., pp. 23–24.

Chapter 16

1. Wilfred L. Knox, *The Acts of the Apostles*, p. 40.
2. A few writers say Galatians 2:1–10 is describing the fourth visit (e.g., John Knox, *Chapters in a Life of Paul* [Cambridge: University Press, 1948], pp. 64–73; and D. T. Rowlinson, "The Jerusalem Conference and Jesus' Nazareth Visit," *Journal of Biblical Literature* 71 [April 1952]:69–74.) This view, however, is generally considered radical and unsatisfactory. To hold it one must accuse Luke of some serious inaccuracies.

3. Cf. T. W. Manson, "St. Paul in Ephesus: The Problem of the
   Epistle to the Galatians," *Bulletin of the John Rylands Library* 24
   (April 1940): 59–80.
4. Enslin accepts none of these alternatives. He believes Luke used a
   "Jerusalem" source and an "Anticohian" account of the apostolic
   council in Jerusalem. He failed to recognize they were two accounts
   of the same event and therefore separated them and made it seem as
   though Paul made two visits to Jerusalem. The famine visit is actually
   the Jerusalem Council viewed from the viewpoint of the church at
   Antioch and the Acts 15 record is the same event from the vantage
   point of the Jerusalem church (Morton Scott Enslin, *Christian
   Beginnings* [New York: Harper, 1938]). This "interpretation" is again
   too extreme and impugns Luke's ability and accuracy.
5. F. F. Bruce, *Commentary on the Book of Acts* (Grand Rapids:
   Eerdmans, 1954), p. 298.
6. Ernest DeWitt Burton, *A Critical and Exegetical Commentary on
   the Epistle of the Galatians*, International Critical Commentary
   (Edinburgh: Clark, 1964), p. 117.
7. Cf. ibid; Oscar Cullmann, *Peter: Disciple, Apostle, Martyr*
   (Philadelphia: Fortress, 1953), pp. 40–52; John Eadie, *Commentary
   on the Epistle of Paul to the Galatians* (Edinburgh: Clark, 1964),
   pp. 140–45; C. F. Hogg and W. E. Vine, *The Epistle to the
   Galatians* (London: Pickering & Inglis, 1921), pp. 123–28; J. G.
   Machen, *The Origin of Paul's Religion*, pp. 78–100; Richard B.
   Rackham, *The Acts of the Apostles* (Grand Rapids: Baker, 1964),
   pp. 238–40; Herman N. Ridderbos, *The Epistle of Paul to the
   Churches of Galatia* (Grand Rapids: Eerdmans, 1953), pp. 78–80.
8. Burton, *A Critical and Exegetical Commentary on the Epistle to
   the Galatians*, p. 115.
9. W. W. Ramsay, *St. Paul the Traveller and the Roman Citizen*
   (London: Hodder and Stoughton, 1925), pp. 52–53.
10. Bruce, *Commentary on the Book of Acts*, pp. 298–300; John Calvin,
    *Commentaries on the Epistles of Paul to the Galatians and
    Ephesians*, trans. William Pringle (Grand Rapids: Eerdmans, 1948),
    pp. 46–48; Martin H. Franzmann, *The Word of the Lord Grows*
    (St. Louis: Concordia, 1961), p. 54; Robert C. Hoerber, "Galatians
    2:1–10 and the Acts of the Apostles," *Concordia Theological
    Monthly* 31 (August 1968): 482–91; Knox, *The Acts of the Apostles*,
    pp. 40–53; Ramsay, *St. Paul the Traveller and the Roman Citizen*,
    pp. 55–60; Douglass Round, *The Date of St. Paul's Epistle to the
    Galatians* (Cambridge: University Press, 1906), p. 21; Merrill C.
    Tenney, *Galatians: The Charter of Christian Liberty* (Grand
    Rapids: Eerdmans, 1950), 76–82.

11. This figure is reached when the ancient method of counting a fractional part of time as a whole is employed. By this method the three years could actually be a year and a half or even less. The 14 years could be 13 and a half years. The total then would be 15.

Chapter 17

1. Oswald T. Allis, *Prophecy and the Church* (Philadelphia: Presbyterian and Reformed, 1945), p. 97.
2. W. Harold Mare, "Paul's Mystery in Ephesians 3," *Bulletin of the Evangelical Theological Society* 8 (Spring 1964): 83.
3. J. Barton Payne, *The Imminent Appearing of Christ* (Grand Rapids: Eerdmans, 1962), p. 126. See also J. Oliver Buswell, *A Systematic Theology of the Christian Religion*, 2 vols. (Grand Rapids: Zondervan, 1962), 2:448–49.
4. J. Dwight Pentecost, *Things to Come* (Findlay, OH: Dunham, 1958), p. 137.
5. Mare, "Paul's Mystery in Ephesians 3," p. 79.
6. Romans 11:25; 16:25; 1 Corinthians 2:7, 4:1; 13:2; 14:2; 15:51; Ephesians 1:9; 3:3–4, 9; 5:32; 6:19; Colossians 1:26–27, 2:2; 4:3; 2 Thessalonians 2:7; 1 Timothy 3:9, 16. There is one other occurrence in certain manuscripts of 1 Corinthians 2:1.
7. This is true of both Allis and Mare in their works previously cited.
8. For elaboration of this point see John F. Walvoord, *The Millennial Kingdom* (Findlay, OH: Dunham, 1959), p. 236.
9. D. F. Salmond, "The Epistle to the Ephesians," in *The Expositor's Greek Testament*, 5 vols. (Grand Rapids: Eerdmans, 1951), 3:304.

Chapter 18

1. Walter Bauer, William F. Arndt, and F. Wilbur Gingrich, *A Greek-English Lexicon of the New Testament and Other Early Christian Literature* (Chicago: University of Chicago Press, 1957), p. 171.
2. G. Coleman Luck, *First Corinthians* (Chicago: Moody, 1958), p. 60.
3. John Calvin, "Commentary on the First Epistle to the Corinthians," in *Calvin's Commentaries*, trans. William Pringle, 22 vols. (Grand Rapids: Baker, 1981), 20:253.
4. This view is clearly presented by Alfred Plummer ("The Pastoral Epistles," in *The Expositor's Bible,* ed. W. Robertson Nicoll [London: Armstrong & Son, 1903], 23:120–21).
5. Ibid., pp. 122–23.
6. George W. Peters, *Divorce and Remarriage* (Chicago: Moody Bible Institute, 1970), p. 32.
7. Bauer, Arndt, and Gingrich, *A Greek-English Lexicon of the New Testament and Other Early Christian Literature*, p. 167.

8. Robert Young, *Young's Analytical Concordance* (Grand Rapids: Associated Publishers and Authors, n.d.), p. 72.
9. H. E. Dana and Julius R. Mantey, *A Manual Grammar of the Greek New Testament* (New York: Macmillan, 1957), p. 74.
10. Ibid., p. 75.
11. John A. Sproule, "Intermediate Greek Notes" (class notes, Grace Theological Seminary, 1979), p. 66.
12. Ibid., p. 68.
13. Young, *Young's Analytical Concordance*, p. 59.
14. A. T. Robertson, *A Grammar of the Greek New Testament in the Light of Historical Research* (Nashville: Broadman, 1934), p. 496.
15. Ibid., p. 502.
16. Newport J. D. White, "The First and Second Epistles to Timothy," in *The Expositor's Greek Testament,* ed. W. Robertson Nicoll, 5 vols. (Grand Rapids: Eerdmans, 1979), 4:111–12.
17. Kenneth S. Wuest, *The Pastoral Epistles in the Greek New Testament* (Grand Rapids: Eerdmans, 1973), p. 53.
18. Ibid.
19. Robertson, *A Grammar of the Greek New Testament in the Light of Historical Research,* p. 794.
20. Dana and Mantey, *A Manual Grammar of the Greek New Testament,* p. 149.
21. Gene A. Getz, *Sharpening the Focus of the Church* (Chicago: Moody, 1975), p. 105.
22. Ralph Earle, "1 Timothy," in *The Expositor's Bible Commentary,* 12 vols. (Grand Rapids: Zondervan, 1978), 11:364.
23. Lewis Sperry Chafer, *Systematic Theology,* 8 vols. (Dallas, TX: Dallas Seminary Press, 1974; reprint [8 vols. in 4], Grand Rapids: Kregel, 1991), 2:270–71.
24. Plummer, "The Pastoral Epistles," p. 119.
25. Ibid.
26. White, "The First and Second Epistles to Timothy," p. 112.
27. John Calvin, "Commentaries on the First Epistle to Timothy," in *Calvin's Commentaries,* trans. William Pringle, 22 vols. (Grand Rapids: Baker, 1981), 21:77.
28. Ibid.
29. R. C. H. Lenski, *The Interpretations of St. Paul's Epistle to the Colossians, to the Thessalonians, to Timothy, to Titus, and to Philemon* (Minneapolis: Augsburg, 1961), p. 580.
30. Ibid., p. 581.
31. Plummer, "The Pastoral Epistles," p. 120.
32. Calvin, "Commentaries on the First Epistle to Timothy," p. 77.

Chapter 19

1. The inclusio form of the warning is clearly seen in the discussion of Melchizedek. See George Wesley Buchanan, *To the Hebrews*, Anchor Bible (Garden City, NY: Doubleday, 1972), p. 116.
2. Philip Edgcumbe Hughes, *A Commentary on the Epistle to the Hebrews* (Grand Rapids: Eerdmans, 1977), p. 189.
3. Brooke Foss Westcott, *The Epistle to the Hebrews: The Greek Text with Notes and Essays* (reprint, Grand Rapids: Eerdmans, 1974), p. 132.
4. Zane C. Hodges, "Hebrews," in *The Bible Knowledge Commentary, New Testament*, ed. John F. Walvoord and Roy B. Zuck (Wheaton, IL: Victor, 1983), pp. 792–93.
5. F. F. Bruce, *The Epistle to the Hebrews* (Grand Rapids: Eerdmans, 1964), p. 112.
6. For an examination of each of the five warnings of Hebrews and their eschatological perspective, see this writer's work, "An Analysis and Exposition of the Eschatology of the Warning Passages in the Book of Hebrews" (ThD diss., Dallas Theological Seminary, 1984).
7. A. T. Robertson, *A Grammar of the Greek New Testament in Light of Historical Research* (Nashville: Broadman, 1930), pp. 777, 785–89.
8. Marcus Dods, "The Epistle to the Hebrews," in *The Expositor's Greek Testament*, ed. W. Robertson Nicoll, 5 vols. (Grand Rapids: Eerdmans, 1961), 4:296.
9. Duane A. Dunham, "An Exegetical Examination of the Warnings in the Epistle to the Hebrews" (ThD diss., Grace Theological Seminary, 1974), p. 159.
10. Hodges, "Hebrews," p. 794.
11. Walter Bauer, William F. Arndt, and F. Wilbur Gingrich, *A Greek-English Lexicon of the New Testament and Other Early Christian Literature* (Chicago: University of Chicago Press, 1957), p. 156.
12. John MacArthur, Jr., *Hebrews*, MacArthur New Testament Commentary (Chicago: Moody, 1983), p. 124.
13. C. Spicq, *L'Epitre aux Hebreux*, 2 vols. (Paris: Librairie Lecoffre, 1952), 2:150–51.
14. For a discussion of the μέτοχος (partner") of Hebrews 1:9, see this writer's work, "The Eschatological Salvation of Hebrews 1:5–2:5," *Bibliotheca Sacra* 145 (January-March 1988): 83–97.
15. Robert Govett, *Govett on Hebrews* (Miami Springs, FL: Conley and Schoettle, 1981), p. 156.
16. For a discussion of the warning as "hypothetical," see Homer A.

Kent, Jr., *The Epistle to the Hebrews* (Grand Rapids: Baker, 1972), pp. 113–14.

17. For a discussion of the believer's confidence and worship function in God's household, see Thomas Kem Oberholtzer, "The Kingdom Rest in Hebrews 3:1–4:13," *Bibliotheca Sacra* 145 (April–June 1988):185–96; also see Hodges, "Hebrews," pp. 794–95.

18. James Moffatt, *A Critical and Exegetical Commentary on the Epistle to the Hebrews,* International Critical Commentary (Edinburgh: Clark, 1924), p. 79.

19. Bauer, Arndt, and Gingrich, *A Greek-English Lexicon of the New Testament and Other Early Christian Literature,* p. 60.

20. Leon Morris, "Hebrews," in *The Expositor's Bible Commentary,* 12 vols. (Grand Rapids: Zondervan, 1981), 12:55.

21. The background and occasion for the writing of Hebrews has parallels similar to those of Qumran. For a discussion of these parallels, see Hughes, *A Commentary on the Epistle to the Hebrews,* pp. 10–11; Spicq, *L'Epitre aux Hebreux,* 1:242ff.; Jean-Baptiste Apollos, "Les Hellenists et Qumran," *Revue de Qumran* 1 (1958–59): 365–90; Yigael Yadin, "The Dead See Scrolls and the Epistle to the Hebrews," in *Scripta Hierosolymitana,* vol. 4 of *Aspects of the Dead Sea Scrolls*, ed. Chaim Rabin and Yigael Yadin (Jerusalem: Magnes, 1965), pp. 36–55.

22. Stanley D. Toussaint, "The Eschatology of the Warning Passages in the Book of Hebrews," *Grace Theological Journal* 3 (Spring 1982): 74.

23. Hodges, "Hebrews," pp. 795–96.

24. Thomas Hewitt, *The Epistle to the Hebrews,* Tyndale New Testament Commentaries (Grand Rapids: Eerdmans, 1960), p. 109.

25. Dods, "The Epistle to the Hebrews," 4:299.

26. Jean Héring, *The Epistle to the Hebrews,* trans. A. W. Heathcote and P. J. Allcock (London: Epworth, 1970), p. 48.

27. For example Toussaint, "The Eschatology of the Warning Passages in the Book of Hebrews," p. 75.

28. Elder Pliny *Historia Naturalis* XVII 300.72.

29. Hodges, "Hebrews," p. 796.

30. Otto Michel, *Der Brief an die Hebräer* (Göttingen: Vandenhoeck & Ruprecht, 1966), pp. 154–55.

Chapter 20

1. H. C. C. Cavallin, "The False Teachers of 2 Pt as Pseudo Prophets," *Novum Testamentum* 21 (July 1979): 263.

2. The author's own translations of the Greek text are used throughout this article.

3. Albert Barnes, *Barnes' Notes on the New Testament* (reprint, Grand Rapids: Kregel, 1964), p. 1454.
4. Ibid.
5. R. C. H. Lenski, *The Interpretations of the Epistles of St. Peter, St. John and St. Jude* (Minneapolis: Augsburg, 1966), p. 329.
6. James Moffatt, *The General Epistles*, Moffatt New Testament Commentary (New York: Harper & Brothers, n.d.), p. 119. The textual problem here is given a "C" rating by the editors of the United Bible Societies Greek New Testament committee. The word in question, ὀλίγως is rare, a New Testament *hapax legomenon*. Metzger argues strongly for its place in the text (Bruce Metzger, *A Textual Commentary on the Greek New Testament* [London: United Bible Societies, 1971], p. 704.
7. Charles Bigg, *A Critical and Exegetical Commentary on the Epistles of St. Peter and St. Jude*, International Critical Commentary (Edinburgh: Clark, 1901), p. 285. See also Johann Huther, *Critical and Exegetical Handbook to the General Epistles of James, Peter, John and Jude*, Meyer's Commentary on the New Testament (New York: Funk and Wagnalls, 1887), p. 416; Lenski, *The Interpretation of the Epistles of St. Peter, St. John and St. Jude*, p. 329; and others.
8. Mayor states that these commentators hold this view: Schott, Keil, Kühl, Hundhausen, Weiss, von Soden, Alford, Plummer, and Plumptre (Joseph B. Mayor, *The Epistle of St. Jude and the Second Epistle of St. Peter* [London: Macmillan, 1907; reprint, Minneapolis: Klock & Klock, 1978], p. 142).
9. Huther, *A Critical and Exegetical Handbook to the General Epistles*, p. 417.
10. Ibid.
11. Mayor, *The Epistle of St. Jude and the Second Epistle of St. Peter*, p. 142.
12. Lenski, *The Interpretation of the Epistles of St. Peter, St. John, and St. Jude*, p. 332.
13. Henry Liddell and Robert Scott, *A Greek-English Lexicon* (Oxford: Clarendon, 1968, pp. 350, 355, 627; Walter Bauer, William F. Arndt, and F. Wilbur Gingrich, *A Greek-English Lexicon of the New Testament and Other Early Christian Literature* (Chicago: University of Chicago Press, 1957), pp. 159–63, 290–91. Bultmann argues that ἐπιγινώσκω, and γινώσκω are used "with no difference in meaning" Theological *Dictionary of the New Testament, s.v.* "γινώσκω, γνῶσις, ἐπιγινώσκω, ἐπίγνωσις," by R. Bultmann, 1:703). It is his view that "the simple and compound forms are used interchangeably" in the papyrus (p. 703). He then argues, "there is no general distinction between the simple and compound

forms in early Christian writings [as] is shown by a comparison of Mark 2:8 with 8:17, Mark 5:30 with Luke 8:46 . . ." and others (p. 704). He then indicates: "Rather curiously, the compound ἐπίγνωσις has become almost a technical term for the decisive knowledge of God which is implied in conversion to the Christian faith. The verb, too, is often used in this sense . . ." (p. 707). However, Schmitz gives a helpful balance to these assertions: "gnosis is regarded as a technical term for the gnostic heresy (cf. 1 Tim. 6:20) and epignosis takes its place, when it refers to Christian knowledge (1 Tim. 2:4; 2 Tim. 2:25; 2:7; Titus 1:1)" (*Dictionary of New Testament Theology,* s.v. "Knowledge, Experience, Ignorance," by Schmitz, 2:405). While it may not be defensible to assume that in every case ἐπίγνωσις means something that γνῶσις does not, it may mean something more, and the context will determine if that is the case.

14. Barnes, *Barnes' Notes on the New Testament,* p. 1454.

15. Ibid.

16. W. H. Griffith Thomas, *The Apostle Peter* (Grand Rapids: Eerdmans, 1946), p. 273.

17. Lenski, *The Interpretation of the Epistles of St. Peter, St. John and St. Jude,* p. 333.

18. Huther, *Critical and Exegetical Handbook to the General Epistles,* p. 418.

19. John Murray argues this point in *The Epistle to the Romans,* 2 vols., New International Commentary on the New Testament (Grand Rapids: Eerdmans, 1959, 1965), 2:77–78.

20. A. R. C. Leaney, *The Letters of Peter and Jude,* Cambridge Bible Commentary on the New English Bible (Cambridge: University Press, 1967), p. 126 (italics his).

21. Henry Alford, *The Greek Testament,* 4 vols. (Chicago: Moody, 1958), 4:411.

22. Huther, *Critical and Exegetical Handbook to the General Epistles,* p. 418.

23. Lenski, *The Interpretation of the Epistles of St. Peter, St. John and St. Jude,* p. 331.

24. Charles Hodge discusses this issue under the topic of perfectionism. He notes that the doctrine of both Lutheran and Reformed branches of the Protestant faith teaches that "sanctification is never perfected in this life; that sin is not in any case entirely subdued; so that the most advanced believer has need as long as he continues in the flesh, daily to pray for the forgiveness of sins" (*Systematic Theology* [reprint, Grand Rapids: Eerdmans, 1906], pp. 245–48). He further notes Paul's comments about himself in Romans 7 and Philippians 3:12–14,

showing that this great apostle still had an inner struggle over temptation to sin. "The characteristic difference between the unrenewed and the renewed is not that the former are entirely sinful, and the latter perfectly holy, but that the former are wholly under the control of their fallen nature, while the latter have the Spirit of God dwelling in them, which leads them to crucify the flesh, and to strive after complete conformity to the image of God" (ibid., p. 248). Strong and Berkhof discuss the problem under sanctification (A. H. Strong, *Systematic Theology* [New York: Revell, 1907], pp. 868–81; Louis Berkhof, *Systematic Theology* [Grand Rapids: Eerdmans, 1939], pp. 527–44). Berkhof rightly reckons that early in the history of the church there was a tendency to confuse justification with sanctification. He adds that Augustine was one of the first to develop more definite ideas of sanctification (ibid., p. 529). This tendency is still present and lies behind some of the difficulties with this passage (2 Peter 2:18–22) and certain others. That this is not an easy topic to resolve is shown by the final chapter, "The End of Sin" in G. C. Berkouwer, *Sin* (Grand Rapids: Eerdmans, pp. 546–67).

25. Joseph H. Thayer indicates this usage (*A Greek-English Lexicon of the New Testament,* 4th ed. [New York: Scribner's Sons, 1901], p. 253), as do several Greek grammars including those by Nigel Turner (*Grammar of New Testament Greek,* vol. 4: *Syntax* [Edinburgh: Clark, 1963], p. 32); F. Blass, A. Debrunner, and Robert W. Funk (*A Greek Grammar of the New Testament* [Chicago: University of Chicago Press, 1961], p. 340; and Maximillan Zerwick (*Biblical Greek* [Rome: Scripta Pontificii Instituti Biblici, 1963], p. 50). Zerwick remarks, "Although in general the comparative form took the place of the superlative one, the opposite was the case for two adjectives, whose superlative form supplanted the comparative one: πρῶτος is used instead of πρότερος and ἔσχατος instead of ὕστερο" (cf. e.g. Matt. 21, 28, 31; 27, 64 . . .)" (ibid.).

26. Bigg, *A Critical and Exegetical Commentary on the Epistles of St. Peter and St. Jude,* p. 287. For a further word on this passage in Matthew, see A. Plummer, *An Exegetical Commentary on the Gospel according to Matthew* (reprint, Minneapolis: James Family, n.d.), pp. 184–85.

27. Many commentaries recognize this, if they comment on the grammar at all. Lenski indicates that Peter used the past to show that the present has not turned out as it should have (*The Interpretation of the Epistles of St. Peter, St. John and St. Jude,* p. 332). Bigg sees it as an elliptical conditional clause which omits

the usual ἀν (*A Critical and Exegetical Commentary on the Epistles of St. Peter and St. Jude*, p. 287). In defense of this position (which Lenski rejected) Bigg cites Goodwin's classical grammar; Blass, Debrunner, and Funk, *A Greek Grammar of the New Testament;* Matthew 26:24; and Romans 9:3. Mayor sides with Bigg (*The Epistle of St. Jude and the Second Epistle of St. Peter*, p. 142). Of some English translations which this writer checked, not one rendered it in an ordinary imperfect. Most chose to indicate a kind of subjunctive aspect, "It would have been. . . ."

28. A. T. Robertson, *A Grammar of the Greek New Testament in the Light of Historical Research* (Nashville: Broadman, 1934), p. 886.

29. C. F. D. Moule, *An Idiom-book of New Testament Greek* (Cambridge: University Press, 1953), p. 9.

30. Herbert Weir Smyth, *Greek Grammar* (Cambridge, MA: Harvard University Press, 1920), p. 424. Alford, commenting on this problem, compared it to Romans 9:3 and added, "The sense of the imperfect in such expressions is the proper and strict one (and no new discovery, but common enough in every schoolboy's reading) . . ." (*The Greek Testament,* 2:403).

31. Thomas Brooks, *Precious Remedies against Satan's Devices* (1652; reprint, London: Banner of Truth, 1968), p. 88.

32. Ralph Venning, *The Plague of Plagues* (1669; reprint, London: Banner of Truth, 1965), p. 170.